LINKERS AND LOADERS

LINKERS AND LOADERS

John R. Levine

MORGAN KAUFMANN PUBLISHERS

An Imprint of Elsevier

SAN FRANCISCO   SAN DIEGO   NEW YORK   BOSTON
LONDON   SYDNEY   TOKYO

Acquisitions Editor Tim Cox
Director of Production and Manufacturing Yonie Overton
Production Editor Edward Wade
Editorial Assistant Sarah Luger
Cover Design Ross Carron Design
Cover Photograph © Greg L. Ryan; Sally Beyer/AllStock/PNI
Text Design, Technical Illustration, and Composition Rebecca Evans & Associates
Copyeditor Jeff Van Bueren
Proofreader Jennifer McClain
Indexer Bruce Tracy
Printer Courier Corporation

Designations used by companies to distinguish their products are often claimed as trademarks or registered trademarks. In all instances where Morgan Kaufmann Publishers is aware of a claim, the product names appear in initial capital or all capital letters. Readers, however, should contact the appropriate companies for more complete information regarding trademarks and registration.

ACADEMIC PRESS
An Imprint of Elsevier
525 B Street, Suite 1900, San Diego, CA 92101-4495, USA
http://www.academicpress.com

Academic Press
24–28 Oval Road, London, NW1 7DX United Kingdom
http://www.hbuk.co.uk/ap/

Morgan Kaufmann Publishers
340 Pine Street, Sixth Floor, San Francisco, CA 94104-3205
http://www.mkp.com

Permissions may be sought directly from Elsevier's Science and Technology Rights Department in Oxford, UK. Phone: (44) 1865 843830, Fax: (44) 1865 853333, e-mail: permissions@elsevier.co.uk. You may also complete your request on-line via the Elsevier homepage: http://www.elsevier.com by selecting "Customer Support" and then "Obtaining Permissions".

Library of Congress Cataloging-in-Publication Data

Levine, John R.
  Linkers and loaders / John R. Levine.
    p. cm.
  ISBN-13:978-1-55860-496-4 ISBN-10:1-55860-496-0
   1. Assembling (Electronic computers) 2. Linkers (Computer programs) 3. Loaders (Computer programs) I. Title.

QA76.76.A87 L48 2000
005.4'56—dc21   99-047127

This book is printed on acid-free paper.

To Tonia and Sarah

Contents

PREFACE

Linkers and loaders have been part of the software toolkit for almost as long as there have been computers. They are the critical tools that permit programs to be built from modules rather than as one big monolith.

As early as 1947, programmers started to use primitive loaders that could take program routines stored on separate tapes and combine and relocate them into one program. By the early 1960s, these loaders had evolved into full-fledged linkage editors. Because program memory remained expensive and limited and computers were (by modern standards) slow, these linkers contained complex features for creating complex memory overlay structures to squeeze large programs into small memory and for re-editing previously linked programs to save the time needed to rebuild a program from scratch.

During the 1970s and 1980s there was little progress in linking technology. Linkers tended to become even simpler, as virtual memory moved much of the job of storage management away from applications and overlays into the operating system; and as computers became faster and disks larger, it became easier to re-create a linked program from scratch to replace a few modules rather than to relink just the changes. In the 1990s linkers have again become more complex, adding support for modern features including dynamically linked shared libraries and the unusual demands of C++. Radical new processor architectures with wide instruction words and compiler-scheduled memory accesses (such as the Intel IA64) will also put new demands on linkers to ensure that the complex requirements of the code are met in linked programs.

WHO IS THIS BOOK FOR?

This book is intended for several overlapping audiences: students, practicing programmers, and computer language designers and developers. Courses in compiler construction and operating systems have generally given scant treatment to linking and loading, often because the linking process seemed trivial or obvious. Although this was arguably true when the languages of interest were Fortran, Pascal, and C, and when operating systems didn't use memory mapping or shared libraries, it's much less true now. C++, Java, and other object-oriented languages require a much more sophisticated linking environment. Memory-mapped executable programs, shared libraries, and dynamic linking affect many parts of an operating system, and an operating system designer disregards linking issues at his or her peril.

Practicing programmers need to be aware of what linkers do, again particularly for modern languages. C++ places unique demands on a linker, and large C++ programs are prone to develop hard-to-diagnose bugs as a result of unexpected occurrences at link time. (The best known of these are static constructors that run in an order the programmer wasn't expecting.) Linker features such as shared libraries and dynamic linking offer great flexibility and power, when used appropriately.

Language designers and developers need to be aware of what linkers do and can do as they build languages and compilers. Programming tasks that had been handled by hand for 30 years are automated in C++, which depends on the linker to handle the details. (Consider what a programmer has to do to get the equivalent of C++ templates in C or to ensure that the initialization routines in each of a hundred C source files are called before the body of the program starts.) Future languages will automate even more program-wide bookkeeping tasks, with more powerful linkers doing the work. Linkers will also be more involved in global program optimization, because the linker is the only stage of the compiler process that handles the entire program's code together and thus can do transformations that affect the entire program as a unit.

People who write linkers also need this book, of course. But all the linker writers in the world could probably fit in one room and half of them already have copies because they reviewed the manuscript.

OVERVIEW

The key points for each chapter are highlighted with dots in the margin like
the ones highlighting this paragraph. If you're inclined to skip over a chapter
or two, please at least look at the highlighted points on your way through.

Chapter 1 provides a short historical overview of the linking process and
discusses the stages of the linking process. It ends with a short but complete
example of a linker run, from input object files to a runnable "Hello, world"
program.

Chapter 2 reviews computer architecture from the point of view of linker
design. It examines SPARC, a representative reduced instruction set architecture; the IBM 360/370, an old but still very viable register-memory architecture; and the Intel x86, which is in a category of its own. Important
architectural aspects include memory architecture, program addressing
architecture, and the layout of address fields in individual instructions.

Chapter 3 examines the internal structure of object and executable files. It
starts with the very simplest files, DOS COM files, and goes on to examine
progressively more complex files including DOS EXE, UNIX a.out and ELF,
MS Windows COFF and PE (EXE and DLL), OS/360 object files, and Intel/
Microsoft OMF.

Chapter 4 covers the first stage of linking—allocating storage to the segments of the linked program—with examples from real linkers.

Chapter 5 covers symbol binding and resolution, the process by which a
symbolic reference in one file to a name in a second file is resolved to a
machine address.

Chapter 6 covers the creation and use of object code libraries, along with
issues of library structure and performance.

Chapter 7 covers address relocation, which is the process of adjusting the
object code in a program to reflect the actual addresses at which it runs. It also
covers position-independent code (PIC)—code created in a way that avoids
the need for relocation—and the costs and benefits of doing so.

Chapter 8 covers the loading process, which involves getting a program
from a file into the computer's memory in order to run it. It also covers tree-
structured overlays, an old but still effective technique to conserve address
space.

Chapter 9 looks at what's required to share a single copy of a library's code
among many different programs. This chapter concentrates on statically
linked shared libraries.

Chapter 10 broadens the discussion of Chapter 9 to dynamically linked shared libraries. It treats two examples in detail, Win32 dynamic-link libraries (DLLs) and UNIX/Linux ELF shared libraries.

Chapter 11 looks at a variety of tasks that sophisticated modern linkers do. It covers new features that C++ requires, including name mangling, global constructors and destructors, template expansion, and duplicate code elimination. Other techniques include incremental linking, link-time garbage collection, link-time code generation and optimization, load-time code generation, and profiling and instrumentation. The chapter concludes with an overview of the Java linking model, which is considerably more semantically complex than any of the other linkers covered.

 ## THE PROJECT

Chapters 3 through 11 have a continuing project to develop a small but functional linker in perl. Although perl is an unlikely implementation language for a production linker, it's an excellent choice for a term project. Perl handles many of the low-level programming chores that bog down programming in languages like C or C++, letting the student concentrate on the algorithms and data structures of the project at hand. Perl is available at no charge on most current computers, including Windows 95/98 and NT, UNIX, and Linux, and many excellent books are available to teach perl to new users. (See the books by Hoffman, Schwartz, and Wall et al. listed in the references at the back of this book.)

The initial project in Chapter 3 builds a linker skeleton that can read and write files in a simple but complete object format, and subsequent chapters add functions to the linker until the final result is a full-fledged linker that supports shared libraries and produces dynamically linkable objects. Perl is quite able to handle arbitrary binary files and data structures, and the project linker could be adapted if desired to handle native object formats.

Object files for the project can be found at the supporting Web site for this book at *linker.iecc.com*.

ACKNOWLEDGMENTS

Many, many people generously contributed their time to reading and reviewing the manuscript of this book, including both the publisher's reviewers and the readers of the *comp.compilers* usenet newsgroup who read and commented on an on-line version of the manuscript. In alphabetical order, they are Mike Albaugh, Rod Bates, Gunnar Blomberg, Robert Bowdidge, Keith Breinholt, Brad Brisco, Andreas Buschmann, David S. Cargo, John Carr, David Chase, Ben Combee, Ralph Corderoy, Paul Curtis, Bjorn De Sutter, Lars Duening, Phil Edwards, Oisin Feeley, Mary Fernandez, Michael Lee Finney, Peter H. Froehlich, Robert Goldberg, James Grosbach, Rohit Grover, Quinn Tyler Jackson, Colin Jensen, Glenn Kasten, Louis Krupp, Terry Lambert, Doug Landauer, Jim Larus, Len Lattanzi, Greg Lindahl, Peter Ludemann, Steven D. Majewski, John McEnerney, Larry Meadows, Jason Merrill, Carl Montgomery, Cyril Muerillon, Sameer Nanajkar, Jacob Navia, Simon Peyton-Jones, Allan Porterfield, Charles Randall, Thomas David Rivers, Ken Rose, Alex Rosenberg, Raymond Roth, Timur Safin, Kenneth G. Salter, Donn Seeley, Aaron F. Stanton, Harlan Stenn, Mark Stone, Robert Strandh, Ian Taylor, Michael Trofimov, Hans Walheim, and Roger Wong.

These people are responsible for most of the true statements in this book. The false ones remain the author's responsibility. (If you find any of the latter, please contact me at the address below so they can be fixed in subsequent printings.)

I particularly thank my editor Tim Cox and editorial assistant Sarah Luger at Morgan Kaufmann for putting up with my interminable delays during the writing process and for pulling all the pieces of this book together.

CONTACT US

This book has a supporting Web site at *linker.iecc.com*. It includes example chapters from the book, samples of perl code and object files for the project, and updates and errata.

You can send email to the author at linker@iecc.com. The author reads all the mail, but because of the volume received may not be able to answer all questions promptly.

LINKING AND LOADING

WHAT DO LINKERS AND LOADERS DO?

The basic job of any linker or loader is simple: It binds more abstract names to more concrete names, which permits programmers to write code using the more abstract names. For example, it takes a name written by a programmer such as getline and binds it to "the location 612 bytes from the beginning of the executable code in module iosys." Or it may take a more abstract numeric address such as "the location 450 bytes beyond the beginning of the static data for this module" and bind it to a numeric address.

1.2 ADDRESS BINDING: A HISTORICAL PERSPECTIVE

A useful way to get some insight into what linkers and loaders do is to look at their part in the development of computer programming systems. The earliest computers were programmed entirely in machine language. Programmers would write out the symbolic programs on sheets of paper, hand-assemble them into machine code, and then toggle the machine code into the computer, or perhaps punch it on paper tape or cards. (Real hotshots could compose code directly at the switches.) If the programmer used symbolic addresses at all, the symbols were bound to addresses as the programmer did his or her hand translation. If it turned out that an instruction had to be added or deleted, the entire program had to be inspected and any addresses affected by the added or deleted instruction adjusted by hand.

The problem was that the names were bound to addresses too early in the process. Assemblers solved that problem by letting programmers write programs in terms of symbolic names, with the assembler binding the names to machine addresses. If the program changed, the programmer had to reassemble it, but the work of assigning the addresses is pushed off from the programmer to the computer.

Libraries of code compound the address assignment problem. Since the basic operations that computers can perform are so simple, useful programs are composed of subprograms that perform higher-level and more complex operations. Computer installations keep a library of prewritten and debugged subprograms that programmers can draw upon for use in new programs they write, rather than requiring programmers to write all their own subprograms. The programmer then loads the subprograms in with the main program to form a complete working program.

Programmers were using libraries of subprograms even before they used assemblers. By 1947, John Mauchly (leader of the ENIAC project) wrote about loading programs along with subprograms selected from a catalog of programs stored on tapes and of the need to relocate the subprograms' code to reflect the addresses at which they were loaded. Perhaps surprisingly, these two basic linker functions—relocation and library search—appear to predate even assemblers, as Mauchly expected both the program and subprograms to be written in machine language. The relocating loader allowed the authors and users of the subprograms to write each subprogram as though it would start at location zero and to defer the actual address binding until the subprograms were linked with a particular main program.

With the advent of operating systems, relocating loaders separate from linkers and libraries became necessary. Before there were operating systems, each program had the machine's entire memory at its disposal, so the program could be assembled and linked for fixed memory addresses, based on the certainty that all addresses in the computer would be available. But with operating systems, the program had to share the computer's memory with the operating system and perhaps even with other programs. This meant that the actual addresses at which the program would be running weren't known until the operating system loaded the program into memory, with final address binding deferred past link time to load time. Linkers and loaders now divided up the work, with linkers doing part of the address binding, assigning relative addresses within each program, and the loader doing a final relocation step to assign actual addresses.

As systems became more complex, they called upon linkers to do more and more complex name management and address binding. Fortran programs used multiple subprograms and common blocks—areas of data shared by multiple subprograms—and it was up to the linker to lay out storage and to assign the addresses both for the subprograms and the common blocks. Linkers increasingly had to deal with object code libraries, including both application libraries written in Fortran and other languages and compiler support libraries that were called implicitly from compiled code to handle I/O and other high-level operations.

Programs quickly became larger than available memory, so linkers provided overlays, a technique that let programmers arrange for different parts of a program to share the same memory, with each overlay loaded on demand when another part of the program called into it. Overlays were widely used on mainframes from the advent of disks around 1960 until the spread of virtual memory in the mid-1970s; they reappeared on microcomputers in the early 1980s in exactly the same form and faded as virtual memory appeared on PCs in the 1990s. Overlays are still used in memory-limited embedded environments, and they may yet reappear in other places where precise programmer or compiler control of memory usage improves performance.

With the advent of hardware relocation and virtual memory, linkers and loaders actually became less complex, because each program could again have an entire address space. Programs could be linked to be loaded at fixed addresses, with hardware rather than software relocation taking care of any load-time relocation. However, computers with hardware relocation invariably run more than one program; frequently they run multiple copies of the same program. When a computer runs multiple copies of one program, some parts of the program—the executable code, in particular—are the same among all running copies, while other parts are unique to each copy. If the parts that don't change can be separated out from the parts that do change, the operating system can use a single copy of the unchanging part, saving considerable storage. Compilers and assemblers were modified to create object code in multiple sections, with one section for read-only code and another section for writable data. The linker had to be able to combine all of the sections of each type so that the linked program would have all the code in one place and all the data in another. This didn't delay address binding any more than before, because addresses were still assigned at link time, but more work was deferred to the linker to assign addresses for all the sections.

Even when different programs are running on a computer, those different programs usually turn out to share a lot of common code. For example, nearly every program written in C uses routines such as `fopen` and `printf`; database applications all use a large access library to connect to the database; and programs running under a graphical user interface (GUI) such as X Windows, MS Windows, or the Macintosh all use pieces of the GUI library. Most systems now provide shared libraries for programs to use, so that all the programs that use a library can share a single copy of it. This both improves run-time performance and saves a lot of disk space; in small programs the common library routines often take up more space than the program itself.

In the simpler static shared libraries, each library is bound to specific addresses at the time the library is built, and the linker binds program references to library routines to those specific addresses at link time. Static libraries turn out to be inconveniently inflexible, because programs potentially have to be relinked every time any part of the library changes, and the details of creating static shared libraries turn out to be very tedious. Systems therefore added dynamically linked libraries in which library sections and symbols aren't bound to actual addresses until the program that uses the library starts running. Sometimes the binding is delayed even further than that; with full-fledged dynamic linking, the addresses of called procedures aren't bound until the first call. Furthermore, programs can bind to libraries as the programs are running, loading libraries in the middle of program execution. This provides a powerful and high-performance way to extend the function of programs. Microsoft Windows in particular makes extensive use of run-time loading of shared libraries—called dynamically linked libraries (DLLs)—to construct and extend programs.

1.3 LINKING VS. LOADING

Linkers and loaders perform several related but conceptually separate actions.

- *Program loading.* They copy a program from secondary storage (which, since about 1968, invariably means a disk) into main memory so it's ready to run. In some cases loading just involves copying the data from disk to memory; in others it involves allocating storage, setting protection bits, or arranging for virtual memory to map virtual addresses to disk pages.

- *Relocation.* Compilers and assemblers generally create each file of object code with the program addresses starting at zero, but few computers let you load your program at location zero. If a program is created from multiple subprograms, all the subprograms have to be loaded at non-overlapping addresses. Relocation is the process of assigning load addresses to the various parts of the program and adjusting the code and data in the program to reflect the assigned addresses. In many systems, relocation happens more than once. It's quite common for a linker to create a program from multiple subprograms and to create one linked output program that starts at zero, with the various subprograms relocated to locations within the big program. Then when the program is loaded, the system picks the actual load address and the linked program is relocated as a whole to the load address.

- *Symbol resolution.* When a program is built from multiple subprograms, the references from one subprogram to another are made using symbols; a main program might use a square root routine called `sqrt`, and the math library defines `sqrt`. A linker resolves the symbol by noting the location assigned to `sqrt` in the library and patching the caller's object code so the call instruction refers to that location.

Although there's considerable overlap between linking and loading, it's reasonable to define a program that does program loading as a loader, and one that does symbol resolution as a linker. Either can do relocation, and there have been all-in-one linking loaders that do all three functions.

The line between relocation and symbol resolution can be fuzzy. Because linkers already can resolve references to symbols, one way to handle code relocation is to assign a symbol to the base address of each part of the program and to treat relocatable addresses as references to the base address symbols.

One important feature that linkers and loaders share is that they both patch object code; as such they are the only widely used programs to do so other than perhaps debuggers. This is a uniquely powerful feature, albeit one that is extremely machine specific in the details and that can lead to baffling bugs if done wrong.

Two-Pass Linking

Now we turn to the general structure of linkers. Linking, like compiling or assembling, is fundamentally a two-pass process. A linker takes as its input a set of input object files, libraries, and perhaps command files, and produces as its result an output object file and perhaps ancillary information such as a load map or a file containing debugger symbols (Figure 1.1).

Each input file contains a set of *segments*, contiguous blocks of code or data to be placed in the output file. Each input file also contains at least one symbol table. Some symbols are exported—defined within the file for use in other files, generally the names of routines within the file that can be called from elsewhere. Other symbols are imported—used in the file but not defined, generally the names of routines called from but not present in the file.

When a linker runs, it first has to scan the input files to find the sizes of the segments and to collect the definitions and references of all of the symbols. It creates a segment table listing all of the segments defined in the input files and a symbol table with all of the symbols imported or exported. Using the data from the first pass, the linker assigns numeric locations to symbols, determines the sizes and location of the segments in the output address space, and figures out where everything goes in the output file.

The second pass uses the information collected in the first pass to control the actual linking process. It reads and relocates the object code, substituting numeric addresses for symbol references and adjusting memory addresses in code and data to reflect relocated segment addresses, and writes the relocated code to the output file. It then writes the output file, generally with header information, the relocated segments, and symbol table information. If the

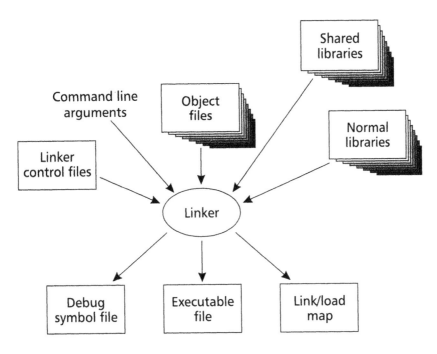

FIGURE **1.1** • The linker process.

program uses dynamic linking, the symbol table contains the information the run-time linker will need to resolve dynamic symbols. In many cases, the linker itself will generate small amounts of code or data in the output file, such as glue code used to call routines in overlays or in dynamically linked libraries or an array of pointers to initialization routines that need to be called at program startup time. Whether or not the program uses dynamic linking, the file may also contain a symbol table for relinking or debugging that isn't used by the program itself but that may be used by other programs that deal with the output file.

Some object formats are relinkable; that is, the output file from one linker run can be used as the input to a subsequent linker run. This requires that the output file contain a symbol table like that in an input file, as well as all of the other auxiliary information present in an input file.

Nearly all object formats have provision for debugging symbols, so that when the program is run under the control of a debugger, the debugger can use those symbols to let the programmer control the program in terms of the line numbers and names used in the source program. Depending on the details of the object format, the debugging symbols may be intermixed in a single symbol table with symbols needed by the linker, or there may be one table for the linker and a separate, somewhat redundant table for the debugger.

A few linkers appear to work in one pass. They do so by first buffering some or all of the contents of the input file in memory or disk during the linking process, then reading the buffered material later. Since this is an implementation trick that doesn't fundamentally affect the two-pass nature of linking, we don't address it further here.

OBJECT CODE LIBRARIES

All linkers support object code libraries in one form or another, with most also providing support for various kinds of shared libraries. The basic principle of an object code library is simple enough (Figure 1.2). A library is little more than a set of object code files. (Indeed, on some systems you can literally catenate a group of object files together and use the result as a link library.) If any imported names remain undefined after the linker processes all of the regular input files, it runs through the library or libraries and links in any of the files in the library that export one or more undefined names.

Shared libraries complicate this task a little by moving some of the work from link time to load time. The linker identifies the shared libraries that resolve the undefined names in a linker run, but rather than linking anything into the program, the linker notes in the output file the names of the libraries in which the symbols were found, so that the shared library can be bound in when the program is loaded. See Chapters 9 and 10 for the details.

RELOCATION AND CODE MODIFICATION

The heart of a linker's or loader's actions is relocation and code modification. When a compiler or assembler generates an object file, it generates the code using the unrelocated addresses of code and data defined within the file and usually zeros for code and data defined elsewhere. As part of the linking process, the linker modifies the object code to reflect the actual addresses assigned. For example, consider the following piece of x86 code that moves the contents of variable a to variable b using the eax register:

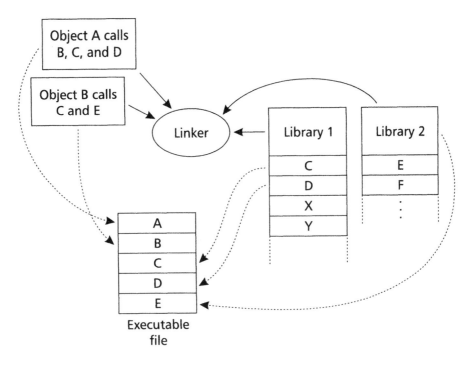

FIGURE **1.2** • Object code libraries.

```
mov a,%eax
mov %eax,b
```

If a is defined in the same file at location hex 1234 and b is imported from somewhere else, the generated object code will be

```
A1 34 12 00 00 mov a,%eax
A3 00 00 00 00 mov %eax,b
```

Each instruction contains a 1-byte operation code followed by a 4-byte address. The first instruction has a reference to 1234 (byte-reversed, because the x86 uses a right-to-left byte order) and the second instruction has a reference to zero because the location of b is unknown.

Now assume that the linker links this code so that the section in which a is located is relocated by hex 10000 bytes, and assume that b turns out to be at hex 9A12. The linker modifies the code to be

```
A1 34 12 01 00 mov a,%eax
A3 12 9A 00 00 mov %eax,b
```

That is, the linker adds 10000 to the address in the first instruction so that now the instruction refers to a's relocated address (11234) and the linker patches in the address for b. These adjustments affect instructions, but any pointers in the data part of an object file have to be adjusted as well.

On older computers with small address spaces and direct addressing, the modification process is fairly simple, because there are only one or two address formats that a linker has to handle. Modern computers, including all RISCs, require considerably more complex code modification. No single instruction contains enough bits to hold a direct address, so the compiler and linker have to use complicated addressing tricks to handle data at arbitrary addresses. In some cases, it's possible to concoct an address using two or three instructions, each of which contains part of the address, and to use bit manipulation to combine the parts into a full address. In such a case, the linker has to be prepared to modify each of the instructions appropriately, inserting some of the bits of the address into each instruction. In other cases, all of the addresses used by a routine or group of routines are placed in an array that is used as an address pool—initialization code sets one of the machine registers to point to that array, and code loads pointers out of the address pool as needed using that register as a base register. The linker may have to create the array from all of the addresses used in a program and then modify instructions that so that they refer to the appropriate address pool entry. We discuss this in Chapter 7.

Some systems require position-independent code that will work correctly regardless of where in the address space it is loaded. Linkers generally have to provide extra tricks to support that, separating out the parts of the program that can't be made position independent and arranging for the two parts to communicate. (See Chapter 8.)

1.4   COMPILER DRIVERS

In most cases, the operation of the linker is invisible to the programmer (or nearly so) because it's run automatically as part of the compilation process. Most compilation systems have a compiler driver that automatically invokes the phases of the compiler as needed. For example, if the programmer has two C language source files, the compiler driver will run a sequence of programs like this on a UNIX system:

1. C preprocessor on file A, creating preprocessed A
2. C compiler on preprocessed A, creating assembler file A
3. Assembler on assembler file A, creating object file A
4. C preprocessor on file B, creating preprocessed B
5. C compiler on preprocessed B, creating assembler file B
6. Assembler on assembler file B, creating object file B
7. Linker on object files A and B and system C library

That is, it compiles each source file to assembler and then object code and links the object code together, including any needed routines from the system C library.

Compiler drivers are often much more clever than this. Many will compare the creation dates of source and object files and only recompile source files that have changed. (The UNIX make program is the classic example.) Particularly when compiling C++ and other object-oriented languages, compiler drivers can play all sorts of tricks to work around limitations in linkers or object formats. For example, C++ templates define a potentially infinite set of related routines, so to find the finite set of template routines that a program actually uses, a compiler driver can link the program's object files together with no template code, read the error messages from the linker to see what's undefined, call the C++ compiler to generate object code for the necessary template routines, and relink. We cover some of these tricks in Chapter 11.

LINKER COMMAND LANGUAGES

Every linker has some sort of command language to control the linking process. At the very least the linker needs the list of object files and libraries to link. Generally there is a long list of possible options: whether to keep debugging symbols, whether to use shared or unshared libraries, which of several possible output formats to use. Most linkers permit some way to specify the address at which the linked code is to be bound, which comes in handy when we are using a linker to link a system kernel or other program that doesn't run under control of an operating system. In linkers that support multiple code and data segments, a linker command language can specify the order in which segments are to be linked, special treatment for certain kinds of segments, and other application-specific options.

There are four common techniques to pass commands to a linker:

1. *Command line.* Most systems have a command line or the equivalent, by which we can pass a mixture of file names and switches. This is the usual approach for UNIX and MS Windows linkers. On systems with limited-length command lines, there's usually a way to direct the linker to read commands from a file and to treat them as though they were on the command line.

2. *Intermixed with object files.* Some linkers, such as IBM mainframe linkers, accept alternating object files and linker commands in a single input file. This dates from the era of card decks, when the programmer would pile up object decks and hand-punched command cards in a card reader.

3. *Embedded in object files.* Some object formats, notably Microsoft's, permit linker commands to be embedded inside object files. This permits a compiler to pass any options needed to link an object file in the file itself. For example, the C compiler passes commands to search the standard C library.

4. *Separate configuration language.* A few linkers have a full-fledged configuration language to control linking. The GNU linker, which can handle an enormous range of object file formats, machine architectures, and address space conventions, has a complex control language that lets a programmer specify the order in which segments should be linked, rules for combining similar segments, segment addresses, and a wide range of other options. Other linkers have less complex languages to handle specific features such as programmer-defined overlays.

1.5 LINKING: A TRUE-LIFE EXAMPLE

We complete our introduction to linking with a small but real linking example. Figure 1.3 shows a pair of C language source files, m.c with a main program

Source file m.c

```
extern void a(char *);
int main(int ac, char **av)
{
  static char string[] = "Hello, world!\ n";
  a(string);
}
```

Source file a.c

```
#include <unistd.h>
#include <string.h>
void a(char *s)
{
  write(1, s, strlen(s));
}
```

FIGURE **1.3** • Source files.

that calls a routine named a and a.c that contains the routine with a call to the library routines strlen and write.

On my Pentium with GCC, the main program m.c compiles into a 165-byte object file in the classic a.out object format (Figure 1.4). That object file includes a fixed-length header, 16 bytes of text segment containing the read-only program code, and 16 bytes of data segment containing the string. Following that are two relocation entries, one that marks the pushl instruction that puts the address of the string on the stack in preparation for the call to a and one that marks the call instruction that transfers control to a. The symbol table exports the definition of _main, imports _a, and contains a couple of other symbols for the debugger. (Each global symbol is prefixed with an underscore, for reasons described in Chapter 5.) Note that the pushl instruction refers to location hex 10, the tentative address for the string, because it's in the same object file, while the call refers to location 0 since the address of _a is unknown.

The subprogram file a.c compiles into a 160-byte object file (Figure 1.5), with the header, a 28-byte text segment, and no data. Two relocation entries mark the calls to strlen and write, and the symbol table exports _a and imports _strlen and _write.

```
Sections:
 Idx Name    Size      VMA       LMA       File off  Algn
  0 .text  00000010  00000000  00000000  00000020  2**3
  1 .data  00000010  00000010  00000010  00000030  2**3
Disassembly of section .text: 00000000 <_main>:
   0:     55                     pushl %ebp
   1:     89 e5                  movl %esp,%ebp
   3:     68 10 00 00 00         pushl $0x10
              4: 32      .data
   8:     e8 f3 ff ff ff         call 0
              9: DISP32 _a
   d:     c9                     leave
   e:     c3                     ret
    ...
```

FIGURE **1.4** • Object code for m.c.

To produce an executable program, the linker combines these two object files with a standard startup initialization routine for C programs and with necessary routines from the C library, as displayed (in part) in Figure 1.6.

The linker combines corresponding segments from each input file, so there is one combined text segment, one combined data segment, and one bss segment (zero-initialized data, which the two input files didn't use). Each segment is padded out to a 4KB boundary to match the x86 page size, so the text segment is 4KB (minus a 32-byte a.out header present in the file but not logically part of the segment); the data and bss segments are also each 4KB.

The combined text segment contains the text of library startup code called start-c, then text from m.o relocated to 10a4, text from a.o relocated to 10b4, and routines linked from the C library relocated to higher addresses in the text segment. The data segment, not displayed in Figure 1.6, contains the combined data segments in the same order as the text segments. Since the code for _main has been relocated to address hex 10a4, that address is patched into the call instruction in start-c. Within the main routine, the reference to the string is relocated to hex 2024, the string's final location in the data segment, and the call is patched to 10b4, the final address of _a. Within _a, the calls to _strlen and _write are patched to the final addresses for those two routines.

```
Sections:
Idx Name      Size      VMA        LMA       File off  Algn
  0 .text    0000001c  00000000  00000000  00000020  2**2
             CONTENTS, ALLOC, LOAD, RELOC, CODE
  1 .data    00000000  0000001c  0000001c  0000003c  2**2
             CONTENTS, ALLOC, LOAD, DATA
Disassembly of section .text: 00000000 <_a>:
   0:    55                      pushl   %ebp
   1:    89 e5                   movl    %esp,%ebp
   3:    53                      pushl   %ebx
   4:    8b 5d 08                movl    0x8(%ebp),%ebx
   7:    53                      pushl   %ebx
   8:    e8 f3 ff ff ff          call    0
             9: DISP32           _strlen
   d:    50                      pushl   %eax
   e:    53                      pushl   %ebx
   f:    6a 01                   pushl   $0x1
  11:    e8 ea ff ff ff          call    0
            12: DISP32           _write
  16:    8d 65 fc                leal    -4(%ebp),%esp
  19:    5b                      popl    %ebx
  1a:    c9                      leave
  1b:    c3                      ret
```

FIGURE **1.5** • Object code for a.c.

The executable program also contains about a dozen other routines from the C library (also not shown) that are called directly or indirectly from the startup code or from _write (error routines, in the latter case). The executable contains no relocation data, because this file format is not relinkable and the operating system loads it at a known fixed address. It contains a symbol table for the benefit of a debugger, although the executable doesn't use the symbols and the symbol table can be stripped off to save space.

In this example, the code linked from the library is considerably larger than the code for the program itself. That's quite common, particularly when programs use large graphics or windowing libraries; this provides the impetus

```
Sections:
  Idx Name     Size      VMA       LMA     File off  Algn
    0 .text   00000fe0  00001020  00001020  00000020  2**3
    1 .data   00001000  00002000  00002000  00001000  2**3
    2 .bss    00000000  00003000  00003000  00000000  2**3
Disassembly of section .text: 00001020 <start-c>:
    ...
    1092:     e8 0d 00 00 00     call   10a4 <_main>
    ...
000010a4 <_main>:
    10a4: 55                     pushl  %ebp
    10a5: 89 e5                  movl   %esp,%ebp
    10a7: 68 24 20 00 00         pushl  $0x2024
    10ac: e8 03 00 00 00         call   10b4 <_a>
    10b1: c9                     leave
    10b2: c3                     ret
000010b4 <_a>:
    10b4: 55                     pushl  %ebp
    10b5: 89 e5                  movl   %esp,%ebp
    10b7: 53                     pushl  %ebx
    10b8: 8b 5d 08               movl   0x8(%ebp),%ebx
    10bb: 53                     pushl  %ebx
    10bc: e8 37 00 00 00         call   10f8 <_strlen>
    10c1: 50                     pushl  %eax
    10c2: 53                     pushl  %ebx
    10c3: 6a 01                  pushl  $0x1
    10c5: e8 a2 00 00 00         call   116c <_write>
    10ca: 8d 65 fc               leal   -4(%ebp),%esp
    10cd: 5b                     popl   %ebx
    10ce: c9                     leave
    10cf: c3                     ret
    ...
000010f8 <_strlen>:
    ...
0000116c <_write>:
    ...
```

FIGURE 1.6 • Selected parts of executable program.

for shared libraries, as discussed in Chapters 9 and 10. The linked program is 8KB, but the identical program linked using shared libraries is only 264 bytes. This is a toy example, of course, but real programs often have equally dramatic space savings.

EXERCISES

EXERCISE • 1.1

What is the advantage of separating linker and loader into separate programs? Under what circumstances would a combined linking loader be useful?

EXERCISE • 1.2

Nearly every programming system produced in the past 50 years includes a linker. Why?

EXERCISE • 1.3

In this chapter we've discussed linking and loading assembled or compiled machine code. Would a linker or loader be useful in a purely interpretive system that directly interprets source language code? How about in an interpretive system that turns the source into an intermediate representation like P-code or the Java Virtual Machine?

ARCHITECTURAL ISSUES

Linkers and loaders—along with compilers and assemblers—are exquisitely sensitive to the architectural details, both the hardware architecture and the architecture conventions required by the operating system of their target computers. In this chapter we cover enough computer architecture to understand the jobs that linkers have to do. The descriptions of the computer architectures in this chapter are deliberately incomplete and leave out the parts that don't affect the linker (such as floating point and I/O).

Two aspects of hardware architecture affect linkers: program addressing and instruction formats. One of the things that a linker does is to modify addresses and offsets both in data memory and in instructions. In both cases, the linker has to ensure that its modifications match the addressing scheme that the computer uses; when modifying instructions it must further ensure that the modifications don't result in an invalid instruction. At the end of the chapter, we also look at address space architecture, that is, what set of addresses a program has to work with.

2.1 APPLICATION BINARY INTERFACES

Every operating system presents an *application binary interface* (ABI) to programs that run under that system. The ABI consists of programming conventions that applications have to follow to run under the operating system. ABIs invariably include a set of system calls and the technique to invoke the system calls, as well as rules about what memory addresses a program can use and often rules about usage of machine registers. From the point of view of an application, the ABI is as much a part of the system architecture as the underlying hardware architecture, because a program will fail equally badly if it violates the constraints of either.

   In many cases, the linker has to do a significant part of the work involved in complying with the ABI. For example, if the ABI requires that each program must contain a table of all of the addresses of static data used by routines in the program, the linker often creates that table, by collecting address information from all of the modules linked into the program. The aspect of the ABI that most often affects the linker is the definition of a standard procedure call, a topic we return to later in this chapter.

2.2 MEMORY ADDRESSES

Every computer includes a main memory. The main memory is an array of storage locations, with each location having a numeric address. The addresses start at zero and run up to some large number determined by the number of bits in an address.

BYTE ORDER AND ALIGNMENT

Each storage location consists of a fixed number of bits. Over the past 50 years computers have been designed with storage locations consisting of as many as 64 bits and as few as 1 bit, but now nearly every computer in production addresses 8-bit bytes. Since many of the data that computers handle, notably program addresses, are bigger than 8 bits, the computers can also handle 16-,

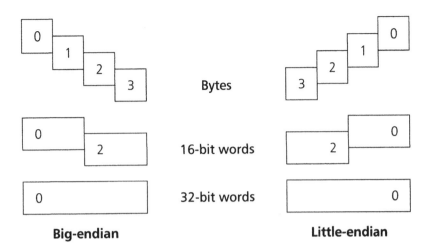

FIGURE **2.1** • Byte-addressable memory.

32-, and often 64- or 128-bit data as well, with multiple adjacent bytes grouped together. On some computers, notably those from IBM and Motorola, the first (numerically lowest-addressed) byte in multibyte data is the most significant byte, while others, notably DEC and Intel, it's the least significant byte (Figure 2.1). In a nod to *Gulliver's Travels*, the IBM/Motorola byte order scheme is known as "big-endian" while the DEC/Intel scheme is called "little-endian."

The relative merits of the two schemes have provoked vehement arguments over the years. In practice the major issue determining the choice of byte order is compatibility with older systems, since it is considerably easier to port programs and data between two machines with the same byte order than between machines with different byte orders. Many recent chip designs can support either byte order, with the choice made either by the way the chip is wired up, by programming at system boot time, or in a few cases it is even selected per application. (On these switch-hitting chips, the byte order of data handled by load and store instructions changes, but the byte order of constants encoded in instructions doesn't. This is the sort of detail that keeps the life of the linker writer interesting.)

Multibyte data must usually be aligned on a natural boundary. That is, 4-byte data should be aligned on a 4-byte boundary, 2-byte on 2-byte, and so forth. Another way to think of it is that the address of any *N*-byte datum should have at least $\log_2 N$ low zero bits. On some systems (Intel x86, DEC VAX, IBM 370/390), misaligned data references work at the cost of reduced performance, while on others (most RISC chips) misaligned data cause a program fault. Even on systems where misaligned data don't cause a fault, the performance loss is usually great enough that it's worth the effort to maintain alignment where possible.

Many processors also have alignment requirements for program instructions. Most RISC chips require that instructions be aligned on 4-byte boundaries.

Each architecture also defines *registers*, a small set of fixed-length high-speed memory locations to which program instructions can refer directly. The number of registers varies from one architecture to another, from as few as eight in the Intel architecture to 32 in some RISC designs. Registers are almost invariably the same size as a program address; that is, on a system with 32-bit addresses, the registers are 32 bits, and on a system with 64-bit addresses, the registers are 64 bits as well.

2.3   ADDRESS FORMATION

As a computer program executes, it loads and stores data to and from memory, as determined by instructions in the program. The instructions are themselves stored in memory, usually a different part of memory from the program's data. Instructions are logically executed in the sequence they are stored, except that *jump* instructions specify a new place in the program to start executing instructions. (Some architectures use the term *branch* for some or all jumps, but we call them all jumps here.) Each instruction that references data memory and each jump specifies the address or addresses of the data to load or store or of the instruction to jump to. All computers have a variety of instruction formats and address formation rules that linkers have to be able to handle as they relocate addresses in instructions.

Although computer designers have come up with innumerable different and complex addressing schemes over the years, most computers currently in production have a relatively simple addressing scheme. (Designers found that it's hard to build a fast version of a complicated architecture, and compilers rarely make good use of complicated addressing features.) We'll use the following three architectures as examples:

- The IBM 360/370/390 (which we'll refer to as the 370). Although this is one of the oldest architectures still in use, its relatively clean design has worn well despite 35 years of added features and has been implemented in chips comparable in performance to modern RISCs.

- SPARC V8 and V9. This is a popular RISC architecture, with fairly simple addressing. V8 uses 32-bit registers and addresses; V9 adds 64-bit registers and addresses. The SPARC design is similar to other RISC architectures such as MIPS and Alpha.

- The Intel 386/486/Pentium (henceforth referred to as the x86). This is one of the most arcane and irregular architectures still in use, but it is undeniably the most popular.

2.4 INSTRUCTION FORMATS

Each architecture has several different instruction formats. We'll only address the format details relative to program and data addressing, because those are the main details that affect the linker. The 370 uses the same format for data references and jumps, while SPARC has different formats and the x86 has some common formats and some different.

Each instruction consists of an opcode, which determines what the instruction does, and operands. An operand may be encoded in the instruction itself (an *immediate* operand) or located in memory. The address of each operand in memory has to be calculated somehow. Sometimes the address is contained in the instruction (*direct addressing*). More often the address is found in one of the registers (*register indirect*) or calculated by adding a constant in the instruction to the contents of a register. If the value in the register is the address of a storage area, and the constant in the instruction is the offset of the desired datum in the storage area, this scheme is known as *based addressing*. If the roles are swapped and the register contains the offset, the scheme is known as *indexed addressing*. The distinction between based and indexed addressing isn't well defined, and many architectures combine them (e.g., the 370 has an addressing mode that adds together two registers and a constant in the instruction, arbitrarily calling one of the registers the base register and the other the index register, although the two are treated the same). Other more complicated address calculation schemes are still in use, but for the most part the linker doesn't have to worry about them because they don't contain any fields the linker has to adjust.

Some architectures use fixed-length instructions, and some use variable-length instructions. All SPARC instructions are 4 bytes long, aligned on 4-byte boundaries. IBM 370 instructions can be 2, 4, or 6 bytes long, with the first 2 bits of the first byte determining the length and format of the instruction. Intel x86 instructions can be anywhere from 1 byte to 14 bytes long. The encoding is quite complex, partly because the x86 was originally designed for limited-memory environments with a dense instruction encoding and partly because the new instructions added in the 286, 386, and later chips had to be shoe-horned into unused bit patterns in the existing instruction set. Fortunately, from the point of view of a linker writer, the address and offset fields that a linker has to adjust all occur on byte boundaries, so the linker generally need not be concerned with the instruction encoding.

2.5 PROCEDURE CALLS AND ADDRESSABILITY

In the earliest computers, memories were small, and each instruction contained an address field large enough to contain the address of any memory location in the computer, a scheme now called direct addressing. By the early 1960s, addressable memory was getting large enough that an instruction set with a full address in each instruction would have large instructions that took up too much of still-precious memory. To solve this problem, computer architects abandoned direct addressing in some or all of the memory reference instructions, using index and base registers to provide most or all of the bits used in addressing. This allowed instructions to be shorter, at the cost of more complicated programming.

On architectures without direct addressing—such as the IBM 370 and SPARC—programs have a bootstrapping problem for data addressing. A routine uses base values in registers to calculate data addresses, but the standard way to get a base value into a register is to load it from a memory location, which is in turn addressed from another base value in a register. The bootstrap problem is to get the first base value into a register at the beginning of the program and subsequently to ensure that each routine has the base values it needs to address the data it uses.

PROCEDURE CALLS

Every ABI defines a standard procedure call sequence, using a combination of hardware-defined call instructions and conventions about register and memory use. A hardware call instruction saves the return address (the address of the instruction after the call) and jumps to the procedure. On architectures with a hardware stack, such as the x86, the return address is pushed on the stack, while on other architectures it's saved in a register, with software having the responsibility to save the register in memory if necessary. Architectures with a stack generally have a hardware return instruction that pops the return address from the stack and jumps to that address, while other architectures use a "branch to address in register" instruction to return.

Within a procedure, data addressing falls into four categories:

1. The caller can pass *arguments* to the procedure.

2. *Local variables* are allocated within the procedure and freed before the procedure returns.

3. *Local static data* is stored in a fixed location in memory and is private to the procedure.

4. *Global static data* is stored in a fixed location in memory and can be referenced from many different procedures.

The piece of stack memory allocated for a single procedure call is known as a *stack frame*. Figure 2.2 shows a typical stack frame. Arguments and local variables are usually allocated on the stack. One of the registers serves as a stack pointer, which can be used as a base register. In a common variant of this scheme, used with SPARC and x86, a separate frame pointer or base pointer register is loaded from the stack pointer at the time a procedure starts. This makes it possible to push variable-sized objects on the stack, changing the value in the stack pointer register to a hard-to-predict value, but still lets the procedure address arguments and locals at fixed offsets from the frame pointer (which doesn't change during a procedure's execution). Assuming that the stack grows from higher to lower addresses and that the frame pointer points to the address in memory where the return address is stored, arguments are at small positive offsets from the frame pointer, and local variables are at negative offsets. The operating system usually sets the initial stack

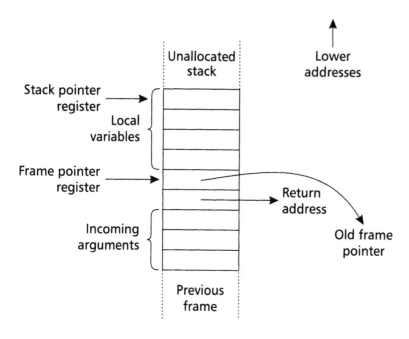

FIGURE **2.2** • Stack frame memory layout.

pointer register before a program starts, so the program need only update the register when it pushes and pops data.

For local and global static data, a compiler can generate a table of pointers to all of the static objects that a routine references. If one of the registers contains a pointer to this table, the routine can address any desired static object by loading the pointer to the object from the table using the table pointer register into another register, then using that second register as the base register to address the object. The trick, then, is to get the address of the table into the first register. On SPARC, the routine can load the table address into the register using a sequence of instructions with immediate operands, and on the 370 the routine can use a variant of a subroutine call instruction to load the program counter (the register that keeps the address of the current instruction) into a base register, although for reasons we discuss later, those techniques cause problems in library code. A better solution is to foist off the job of loading the table pointer on the routine's caller, because the caller will have its own table

```
... push arguments on the stack ...
store Rt -> xxx(Rf) ; save caller's table pointer in caller's stack frame
load Rx <- MMM(Rt)  ; load address of called routine into temp register
load Rt <- NNN(Rt)  ; load called routine's table pointer
call (Rx) ; call routine at address in Rx
load Rt <- xxx(Rf)  ; restore caller's table pointer
```

FIGURE **2.3** • Idealized calling sequence.

pointer already loaded and can get the address of the called routine's table from its own table.

Figure 2.3 shows a typical routine calling sequence. Rf is the frame pointer, Rt is the table pointer, and Rx is a temporary scratch register. The caller saves its own table pointer in its own stack frame, then loads both the address of the called routine and the called routine's pointer table into registers, then makes the call. The called routine can then find all of its necessary data using the table pointer in Rt, including addresses and table pointers for any routines that it in turn calls.

Several optimizations are often possible. In many cases, all of the routines in a module share a single pointer table, in which case intramodule calls needn't change the table pointer. The SPARC convention is that an entire library shares a single table—created by the linker—so the table pointer register can remain unchanged in intramodule calls. Calls within the same module can usually be made using a version of the call instruction with the offset to the called routine encoded in the instruction, which avoids the need to load the address of the routine into a register. With both of these optimizations, the calling sequence to a routine in the same module reduces to a single call instruction.

To return to the address bootstrap question, how does this chain of table pointers get started? If each routine gets its table pointer loaded by the preceding routine, where does the initial routine get its pointer? The answer varies, but it always involves special-case code. The main routine's table may be stored at a fixed address, or the initial pointer value may be tagged in the executable file so the operating system can load it before the program starts. No matter what the technique is, it invariably needs some help from the linker.

2.6   DATA AND INSTRUCTION REFERENCES

We now look more concretely at the way that programs in our three architectures address data values.

IBM 370

The 1960s-vintage System/360 started with a very straightforward data addressing scheme, which has become somewhat more complicated over the years as the 360 evolved into the 370 and 390. Every instruction that references data memory calculates the address by adding a 12-bit unsigned offset in the instruction to a base register and maybe to an index register. There are 16 general registers, each 32 bits, numbered from 0 to 15, all but one of which can be used as index registers. If register 0 is specified in an address calculation, the value 0 is used rather than the register contents. (Register 0 exists for arithmetic, but not for addressing.) In instructions that take the target address of a jump from a register, register 0 means don't jump.

Figure 2.4 shows the major instruction formats. An RX instruction contains a register operand and a single memory operand, whose address is calculated by adding the offset in the instruction to a base register and an index register. More often than not, the index register is zero so the address is just base plus offset. In the RS, SI, and SS formats, the 12-bit offset is added to a base register. An RS instruction has one memory operand, with one or two other operands being in registers. An SI instruction has one memory operand, the other operand being an immediate 8-bit value in the instruction. An SS instruction has two memory operands, for storage-to-storage operations. The RR format has two register operands and no memory operands at all, although some RR instructions interpret one or both of the registers as pointers to memory. The 370 and 390 added some minor variations on these formats, but none with different data addressing formats.

Instructions can directly address the lowest 4096 locations in memory by specifying base register zero. This ability is essential in low-level system programming but is never used in application programs, all of which use base register addressing.

Note that in all three instruction formats, the 12-bit address offset is always stored as the low 12 bits of a 16-bit aligned halfword. This makes it

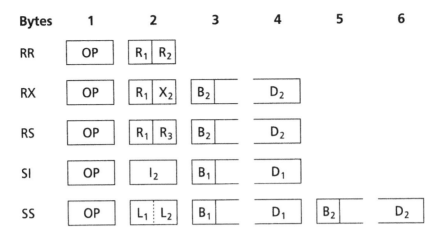

FIGURE **2.4** • IBM 370 instruction formats.

possible to specify fixups to address offsets in object files without any reference to instruction formats, because the offset format is always the same.

The original 360 had 24-bit addressing, with an address in memory or a register being stored in the low 24 bits of a 32-bit word and the high 8 bits disregarded. The 370 extended addressing to 31 bits. Unfortunately, many programs—including OS/360, the most popular operating system—stored flags or other data in the high byte of 32-bit address words in memory, so it wasn't possible to extend the addressing to 32 bits in the obvious way and still support existing object code. Instead, the system has 24-bit and 31-bit modes, and at any moment a CPU interprets 24-bit addresses or 31-bit addresses. A convention enforced by a combination of hardware and software states that an address word with the high bit set contains a 31-bit address in the rest of the word, while one with the high bit clear contains a 24-bit address. As a result, a linker has to be able to handle both 24-bit and 31-bit addresses because programs can and do switch modes depending on how long ago a particular routine was written. For historical reasons, 370 linkers also handle 16-bit addresses, because early small models in the 360 line often had 64KB or less of main memory and programs used load and store halfword instructions to manipulate address values.

Later models of the 370 and 390 added segmented address spaces somewhat like those of the x86 series. These features let the operating system define multiple 31-bit address spaces that a program can address, with extremely complex rules defining access controls and address space switching. As far as I can tell, there is no compiler or linker support for these features, which are primarily used by high-performance database systems, so we won't address them further.

Instruction addressing on the 370 is also relatively straightforward. In the original 360, the jumps (always referred to as branch instructions) are all RR or RX format. In RR jumps, the second register operand contains the jump target, with register 0 meaning don't jump. In RX jumps, the memory operand is the jump target. The procedure call is branch and link (supplanted by the later branch and save for 31-bit addressing), which stores the return address in a specified register and then jumps to the address in the second register in the RR form or to the second operand address in the RX form.

For jumping around within a routine, the routine has to establish address-ability, that is, a base register that points to (or at least close to) the beginning of the routine that RX instructions can use. By convention, register 15 contains the address of the entry point to a routine and can be used as a base register. Alternatively, an RR branch and link or branch and save with a second register of 0 stores the address of the subsequent instruction in the first oper-and register but doesn't jump; this can be used to set up a base register if the prior register contents are unknown. Since RX instructions have a 12-bit offset field, a single base register covers a 4KB piece of code. If a routine is bigger than that, it has to use multiple base registers to cover all of the routine's code.

The 390 added relative forms of most of the jumps. In these new forms, the instruction contains a signed 16-bit offset that is logically shifted left 1 bit (because instructions are aligned on even bytes) and that is added to the address of the instruction to get the address of the jump target. These new for-mats use no register to compute the address and permit jumps within ± 64KB; this is enough for intraroutine jumps in all but the largest routines.

SPARC

SPARC has four major instruction formats and 31 minor instruction formats (Figure 2.5), four jump formats, and two data addressing modes.

SPARC comes close to living up to its billing as a reduced instruction set processor, although as the architecture has evolved through several versions, the original simple design has grown somewhat more complex. SPARC versions through V8 are 32-bit architectures. SPARC V9 expands the architecture to 64 bits.

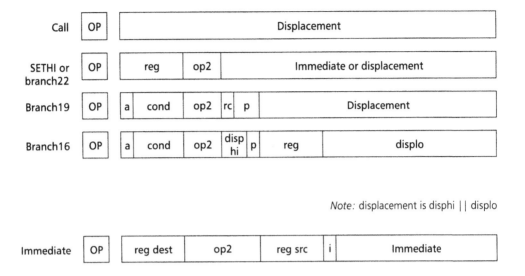

FIGURE **2.5** • SPARC.

SPARC V8

In SPARC V8, there are 31 general-purpose registers, each 32 bits, numbered from 1 to 31. Register 0 is a pseudo-register that always contains the value zero.

An unusual *register window* scheme attempts to minimize the amount of register saving and restoring at procedure calls and returns. The windows have little effect on linkers, so we won't discuss them further. (Register windows originated in the Berkeley RISC design from which SPARC is influenced.)

Data references use one of two addressing modes. One mode computes the address by adding the values in two registers together. (One of the registers can be register 0 if the other register already contains the desired address.) The other mode adds a 13-bit signed offset in the instruction to a base register.

SPARC assemblers and linkers support a pseudo-direct addressing scheme using a two-instruction sequence. The two instructions are SETHI, which loads its 22-bit immediate value into the high 22 bits of a register and zeros the lower 10 bits, followed by OR-immediate, which ORs its 13-bit immediate value into the low part of the register. The assembler and linker arrange to put the high and low parts of the desired 32-bit address into the two instructions.

The procedure call instruction and most conditional jump instructions (referred to as branches in SPARC literature) use relative addressing with various-size branch offsets ranging from 16 to 30 bits. Whatever the offset size, the jump shifts the offset 2 bits left (because all instructions have to be at 4-byte word addresses), sign-extends the result to 32 or 64 bits, and adds that value to the address of the jump or call instruction to get the target address. The call instruction uses a 30-bit offset, which means it can reach any address in a 32-bit V8 address space. Calls store the return address in register 15. Various kinds of jumps use a 16-, 19-, or 22-bit offset, which is large enough to jump anywhere in any plausibly sized routine. The 16-bit format breaks the offset into a 2-bit high part and a 14-bit low part stored in different parts of the instruction word, but that doesn't cause any great trouble for the linker.

SPARC also has a jump and link instruction that computes the target address the same way that data reference instructions do, by adding together either two source registers or a source register and a constant offset. It also can store the return address in a target register.

Procedure calls use call or jump and link, which store the return address in register 15 and jump to the target address. Procedure return uses JMP 8[r15] to return two instructions after the call. (SPARC calls and jumps are delayed and optionally execute the instruction following the jump or call before jumping.)

SPARC V9

SPARC V9 expands all of the registers to 64 bits, using the low 32 bits of each register for old 32-bit programs. All existing instructions continue to work as before, except that register operands are now 64 rather than 32 bits. New load and store instructions handle 64-bit data, and new branch instructions can test either the 32- or 64-bit result of a previous instruction. SPARC V9 adds no new instructions for synthesizing full 64-bit addresses, nor is there a new call instruction. Full addresses can be synthesized by means of lengthy sequences that create the two 32-bit halves of the address in separate registers using SETHI and OR, shift the high-half 32 bits to the left, and OR the two parts together. In practice, 64-bit addresses are loaded from a pointer table, and intermodule calls load the address of the target routine from the table into a register and then use jump and link to make the call.

INTEL X86

The Intel x86 architecture is by far the most complex of the three that we discuss. It features an asymmetrical instruction set and segmented addresses.

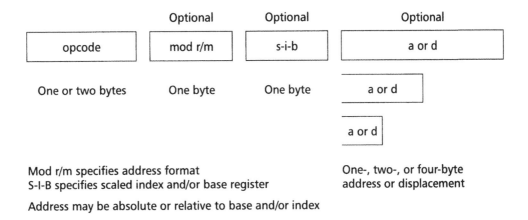

FIGURE **2.6** • Generalized x86 instruction format.

There are six 32-bit general-purpose registers named EAX, EBX, ECX, EDX, ESI, and EDI; two 32-bit registers used primarily for addressing, EBP and ESP; and six specialized 16-bit segment registers, CS, DS, ES, FS, GS, and SS. The low half of each of the 32-bit registers can be used as 16-bit registers, called AX, BX, CX, DX, SI, DI, BP, and SP, respectively. The low and high bytes of each of the AX through DX registers are 8-bit registers called AL, AH, BL, BH, CL, CH, DL, and DH. On the 8086, 186, and 286 chips, many instructions required their operands to be in specific registers, but on the 386 and later chips, most but not all of the functions that required specific registers have been generalized to use any register. The ESP is the hardware stack pointer and always contains the address of the current stack. The EBP pointer is usually used as a frame register that points to the base of the current stack frame. (The instruction set encourages but doesn't require this.)

At any moment an x86 is running in one of three modes: real mode, which emulates the original 16-bit 8086; 16-bit protected mode, which was added on the 286; or 32-bit protected mode, which was added on the 386. Here we primarily discuss 32-bit protected mode. Protected mode involves the x86's notorious segmentation, but we'll discuss that subject later (Section 2.8).

Most instructions that address data in memory use a common instruction format (Figure 2.6). (The ones that don't use specific architecture-defined registers; for example, the push and pop instructions always use ESP to address the stack.) Addresses are calculated by adding together any or all of a signed 1-, 2-, or 4-byte displacement value in the instruction; a base register, which can be any of the 32-bit registers; and an optional index register, which can be any of the 32-bit registers except ESP. The index can be logically shifted left 0, 1, 2, or 3 bits to make it easier to index arrays of values.

Although it's possible for a single instruction to include all of the displacement, base, and index, most just use a 32-bit displacement, which provides direct addressing, or a base with a 1- or 2-byte displacement, which provides stack addressing and pointer dereferencing. From a linker's point of view, direct addressing permits an instruction or data address to be embedded anywhere in the program on any byte boundary.

Conditional and unconditional jumps and subroutine calls all use relative addressing. Any jump or call instruction can have a 1-, 2-, or 4-byte offset, which is added to the address of the instruction following the instruction to get the target address. This permits jumps and calls anywhere in the current 32-bit address space. Unconditional jumps and calls also can compute the target address using the full data address calculation described above; most often this is used to jump or call to an address stored in a register. Call instructions push the return address on the stack pointed to by ESP. Unconditional jumps and calls can also have a full 6-byte segment/offset address in the instruction or can calculate the address at which the segment/offset target address is stored. These call instructions push both the return address and the caller's segment number, to permit intersegment calls and returns.

2.7 PAGING AND VIRTUAL MEMORY

On most modern computers, each program can potentially address a vast amount of memory (4GB on a typical 32-bit machine). Few computers actually have that much memory, and even the ones that do need to share it among multiple programs. Paging hardware divides a program's address space into fixed-size *pages*, typically 2KB or 4KB in size, and divides the physical memory of the computer into *page frames* of the same size. The hardware contains *page tables* with an entry for each page in the address space, as shown in Figure 2.7.

A page table entry can contain the real memory page frame for the page, or it can contain flag bits to mark the page as not present. When an application program attempts to use a page that is not present, hardware generates a *page fault*, which is handled by the operating system. The operating system can load a copy of the contents page from disk into a free page frame, then let the

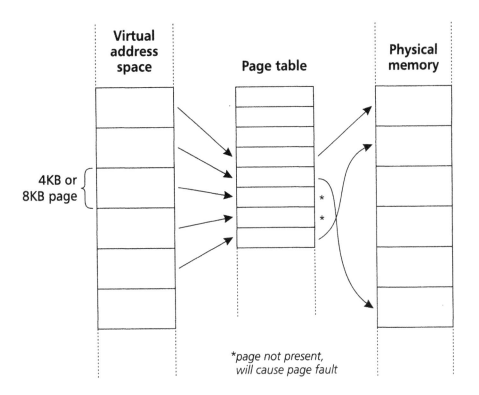

FIGURE 2.7 • Page mapping.

application continue. By moving pages back and forth between main memory and disk as needed, the operating system can provide *virtual memory*, which appears to the application to be far larger than the real memory in use.

Virtual memory comes at a cost, however. Individual instructions execute in a fraction of a microsecond, but a page fault and consequent page in or page out (transfer from disk to main memory or vice versa) takes several milliseconds because it requires a disk transfer.

The more page faults a program generates, the slower it runs, with the worst case being thrashing—all page faults with no useful work getting done. The fewer pages a program needs, the fewer page faults it will generate. If the linker can pack related routines into a single page or a small group of pages, paging performance improves.

If pages can be marked as read-only, performance also improves. Read-only pages don't need to be paged out because they can be reloaded from wherever they came from originally. If identical pages logically appear in multiple address spaces (which often happens when multiple copies of the same program are running), a single physical page suffices for all of the address spaces.

An x86 with 32-bit addressing and 4KB pages would need a page table with 2^{20} entries to map an entire address space. Because each page table entry is usually 4 bytes, this would make the page tables an impractical 4MB long. As a result, paged architectures page the page tables, with upper-level page tables that point to lower-level page tables that point to the actual page frames corresponding to virtual addresses. On the 370, each entry in the upper-level page table (called the segment table) maps 1MB of address space, so the segment table in 31-bit address mode may contain up to 2048 entries. Each entry in the segment table may be empty (in which case the entire segment is not present) or may point to a lower-level page table that maps the pages in that segment. Each lower-level page table has up to 256 entries, one for each 4KB chunk of address space in the segment. The x86 divides up its page tables similarly, although the boundaries are different. Each upper-level page table (called a page directory) maps 4MB of address space, so the upper-level page table contains 1024 entries. Each lower-level page table also contains 1024 entries, to map the 1024 4KB pages in the 4MB of address space corresponding to that page table. The SPARC architecture defines the page size as 4KB and has three levels of page tables rather than two.

The two- or three-level nature of page tables is invisible to applications with one important exception: The operating system can change the mapping for a large chunk of the address space (1MB on the 370, 4MB on the x86, 256KB or 16MB on SPARC) by changing a single entry in an upper-level page table, so for efficiency reasons the address space is often managed in chunks of that size by replacing individual second-level page table entries rather than by reloading the whole page table on process switches.

THE PROGRAM ADDRESS SPACE

Every application program runs in an address space defined by a combination of the computer's hardware and operating system. The linker or loader needs to create a runnable program that matches that address space.

The simplest kind of address space was that provided by PDP-11 versions of UNIX. The address space was 64KB, starting at location zero. The read-only code of the program was loaded at location zero, with the read/write data following the code. The PDP-11 had 8KB pages, so the data started on the 8KB boundary after the code. The stack grew downward, starting at 64KB – 1, and as the stack and data grew, the respective areas were enlarged; if they met, the program ran out of space. UNIX on the VAX—the follow-on to the PDP-11—used a similar scheme. The first 2 bytes of every VAX UNIX program were zero (a register save mask indicating not to save anything). As a result, a null all-zero pointer was always valid, and if a C program used a null value as a string pointer, the zero byte at location zero was treated as a null string. As a result, a generation of UNIX programs in the 1980s contained hard-to-find bugs involving null pointers, and for many years, UNIX ports to other architectures provided a zero byte at location zero because it was easier than finding and fixing all the null pointer bugs.

UNIX systems put each application program in a separate address space, and they put the operating system in an address space logically separate from the applications. Other systems put multiple programs in the same address space, making the linker's and particularly the loader's job more complex because a program's actual load address isn't known until the program is about to be run.

DOS on x86 systems uses no hardware protection, so the system and running applications share the same address space. When the system runs a program, it finds the largest piece of free memory, which may be anywhere in the address space, loads the program into it, and starts it. IBM mainframe operating systems do roughly the same thing, loading a program into an available chunk of address space. In both cases, either the program loader or in some cases the program itself has to adjust to the location where the program is loaded.

MS Windows has an unusual loading scheme. Each program is linked to load at a standard starting address, but the executable program file contains relocation information. When MS Windows loads the program, it places the program at that starting address if possible, but it may load it somewhere else if the preferred address isn't available.

MAPPED FILES

Virtual memory systems move data back and forth between real memory and disk, paging data to disk when it doesn't fit in real memory. Originally, paging all went to anonymous disk space separate from the named files in the file system. Soon after the invention of paging, however, designers noticed that it was

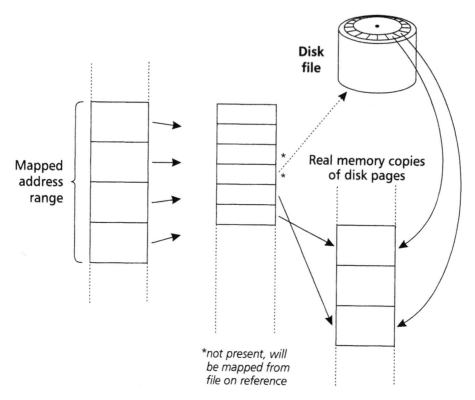

**Disk
file**

Mapped
address
range

Real memory copies
of disk pages

*not present, will
be mapped from
file on reference

FIGURE **2.8** • Mapping a file.

possible to unify the paging system and the file system by using the paging
system to read and write named disk files. When a program maps a file to a
part of the program's address space, the operating system marks all of the
pages in that part of the address space as not present and uses the file as the
paging disk for that part of the address space (Figure 2.8). The program can
read the file merely by referencing that part of the address space, at which
point the paging system loads the necessary pages from disk.

There are three different approaches to handling writes to mapped files.
The simplest is to map a file as read-only (RO), so that any attempts to store
into the mapped region fail (usually causing the program to abort). The second is to map the file as read/write (RW), so that changes to the memory copy
of the file are paged back to the disk by the time the file is unmapped. The third
is to map the file as copy-on-write (COW, not the most felicitous acronym).
This maps each page as read-only until the program attempts to store into the

page. At that time, the operating system makes a copy of the page, which is then treated as a private page that is not mapped from a file. From the program's point of view, mapping a file as COW is very similar to allocating a fresh area of anonymous memory and reading the file's contents into that area, because changes the program makes are visible to that program but not to any other program that might have mapped the same file.

SHARED LIBRARIES AND PROGRAMS

In nearly every system that handles multiple programs simultaneously, each program has a separate set of page tables, giving each program a logically separate address space. This makes a system considerably more robust, because buggy or malicious programs can't damage or spy on other programs, but it could potentially cause performance problems. If a single program or single program library is in use in more than one address space, the system can save a great deal of memory if all of the address spaces share a single physical copy of the program or library. This is relatively straightforward for the operating system to implement—just map the executable file into each program's address space. Unrelocated code and read-only data are mapped RO; writable data are mapped COW. The operating system can use the same physical page frames for RO and unwritten COW data in all the processes that map the file. (If the code has to be relocated at load time, the relocation process changes the code pages and they have to be treated as COW, not RO.)

Considerable linker support is needed to make this sharing work. In the executable program, the linker needs to group all of the executable code into one part of the file that can be mapped RO and the data into another part that can be mapped COW. Each section has to start on a page boundary, both logically in the address space and physically in the file. When several different programs use a shared library, the linker needs to mark each program so that when each starts, the library is mapped into the program's address space.

POSITION-INDEPENDENT CODE

When a program is in use in several different address spaces, the operating system can usually load the program at the same place in each of the address spaces in which it appears. This makes the linker's job much easier, because it

can bind all of the addresses in the program to fixed locations and no relocation needs to be done at the time the program is loaded.

Shared libraries complicate this situation considerably. In some simple
shared-library designs, each library is assigned a globally unique memory address either at system boot time or at the time the libraries are created. This puts
each library at a fixed address, but at the cost of creating a serious bottleneck
to shared-library administration, because the global list of library memory
addresses has to be maintained by the system manager. Furthermore, if a new
version of a library appears that is larger than the previous version and doesn't
fit into the address space assigned, then the entire set of shared libraries and,
potentially, all of the programs that reference them may need to be relinked.

The alternative is to permit different programs to map a library to different places in the address space. This eases library administration, but the
compiler, the linker, and the program loader need to cooperate so that the
library will work regardless of where in the address space it appears.

One simple approach is to include standard relocation information with
the library; when the library is mapped into each address space, the loader
can fix up any relocatable addresses in the program to reflect the loaded
addresses. Unfortunately, the process of fixing up the addresses involves writing into the library's code and data, which means that the pages will no longer
be shared if they're mapped as COW or the program will crash if the pages are
mapped as RO.

To avoid this problem, shared libraries use *position-independent code*
(PIC), code that will work regardless of where in memory it is loaded. All the
code in shared libraries is usually PIC, so the code can be mapped as read-
only. Data pages still usually contain pointers that need relocation, but
because data pages are mapped COW anyway, there's little sharing lost.

For the most part, PIC is pretty easy to create. All three of the architectures
we have discussed in this chapter use relative jumps, so that jump instructions within the routines need no relocation. References to local data on the
stack use based addressing relative to a base register, which doesn't need any
relocation either. The only challenges are calls to routines not in the shared
library and references to global data. Direct data addressing and the SPARC
high/low register loading trick won't work, because they both require run-
time relocation. Fortunately, there are a variety of tricks we can use to let PIC
code handle interlibrary calls and global data. We discuss them when we cover
shared libraries in detail in Chapters 9 and 10.

2.8 INTEL 386 SEGMENTATION

Next we turn to the notorious Intel architecture segmentation system. The x86 series is the only segmented architecture still in common use—other than some legacy ex-Burroughs Unisys mainframes—but because it's so popular, we have to deal with it. Although 32-bit operating systems don't make any significant use of segmentation, older systems and the very popular 16-bit embedded versions of the x86 series use it extensively.

The original 8086 was intended as a follow-on to Intel's quite popular 8-bit 8080 and 8085 microprocessors. The 8080 had a 16-bit address space, and the 8086 designers were torn between keeping the 16-bit address space—which made translation of 8085 programs easier and permitted more compact code—and providing a larger address space to give headroom for future applications in larger programs. They compromised by providing multiple 16-bit address spaces. Each 16-bit address space was known as a *segment.*

A running x86 program has four active segments defined by the four segment registers. The CS register defines the code segment, from which instructions are fetched. The DS register defines the data segment, from which most data are loaded and stored. The SS register defines the stack segment; it is used for the operands of push and pop instructions, the program address values pushed and popped by call and return instructions, and any data reference made using the EBP or ESP as a base register. The ES register defines the extra segment, used by a few string manipulation instructions. The 386 and later chips define two more segment registers, FS and GS. Any data reference can be directed into a specific segment by using a segment override. For example, the instruction MOV EAX,CS:TEMP fetches a data value from the location TEMP in the code segment rather than the data segment. The FS and GS segments are only used by means of segment overrides.

The segment values need not all be different. Most programs set the DS and SS values the same, so that pointers to stack variables and global variables can be used interchangeably. Some small programs set all four segment registers the same, providing a single address space known as the *tiny model.*

On the 8086 and 186, the architecture defined a fixed mapping from segment numbers to memory addresses by shifting the segment number 4 bits to the left. For example, segment number 0x123 would start at memory location 0x1230. This simple addressing is known as *real mode.* Programmers often refer informally to *paragraphs*, 16-byte units of memory that a segment number can address.

The 286 added a protected mode, in which the operating system can map segments to arbitrary places in real memory and can mark segments as not present, providing segment-based virtual memory. Each segment can be marked executable, readable, or read/write, providing segment-level protection. The 386 extended protected mode to 32-bit addressing, so that each segment can be up to 4GB in size rather than only 64KB.

With 16-bit addressing, all but the smallest programs have to handle segmented addresses. Changing the contents of a segment register is quite slow (9 clock cycles on a 486 compared to 1 clock cycle to change the contents of a general-purpose register). As a result, programs and programmers go to great lengths to pack code and data into as few segments as possible to avoid having to change the contents of the segment registers. Linkers aid this process by providing "groups" that can collect related code or data into a single segment at link time. Code and data pointers can be either near (with an offset value but no segment number) or far (with both segment number and offset value).

Compilers can generate code for various memory models that determine whether code and data addresses are near or far by default. *Small model* code makes all pointers near and has one code and one data segment. *Medium model* code has multiple code segments (one per program source file) using far calls, but a single default data segment. *Large model* code has multiple code and data segments and all pointers are far by default. Writing efficient segmented code is very tricky and has been well documented elsewhere.

Segmented addressing places significant demands on the linker. Every address in a program has both a segment and an offset. Object files consist of multiple blocks of code that the linker packs into segments. Executable programs to be run in real mode have to mark all of the segment numbers that occur in the program so they can be relocated to the actual segments where the program is loaded. In addition, executable programs to be run in protected mode have to mark what data is to be loaded into what segment and the protection level (code, read-only data, read/write data) for each segment.

Although the 386 supports all of the 16-bit segmentation features of the 286, as well as 32-bit versions of all of the segmentation features, most 32-bit programs don't use segmentation at all. Paging, also added in the 386, provides most of the practical benefits of segmentation without the performance cost and the extra complications of writing segment manipulation code. Most

386 operating systems run applications in the tiny model, more often known as the *flat model* (a segment on a 386 is no longer tiny). They create a single code segment and a single data segment, each 4GB long, mapping them both to the full 32-bit paged address space. Even though the program is only using a single segment, that segment can be the full size of the address space.

The 386 makes it possible to use both 16-bit and 32-bit segments in the same program; a few operating systems, notably Windows 95 and 98, take advantage of that ability. Windows 95 and 98 run a lot of legacy Windows 3.1 code in 16-bit segments in a shared address space, while each new 32-bit program runs in its own flat model address space, with the 16-bit programs' address space mapped in to permit calls back and forth.

2.9 EMBEDDED ARCHITECTURES

Linking for embedded systems poses a variety of problems that rarely occur in other environments. Embedded chips have limited amounts of memory and limited performance, but because an embedded program may be built into chips in thousands or millions of devices, there are great incentives to make programs run as fast as possible using as little memory as possible. Some embedded systems use low-cost versions of general-purpose chips, such as the Intel 80186, while others use specialized processors such as the Motorola 56000 series of digital signal processors (DSPs).

ADDRESS SPACE QUIRKS

Embedded systems have small address spaces with quirky layouts. A 64KB address space can contain combinations of fast on-chip ROM and RAM, slow off-chip ROM and RAM, on-chip peripherals, and off-chip peripherals. There may be several noncontiguous areas of ROM or RAM. The 56000 has three address spaces of 64KB 24-bit words, each with combinations of RAM, ROM, and peripherals.

Embedded-chip development uses system boards that contain the processor chip along with supporting logic and chips. Frequently, different development boards for the same processor will have different memory layouts.

Different models of chips have differing amounts of RAM and ROM, so programmers have to trade off the effort to squeeze a program into a smaller memory versus the extra cost of using a more expensive version of the chip with more memory. A linker for an embedded system needs a way to specify the layout of the linked program in great detail, by assigning particular kinds of code or data or even individual routines and variables to specific addresses.

Non-uniform Memory

References to on-chip memory are faster than those to off-chip memory, so in a system with both kinds, the most time-critical routines need to be placed in the fast memory. Sometimes it's possible to squeeze all of the program's time-critical code into the fast memory at link time. Other times it makes more sense to copy code or data from slow memory to fast memory as needed, so several routines can share the same fast memory at different times. To accomplish this trick, it's very useful to be able to tell a linker to "put this code at location XXXX but link it as though it's at location YYYY," so the code will be correct when it's copied from XXXX in slow memory to YYYY in fast memory at run time.

Memory Alignment

DSPs frequently have stringent memory alignment requirements for certain kinds of data structures. The Motorola 56000 series, for example, has an addressing mode to handle circular buffers very efficiently, so long as the base address of the buffer is aligned on a power-of-two boundary at least as large as the buffer size (for example, a 50-word buffer would need to be aligned on a 64-word boundary). The Fast Fourier Transform (FFT), an extremely important calculation for signal processing, depends on address bit manipulations that also require that the data on which an FFT operates be power-of-two aligned. Unlike on conventional architectures, the alignment requirements depend on the sizes of the data arrays, so that packing them efficiently into available memory can be tricky and tedious.

EXERCISE • 2.1

Use these SPARC program instructions to answer the following questions. (These instructions aren't intended as a useful program, just as some instruction format examples.)

```
Loc  Hex                Symbolic
1000 40 00 03 00        CALL X
1004 01 00 00 00        NOP  ; no operation, for delay
1008 7F FF FE ED        CALL Y
100C 01 00 00 00        NOP
1010 40 00 00 02        CALL Z
1014 01 00 00 00        NOP
1018 03 37 AB 6F        SETHI r1,3648367 ; set high 22 bits of r1
101C 82 10 62 EF        ORI r1,r1,751    ; OR in low 10 bits of r1
```

a. In a CALL instruction, the high 2 bits are the instruction code and the low 30 bits are a signed word (not byte) offset. What are the hex addresses for X, Y, and Z?

b. What does the call to Z at location 1010 accomplish?

c. The two instructions at 1018 and 101C load a 32-bit address into register 1. The SETHI loads the low 22 bits of the instruction into the high 22 bits of the register, and the ORI logically ORs the low 13 bits of the instruction into the register. What address will register 1 contain?

d. If the linker moves X to be at location hex 2504 but doesn't change the location of the code in the example, to what will it change the instruction at location 1000 so that it still refers to X?

EXERCISE • 2.2

Use these Pentium program instructions to answer the following questions. Don't forget that the x86 is little-endian.

```
Loc  Hex                    Symbolic
1000 E8 12 34 00 00         CALL A
1005 E8 ?? ?? ?? ??         CALL B
100A A1 12 34 00 00         MOV %EAX,P
100F 03 05 ?? ?? ?? ??      ADD %EAX,Q
```

a. At what location are routine A and data word P located? (*Tip:* On the x86, relative addresses are computed relative to the byte address *after* the instruction.)

b. If routine B is located at address 0F00 and data word Q is located at address 3456, what are the byte values of the ?? bytes in the example?

EXERCISE • 2.3

Does a linker or loader need to understand every instruction in the target architecture's instruction set? If a new model of the target adds new instructions, will the linker need to be changed to support them? What if the model adds new addressing modes to existing instructions, as the 386 did relative to the 286?

EXERCISE • 2.4

Back in the Golden Age of computing, when programmers worked in the middle of the night because that was the only time they could get computer time, rather than because that's when they were awake, many computers used word rather than byte addresses. The PDP-6 and -10, for example, had 36-bit words and 18-bit addressing, in which each instruction was a word with the operand address in the low half of the word. (Programs could also store addresses in the high half of a data word, although there was no direct instruction set support for that.) How different is linking for a word-addressed architecture compared to linking for a byte-addressed architecture?

EXERCISE • 2.5

How hard would it be to build a retargetable linker, that is, one that could be built to handle different target architectures by changing a few specific parts of the source code for the linker? How about a multitarget linker, to handle code for a variety of different architectures (although not in the same linker job)?

OBJECT FILES

Compilers and assemblers create object files containing the generated binary code and data for a source file. Linkers combine multiple object files into one file; loaders take object files and load them into memory. (In an integrated programming environment, the compilers, assemblers, and linkers are run implicitly when the user tells it to build a program, but they're there under the covers.) In this chapter we delve into the details of object file formats and contents.

3.1 WHAT GOES INTO AN OBJECT FILE?

An object file contains five basic kinds of information. (Some object files contain even more than this, but these categories are plenty to keep us occupied in this chapter.)

1. *Header information:* This is overall information about the file, such as the size of the code, the name of the source file it was translated from, and the creation date.

2. *Object code:* This is binary instructions and data generated by a compiler or assembler.

3. *Relocation information:* This is a list of the places in the object code that have to be fixed up when the linker changes the addresses of the object code.

4. *Symbols:* These include global symbols defined in this module and symbols to be imported from other modules or defined by the linker.

5. *Debugging information:* This includes other information about the object code that is not needed for linking but that is of use to a debugger, such as source file and line number information, local symbols, and descriptions of data structures used by the object code such as C structure definitions.

Not all object formats contain all of these kinds of information, and it's possible to have quite useful formats with little or no information beyond the object code.

DESIGNING AN OBJECT FORMAT

The design of an object format is a compromise driven by the various uses to which an object file will be put. A file may be *linkable*, used as input by a link editor or linking loader; *executable*, capable of being loaded into memory and run as a program; *loadable*, capable of being loaded into memory as a library along with a program; or any combination of the three. Some formats support just one or two of these uses, others support all three.

A linkable file contains extensive symbol and relocation information needed by the linker along with the object code. The object code is often divided up into many small logical segments that will be treated differently by the linker. An executable file contains object code—usually page aligned to permit the file to be mapped into the address space—but doesn't need any symbols (unless it will do run-time dynamic linking) and needs little or no relocation information. The object code is a single large segment or a small set of segments that reflect the hardware execution environment (most often read-only vs. read/write pages). Depending on the details of a system's run-time environment, a loadable file may consist solely of object code, or it may contain complete symbol and relocation information to permit run-time symbolic linking.

There is some conflict among these applications. The logically oriented grouping of linkable segments rarely matches the hardware-oriented grouping of executable segments. Particularly on smaller computers, linkable files are read and written by the linker a piece at a time, while executable files are loaded in their entirety into main memory. This distinction is most obvious in the completely different DOS linkable OMF format and executable EXE format.

We'll tour a series of popular formats, starting with the simplest and working up to the most complicated.

3.2 THE NULL OBJECT FORMAT: DOS COM FILES

It's quite possible to have a usable object file with no information in it whatsoever other than the runnable binary code. The DOS COM format is the best-known example. A COM file literally consists of nothing other than binary code. When the operating system runs a COM file, it merely loads the contents of the file into a block of free memory starting at offset 0x100 (0–FF are for the Program Segment Prefix (PSP) with command line arguments and other parameters), sets the x86 segment registers all to point to the PSP, sets the stack pointer (SP) register to the end of the segment because the stack grows downward, and jumps to the beginning of the loaded program.

The segmented architecture of the x86 makes this work. Because all x86 program addresses are interpreted relative to the base of the current segment and the segment registers all point to the base of the segment, the program is always loaded at segment-relative location 0x100. Hence, for a program that fits in a single segment, no fixups are needed because segment-relative addresses can be determined at link time.

For programs that don't fit in a single segment, the fixups are the programmer's problem, and there are indeed programs that start out by fetching one of their segment registers and adding its contents to stored segment values elsewhere in the program. Of course, this is exactly the sort of tedium that linkers and loaders are intended to automate, and DOS does that with EXE files, described later in this chapter.

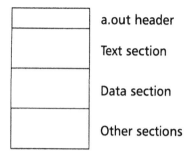
a.out header

Text section

Data section

Other sections

FIGURE **3.1** • Simplifed a.out.

3.3 CODE SECTIONS: UNIX A.OUT FILES

Computers with hardware memory relocation (nearly all of them, these days) usually create a new process with an empty address space for each newly run program, in which case programs can be linked to start at a fixed address and require no relocation at load time. The UNIX a.out object format handles this situation.

In the simplest case, an a.out file consists of a small header followed by the executable code (called the text section for historical reasons) and the initial values for static data (Figure 3.1). The PDP-11 had only 16-bit addressing, which limited programs to a total of 64KB. This limit quickly became too small, so later models in the PDP-11 line provided separate address spaces for code (I for Instruction space) and data (D space), so a single program could contain both 64KB of code and 64KB of data. To support this feature, the compilers, assembler, and linker were modified to create two-section object files, with the code located in the first section and the data in the second section; the program loader loaded the first section into a process's I space and the second into the D space.

Separate I and D space had another performance advantage: Because a program couldn't change its own I space, multiple copies of a single program could share a single copy of a program's code while keeping separate copies of the program's data. On a timeshared system like UNIX, multiple copies of the shell (the command interpreter) and the network daemons are common, and shared program code saves considerable real memory.

The only currently common computer that still uses separate addressing for code and data is the 286 (or the 386 in 16-bit protected mode). Even on

```
int a_magic;    // magic number
int a_text;     // text segment size
int a_data;     // initialized data size
int a_bss;      // uninitialized data size
int a_syms;     // symbol table size
int a_entry;    // entry point
int a_trsize;   // text relocation size
int a_drsize;   // data relocation size
```

FIGURE 3.2 • Header of an a.out file.

more modern machines with large address spaces, the operating system can handle shared read-only code pages in virtual memory much more efficiently than read/write pages, so all modern loaders support them. This means that linker formats must at the very least mark read-only versus read/write sections. In practice, most linker formats have many sections, such as read-only data, symbols and relocation for subsequent linking, debugging symbols, and shared-library information. (UNIX terminology confusingly calls the file sections segments, so we use that term in discussions of UNIX file formats.)

HEADER OF AN A.OUT FILE

The header varies somewhat from one version of UNIX to another, but the version in BSD UNIX (Figure 3.2) is typical. (In the examples in this chapter, int values are 32 bits and short values are 16 bits.)

The magic number a_magic indicates what kind of executable file this is.[1] Different magic numbers tell the operating system program loader to load the file into memory differently; we discuss these variations below. The text and data segment sizes a_text and a_data are the sizes in bytes of the read-only code and read/write data that follow the header. Because UNIX automatically initializes newly allocated memory to zero, any data with an initial content of

---

1. Historically, the magic number on the original PDP-11 was octal 407, which was a branch instruction that would jump over the next seven words of the header to the beginning of the text segment. That permitted a primitive form of position-independent code. A bootstrap loader could load the entire executable including the file header into memory, usually at location zero, and then jump to the beginning of the loaded file to start the program. Only a few stand-alone programs ever used this ability, but the magic number 407 is still with us 25 years later.

zero or whose contents don't matter need not be present in the a.out file. The uninitialized size a_bss identifies how much uninitialized (really zero-initialized) data logically follows the data in the a.out file.

The a_entry field gives the starting address of the program, while a_syms, a_trsize, and a_drsize specify how much symbol table and relocation information follows the data segment in the file. Programs that have been linked and are ready to run need neither symbol nor relocation information, so these fields are zero in runnable files unless the linker has included symbols for the debugger.

Interactions with Virtual Memory

The process involved (illustrated in Figure 3.3) when the operating system loads and starts a simple two-segment file is straightforward:

1. Read the a.out header to get the segment sizes.

2. Check to see if there's already a sharable code segment for this file. If so, map that segment into the process's address space. If not, create one, map it into the address space, and read the text segment from the file into the new memory segment.

3. Create a private data segment large enough for the combined data and bss, map it into the process, and read the data segment from the file into the data segment. Zero out the bss segment.

4. Create and map in a stack segment (usually separate from the data segment, because the data heap and stack grow separately). Place arguments from the command line or calling program on the stack.

5. Set registers appropriately and jump to the starting address.

This scheme (known as NMAGIC, where the N means new, as of about 1975) works quite well, and PDP-11 and early VAX UNIX systems used it for years for all object files, and linkable files used it throughout the life of the a.out format into the 1990s. When UNIX systems gained virtual memory, several improvements to this simple scheme sped up program loading and saved considerable real memory.

On a paging system, the simple scheme above allocates fresh virtual memory for each text segment and data segment. Because the a.out file is

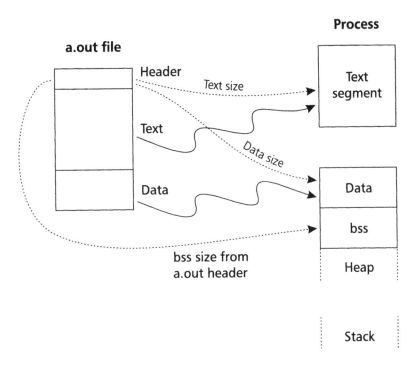

FIGURE 3.3 • Loading an a.out into a process.

already stored on the disk, the object file itself can be mapped into the process's address space. This saves disk space, because new disk space for virtual memory need only be allocated for pages that the program writes into, and it can speed program startup, because the virtual memory system need only load in from disk the pages that the program is actually using, not the whole file.

A few changes to the a.out format make this possible (Figure 3.4) and create what's known as ZMAGIC format. These changes align the segments in the object file on page boundaries. On systems with 4KB pages, the a.out header is expanded to 4KB and the text segment's size is rounded up to the next 4KB boundary. There's no need to round up the size of the data segment, since the bss segment logically follows the data segment and is zeroed by the program loader anyway.

ZMAGIC files reduce unneeded paging, but they do it at the cost of wasting a lot of disk space. The a.out header is only 32 bytes long, yet an entire 4KB of disk space is allocated. The gap between the text and the data also wastes 2KB (half a 4KB page) on average. Both of these are fixed in the compact pageable format known as QMAGIC.

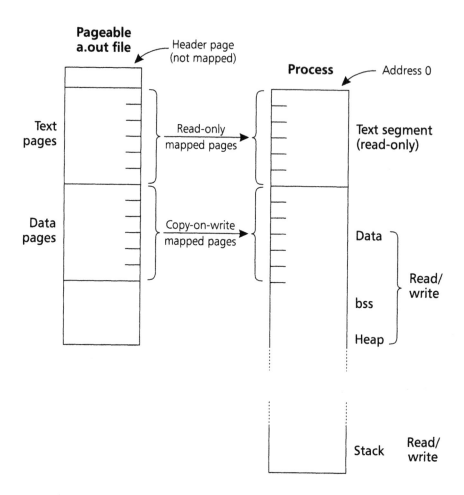

FIGURE 3.4 • Mapping a ZMAGIC a.out file into a process.

Compact pageable files consider the a.out header to be part of the text segment, because there's no particular reason that the code in the text segment has to start at location zero. Indeed, program location zero is a particularly bad place to load a program because uninitialized pointer variables often contain zero. The code actually starts immediately after the header, and the whole page is mapped into the second page of the process, leaving the first page unmapped so that pointer references to location zero will fail (Figure 3.5). This has the harmless side effect of mapping the header into the process as well.

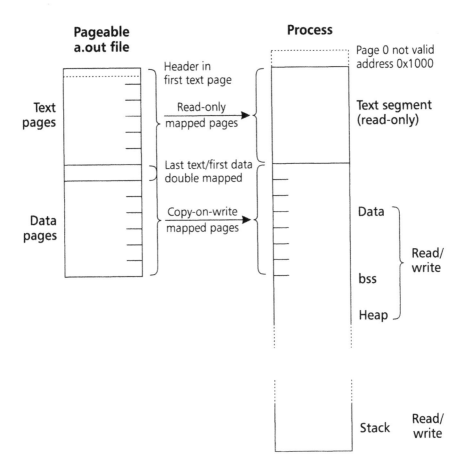

FIGURE 3.5 • Mapping a compact QMAGIC a.out into a process.

The text and data segments in a QMAGIC executable are each rounded up to a full page, so the system can easily map file pages to address space pages. The last page of the data segment is padded out with zeros for bss data; if more bss data exist than fit in the padding area, the a.out header contains the size of the remaining bss area to allocate.

Although BSD UNIX loads programs at location zero (or 0x1000 for QMAGIC), other versions of UNIX load programs at other addresses. For example, System V for the Motorola 68000 series loads at 0x80000000 and for the 386 loads at 0x8048000. It doesn't matter where the load address is so long as it's page aligned and the linker and operating system can permanently agree what it is.

3.4 RELOCATION: DOS EXE FILES

The a.out format is quite adequate for systems that assign a fresh address space to each process so that every program can be loaded at the same logical address. Many systems are not so fortunate. Some load all the programs into the same address space. Others give each program its own address space but don't always load the program at the same address. (The 32-bit versions of MS Windows fall into this latter category.)

In these cases, executable files contain *relocation entries*, often called *fixups*, that identify the places in the program where addresses need to be modified when the program is loaded. One of the simplest formats with fixups is the DOS EXE format.

As we saw with the COM format above, DOS loads a program into a contiguous chunk of available real-mode memory. If the program doesn't fit in one 64KB segment, the program has to use explicit segment numbers to address program and data, and at load time the segment numbers in the program have to be fixed up to match the address where the program is actually loaded. The segment numbers in the file are stored as though the program will be loaded at location zero, so the fixup action is to add to every stored segment number the base paragraph number at which the program is actually loaded (that is, if the program is loaded at location 0x5000, which is paragraph 0x500, a reference to segment 12 is relocated to be a reference to segment 512). The offsets within the segments don't change, because the program is relocated as a unit, so the loader needn't adjust anything other than the segment numbers.

Each EXE file starts with a header as shown in Figure 3.6. Following the header is some extra information of variable length (used for overlay loaders, self-extracting archives, and other application-specific hackery) and a list of the fixup addresses in 32-bit segment:offset format. The fixup addresses are relative to the base of the program, so the fixups themselves have to be relocated to find the addresses in the program to change. After the fixups comes the program code. There may be more information, ignored by the program loader, after the code. (In the example below, far pointers are 32 bits with a 16-bit segment number and a 16-bit offset.)

Loading an EXE file is only slightly more complicated than loading a COM file, requiring the following steps:

1. Read in the header and check the magic number for validity.

```
char signature[2] = "MZ"; // magic number
short lastsize;           // # bytes used in last block
short nblocks;            // number of 512-byte blocks
short nreloc;             // number of relocation entries
short hdrsize;            // size of file header in 16-byte paragraphs
short minalloc;           // minimum extra memory to allocate
short maxalloc;           // maximum extra memory to allocate
void far *sp;             // initial stack pointer
short checksum;           // ones complement of file sum
void far *ip;             // initial instruction pointer
short relocpos;           // location of relocation fixup table
short noverlay;           // Overlay number, 0 for program
char extra[];             // extra material for overlays, etc.
void far *relocs[];       // relocation entries, starts at relocpos
```

FIGURE 3.6 • Format of EXE file header.

2. Find a suitable area of memory. The minalloc and maxalloc fields identify the minimum and maximum number of extra paragraphs of memory to allocate beyond the end of the loaded program. (Linkers invariably default the minimum to the size of the program's bss-like uninitialized data and the maximum to 0xFFFF.)

3. Create a PSP (the control area at the head of the program).

4. Read in the program code immediately after the PSP. The nblocks and lastsize fields define the length of the code.

5. Start reading nreloc fixups at relocpos. For each fixup, add the base address of the program code to the segment number in the fixup, then use the relocated fixup as a pointer to a program address at which to add the base segment address of the program code.

6. Set the stack pointer to sp, relocated, and jump to ip, relocated, to start the program.

Other than the peculiarities associated with segmented addressing, this is a fairly typical setup for program loading. In a few cases, different pieces of the program are relocated differently. In 286 protected mode, which EXE files do not support, each segment of code or data in the executable file is loaded into a separate segment in the system, but for architectural reasons the segment numbers cannot be consecutive. Each protected mode executable has a table near the beginning listing all of the segments that the program will require. The system makes a table of actual segment numbers corresponding to each segment in the executable. When processing fixups, the system looks up the logical segment number in that table and replaces it with the actual segment number, a process more akin to symbol binding than to relocation. (Some systems permit symbol resolution at load time as well, but we save that topic for Chapter 10.)

3.5 SYMBOLS AND RELOCATION

The object formats we've considered so far are all loadable; that is, they can be loaded into memory and run directly. Most object files aren't loadable, but rather are intermediate files passed from a compiler or assembler to a linker or library manager. These linkable files can be considerably more complex than runnable ones. Runnable files have to be simple enough to run on the "bare metal" of the computer, while linkable files are processed by a layer of software that can do very sophisticated processing. In principle, a linking loader could do all of the functions of a linker as a program was being loaded, but for efficiency reasons the loader is generally as simple as possible to speed program startup. (Dynamic linking, which we cover in Chapter 10, moves a lot of the function of the linker into the loader, with attendant performance loss, but modern computers are fast enough that the gains from dynamic linking outweigh the performance penalty.)

We look at five formats of increasing complexity: relocatable a.out used on BSD UNIX systems, ELF used on System V, IBM 360 objects, the extended COFF linkable and PE executable formats used on 32-bit MS Windows, and the OMF linkable format used on pre-COFF MS Windows systems.

3.6 RELOCATABLE A.OUT

UNIX systems have always used a single object format for both runnable and linkable files, with the runnable files leaving out the sections of use only to the

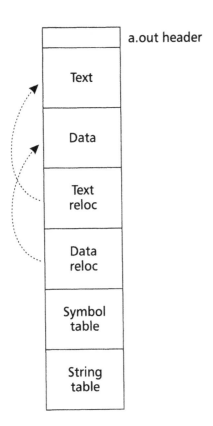

FIGURE 3.7 • Simplified relocatable a.out.

linker. The a.out header format we saw in Figure 3.2 includes several fields used by the linker. The sizes of the relocation tables for the text and data segments are in a_trsize and a_drsize, and the size of the symbol table is in a_syms. The three sections follow the text and data (Figure 3.7).

RELOCATION ENTRIES

Relocation entries serve two functions. When a section of code is relocated to a different base address, relocation entries mark the places in the code that have to be modified. In a linkable file, there are also relocation entries that mark references to undefined symbols, so the linker knows where to patch in the symbol's value when the symbol is finally defined.

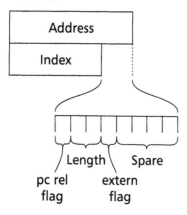

FIGURE **3.8** • Relocation entry format.

Figure 3.8 shows the format of a relocation entry. Each entry contains the address within the text or data section to be relocated, along with information that defines what to do. The address is the offset from the beginning of the text or data segment of a relocatable item. The length field identifies how long the item is; values zero through three mean 1, 2, 4, or (on some architectures) 8 bytes. The pc rel flag means that this is a PC-relative item, that is, that it is used in an instruction as a relative address.

The extern flag controls the interpretation of the index field to determine which segment or symbol the relocation refers to. If the extern flag is off, this is a plain relocation item, and the index tells which segment (text, data, or bss) the item is addressing. If the extern flag is on, this is a reference to an external symbol, and the index is the symbol number in the file's symbol table.

This relocation format is adequate for most machine architectures, but some of the more complex ones need extra flag bits to indicate such details as 3-byte address constants on the 370 or high- and low-half constants on SPARC.

SYMBOLS AND STRINGS

The final section of an a.out file is the symbol table. Each entry is 12 bytes and describes a single symbol (Figure 3.9).

UNIX compilers permit arbitrarily long identifiers, so the name strings are all in a string table that follows the symbol table. The first item in a symbol

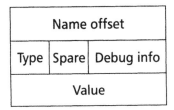

Name offset		
Type	Spare	Debug info
Value		

FIGURE 3.9 • Symbol format.

table entry is the offset in the string table of the null-terminated name of the symbol. In the type byte, if the low bit is set the symbol is external (this is a misnomer; it would more accurately be called global, meaning visible to other modules). Non-external symbols are not needed for linking but can be used by debuggers. The rest of the bits specify the symbol type. (These symbol types are adequate for older languages such as C and Fortran and, just barely, for C++.) The most important types include the following:

- *text, data,* or *bss:* This is a symbol defined in this module. The external bit may or may not be on. Its value is the relocatable address in the module corresponding to the symbol.

- *abs:* This is an absolute nonrelocatable symbol (rare outside of debugger information). The external bit may or may not be on. Its value is the absolute value of the symbol.

- *undefined:* This is a symbol not defined in this module. The external bit must be on. Its value is usually zero.[2]

A.OUT SUMMARY

The a.out format is a simple and effective one for relatively simple systems with paging. It has fallen out of favor because it doesn't easily support

---

2. As a special case, a compiler can use an undefined symbol to request that the linker reserve a block of storage by that symbol's name. If an undefined external symbol has a nonzero value, that value is a hint to the linker as to how large a block of storage the program expects the symbol to address. At link time, if there is no definition of the symbol, the linker creates a block of storage by that name in the bss segment with the size being the largest hint value found in any of the linked modules. If the symbol is defined in any module, the linker uses the definition and ignores the size hints. This "common block hack" supports typical (albeit nonstandard) usage of Fortran common blocks and uninitialized C external data.

dynamic linking. Also, a.out doesn't support C++ very well, which requires special treatment of initializer and finalizer code.

3.7 UNIX ELF

The traditional a.out format served the UNIX community for over a decade, but with the advent of UNIX System V, AT&T decided that it needed something better to support cross-compilation, dynamic linking, and other modern system features. Early versions of System V used Common Object File Format (COFF), which was originally intended for cross-compiled embedded systems and didn't work all that well for a timesharing system because it couldn't support C++ or dynamic linking without extensions. In later versions of System V, COFF was superseded by Executable and Linking Format (ELF). ELF has been adopted by the popular freeware Linux and by BSD variants of UNIX as well. ELF has an associated debugging format called DWARF. In this discussion we examine the 32-bit version of ELF. There are 64-bit variants that extend sizes and addresses to 64 bits in a straightforward way.

ELF files come in three slightly different flavors: relocatable, executable, and shared object. Relocatable files are created by compilers and assemblers but need to be processed by the linker before running. Executable files have all relocation done and all symbols resolved except perhaps shared-library symbols that must be resolved at run time. Shared objects are shared libraries, containing both symbol information for the linker and directly runnable code for run time.

ELF files have an unusual dual nature (Figure 3.10). Compilers, assemblers, and linkers treat the file as a set of logical sections described by a section header table, while the system loader treats the file as a set of segments described by a program header table. A single segment will usually consist of several sections. For example, a loadable read-only segment could contain sections for executable code, read-only data, and symbols for the dynamic linker. Relocatable files have section tables, executable files have program header tables, and shared objects have both. The sections are intended for further processing by a linker, while the segments are intended to be mapped into memory.

ELF files all start with the ELF header (Figure 3.11). The header is designed to be decodable even on machines with a different byte order from the file's

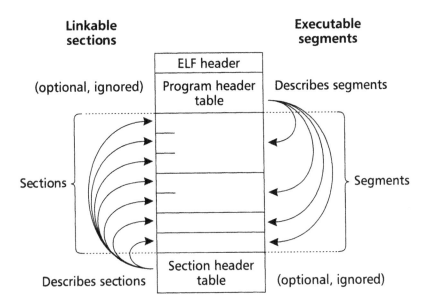

FIGURE **3.10** • Two views of an ELF file.

target architecture. The first 4 bytes are the magic number identifying an ELF file, followed by 3 bytes describing the format of the rest of the header. Once a program has read the `class` and `byteorder` flags, it knows the byte order and word size of the file and can do the necessary byte swapping and size conversions. Other fields provide the size and location of the section header and program header, if present.

RELOCATABLE FILES

A relocatable or shared-object file is considered to be a collection of sections, as defined in section headers (Figure 3.12). Each section contains a single type of information, such as program code, read-only or read/write data, relocation entries, or symbols. Every symbol defined in the module is defined relative to a section, so a procedure's entry point would be relative to the program code section that contains that procedure's code. There are also two pseudosections, SHN_ABS (number 0xfff1) that logically contains absolute nonrelocatable symbols and SHN_COMMON (number 0xfff2) that contains uninitialized data blocks and is the descendant of the a.out common block hack. Section zero is always a null section, with an all-zero section table entry.

```
char magic[4] = "\177ELF"; // magic number
char class;                // address size, 1 = 32-bit, 2 = 64-bit
char byteorder;            // 1 = little-endian, 2 = big-endian
char hversion;             // header version, always 1
char pad[9];
short filetype;            // file type: 1 = relocatable, 2 = executable,
                           // 3 = shared object, 4 = core image
short archtype;            // 2 = SPARC, 3 = x86, 4 = 68K, etc.
int fversion;              // file version, always 1
int entry;                 // entry point if executable
int phdrpos;               // file position of program header or 0
int shdrpos;               // file position of section header or 0
int flags;                 // architecture-specific flags, usually 0
short hdrsize;             // size of this ELF header
short phdrent;             // size of an entry in program header
short phdrcnt;             // number of entries in program header or 0
short shdrent;             // size of an entry in section header
short shdrcnt;             // number of entries in section header or 0
short strsec;              // section number that contains section name strings
```

FIGURE 3.11 • ELF header.

Section types include the following:

- PROGBITS: This holds program contents including code, data, and debugger information.

- NOBITS: This is similar to PROGBITS but no space is allocated in the file itself. It is used for bss data allocated at program load time.

- SYMTAB and DYNSYM: These hold symbol tables, which are described in more detail later in this chapter. The SYMTAB table contains all symbols and is intended for the regular linker, while DYNSYM is just the symbols for dynamic linking. (The latter table has to be loaded into memory at run time, so it's kept as small as possible.)

- STRTAB: This is a string table, analogous to the one in a.out files. Unlike a.out files, ELF files can and often do contain separate string tables for separate purposes (e.g., section names, regular symbol names, and dynamic linker symbol names).

```
int sh_name;      // name, index into the string table
int sh_type;      // section type
int sh_flags;     // flag bits, below
int sh_addr;      // base memory address, if loadable, or zero
int sh_offset;    // file position of beginning of section
int sh_size;      // size in bytes
int sh_link;      // section number with related info or zero
int sh_info;      // more section-specific info
int sh_align;     // alignment granularity if section is moved
int sh_entsize;   // size of entries if section is an array
```

FIGURE 3.12 • Section header.

- REL and RELA: These hold relocation information. REL entries add the relocation value to the base value stored in the code or data, while RELA entries include the base value for relocation in the relocation entries themselves. (For historical reasons, x86 objects use REL relocation and 68000 objects use RELA.) There are a number of relocation types for each architecture, similar to (and derived from) the a.out relocation types.

- DYNAMIC and HASH: These hold dynamic linking information and the run-time symbol hash table.

There are three flag bits used: ALLOC, which means that the section occupies memory when the program is loaded; WRITE, which means that the section when loaded is writable; and EXECINSTR, which means that the section contains executable machine code.

A typical relocatable executable has about a dozen sections. Many of the section names are meaningful to the linker, which looks for the section types it knows about for specific processing, while either discarding or passing through unmodified sections (depending on flag bits) that it doesn't know about.

Sections include the following:

- .text, which is type PROGBITS with attributes ALLOC+EXECINSTR. It's the equivalent of the a.out text segment.

- .data, which is type PROGBITS with attributes ALLOC+WRITE. It's the equivalent of the a.out data segment.

- .rodata, which is type PROGBITS with attribute ALLOC. It's read-only data, hence no WRITE.

- .bss, which is type NOBITS with attributes ALLOC+WRITE. The .bss section takes no space in the file, hence NOBITS, but is allocated at run time, hence ALLOC.

- .rel.text, .rel.data, and .rel.rodata, each of which is type REL or RELA. This contains the relocation information for the corresponding text or data section.

- .init and .fini, each of type PROGBITS with attributes ALLOC+ EXECINSTR. These are similar to .text, but they are code to be executed when the program starts up or terminates, respectively. C and Fortran don't need these, but they're essential for C++, which has global data with executable initializers and finalizers.

- .symtab and .dynsym, of types SYMTAB and DYNSYM, respectively. These are regular and dynamic linker symbol tables. The dynamic linker symbol table is ALLOC set, because it's loaded at run time.

- .strtab and .dynstr, both of type STRTAB. These are tables of name strings for a symbol table or the section names for the section table. The dynstr section, the strings for the dynamic linker symbol table, has ALLOC set because it's loaded at run time.

There are also some specialized sections like .got and .plt, the global offset table and procedure linkage table, that are used for dynamic linking (covered in Chapter 10); .debug, which contains symbols for the debugger; .line, which contains mappings from source line numbers to object code locations, again for the debugger; and .comment, which contains documentation strings (usually version control numbers).

An unusual section type is .interp, which contains the name of a program to use as an interpreter. If this section is present, rather than running the program directly, the system runs the interpreter and passes it the ELF file as an argument. For many years now, UNIX has had self-running interpreted text files, using

```
#! /path/to/interpreter
```

```
int name;      // position of name string in string table
int value;     // symbol value, section relative in reloc,
               // absolute in executable
int size;      // object or function size
char type:4;   // data object, function, section, or special-case file
char bind:4;   // local, global, or weak
char other;    // spare
short sect;    // section number, ABS, COMMON, or UNDEF
```

FIGURE 3.13 • ELF symbol table.

as the first line of the file. ELF extends this facility to interpreters that run nontext programs. In practice this is used to call the run-time dynamic linker to load the program and to link in any required shared libraries.

The ELF symbol table is similar to the a.out symbol table. It consists of an array of entries (Figure 3.13). The a.out symbol entry is fleshed out with a few more fields. The size field tells how large a data object is (particularly for undefined bss; this is the common block hack again). A symbol's binding can be local, just visible in this module, global, visible everywhere, or weak. A weak symbol is a half-hearted global symbol: If a definition is available for an undefined weak symbol, the linker will use it, but if not, the value defaults to zero.

The symbol's type is normally data or function. There is a section symbol defined for each section, usually with the same name as the section itself, for the benefit of relocation entries. (ELF relocation entries are all relative to symbols, so a section symbol is necessary to indicate that an item is relocated relative to one of the sections in the file.) A file entry is a pseudo-symbol containing the name of the source file.

The section number is the section relative to which the symbol is defined (e.g., function entry points are defined relative to .text). Three special pseudo-sections also appear, UNDEF for undefined symbols, ABS for nonrelocatable absolute symbols, and COMMON for common blocks that are not yet allocated. (The value of a COMMON symbol gives the required alignment granularity, and the size gives the minimum size. Once allocated by the linker, COMMON symbols move into the .bss section.)

A typical complete ELF file (Figure 3.14) contains quite a few sections for code, data, relocation information, linker symbols, and debugger symbols. If the file is a C++ program, it will probably also contain .init, .fini, .rel.init, and .rel.fini sections as well.

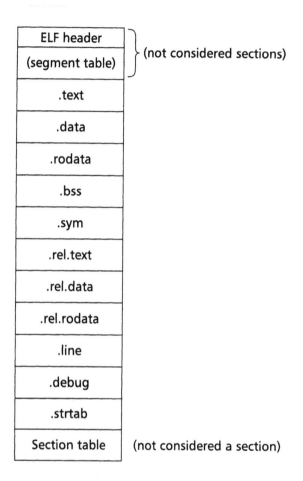

ELF header	} (not considered sections)
(segment table)	
.text	
.data	
.rodata	
.bss	
.sym	
.rel.text	
.rel.data	
.rel.rodata	
.line	
.debug	
.strtab	
Section table	(not considered a section)

FIGURE **3.14** • Sample relocatable ELF file.

ELF EXECUTABLE FILES

An executable ELF file has the same general format as a relocatable ELF file, but the data are arranged so that the file can be mapped into memory and run. The file contains a program header that follows the ELF header in the file. The program header defines the segments to be mapped. The program header (Figure 3.15) is an array of segment descriptions.

An executable usually has only a handful of segments, a read-only one for the code and read-only data and a read/write one for read/write data. All of

```
int type;        // loadable code or data, dynamic linking info, etc.
int offset;      // file offset of segment
int virtaddr;    // virtual address to map segment
int physaddr;    // physical address, not used
int filesize;    // size of segment in file
int memsize;     // size of segment in memory (bigger if contains bss)
int flags;       // Read, Write, Execute bits
int align;       // required alignment, invariably hardware page size
```

FIGURE **3.15** • ELF program header.

	File offset	Load address	Type header
ELF header	0	0x8000000	
Program header	0x40	0x8000040	
Read-only text (size 0x4500)	0x100	0x8000100	LOAD, read/execute
Read/write data (file size 0x2200, memory size 0x3500)	0x4600	0x8005600	LOAD, read/write/execute

Nonloadable information and optional section headers

FIGURE **3.16** • ELF loadable segments.

the loadable sections are packed into the appropriate segments so the system can map the file with one or two operations.

ELF files extend the "header in the address space" trick used in QMAGIC a.out files to make the executable files as compact as possible at the cost of some unused space in the address space. A segment can start and end at arbitrary file offsets, but the virtual starting address for the segment must have the same low bits modulo the alignment as the starting offset in the file (i.e., it must start at the same offset on a page). The system maps in the entire range from the page where the segment starts to the page where the segment ends, even if the segment logically only occupies part of the first and last pages mapped. Figure 3.16 shows a typical segment arrangement.

The mapped text segment consists of the ELF header, the program header, and read-only text, since the ELF and program headers are in the same page as the beginning of the text. The read/write data segment in the file starts immediately after the text segment. The page from the file is mapped both read-only as the last page of the text segment in memory and copy-on-write as the first page of the data segment. In this example, if a computer has 4KB pages, and in an executable file the text ends at 0x80045ff, then the data start at 0x8005600. The file page is mapped into the last page of the text segment at location 0x8004000 where the first 0x600 bytes contain the text from 0x8004000–0x80045ff, and into the data segment at 0x8005000 where the rest of the page contains the initial contents of data from 0x8005600–0x80056ff.

Again, the bss section is logically continuous with the end of the read/write sections in the data segment (in this case 0x1300 bytes, the difference between the file size and the memory size). The last page of the data segment is mapped in from the file, but as soon as the operating system starts to zero the bss segment, the copy-on-write system makes a private copy of the page.

If the file contains .init or .fini sections, those sections are part of the read-only text segment; the linker inserts code at the entry point to call the .init section code before it calls the main program and to call the .fini section code after the main program returns.

An ELF shared object contains all the baggage of a relocatable and an executable file. It has the program header table at the beginning, followed by the sections in the loadable segments, including dynamic linking information. After the sections consisting of the loadable segments are the relocatable symbol table and other information that the linker needs while creating executable programs that refer to the shared object. The section table is located at the end.

ELF SUMMARY

ELF is a moderately complex format, but it serves its purposes well. It's a flexible enough relocatable format to support C++, while still being an efficient executable format for a virtual memory system with dynamic linking; ELF makes it easy to map executable pages directly into the program address space. It also permits cross-compilation and cross-linking from one platform to another, with enough information in each ELF file to identify the target architecture and byte order.

3.8 IBM 360 Object Format

The IBM 360 object format was designed in the early 1960s but remains in use today. It was originally designed for 80-column punch cards, but it has been adapted for disk files on modern systems. Each object file contains a set of control sections (csects), which may be named or not and are separately relocatable blocks of code and/or data. Typically each source routine is compiled into one csect or perhaps into one csect for code and another for data. A csect's name, if it has one, can be used as a symbol that addresses the beginning of the csect; other types of symbols include those defined within a csect, undefined external symbols, common blocks, and a few others. Each symbol defined or used in an object file is assigned a small integer External Symbol ID (ESID). An object file is a sequence of 80-byte records in a common format (Figure 3.17). The first byte of each record is 0x2, a value that marks the record as part of an object file. (A record that starts with a blank is treated as a command by the linker.) Bytes 2–4 are the record type, TXT for program code or text, ESD for an external symbol directory that defines symbols and ESIDs, RLD for Relocation Directory, and END for the last record that also defines the starting point. The rest of the record up through byte 72 is specific to the record type. Bytes 73–80 are ignored. On actual punch cards they were usually a sequence number.

An object file starts with some ESD records that define the csects and all symbols, then the TXT records, then the RLD records, and finally the END. There's quite a lot of flexibility in the order of the records. Several TXT records can redefine the contents of a single location, with the last one in the file winning. This made it possible (and not uncommon) to punch a few "patch" cards to place at the end of an object deck, rather than reassembling or recompiling.

ESD Records

Each object file starts with ESD records (Figure 3.18) that define the csects and symbols used in the file and give them all ESIDs. Each ESD record defines up to three symbols with sequential ESIDs. Symbols are up to eight EBCDIC characters. The symbol types are as follows:

- SD (section definition) and PC (private code). These define a csect. The csect origin is the logical address of the beginning of the csect (usually

```
char flag = 0x2;
char rtype[3];              // three-letter record type
char data[68];              // format-specific data
char seq[8];                // ignored, usually sequence numbers
```

FIGURE **3.17** • IBM object record format.


```
char flag = 0x2;          // 1
char rtype[3] = "ESD";    // 2-4 three-letter type
char pad1[6];
short nbytes;             // 11-12 number of bytes of info: 16, 32, or 48
char pad2[2];
short esid;               // 15-16 ESID of first symbol

{                         // 17-72, up to 3 symbols
  char name[8];           // blank padded symbol name
  char type;              // symbol type
  char base[3];           // csect origin or label offset
  char bits;              // attribute bits
  char len[3];            // length of object or csect ESID
}
```

FIGURE **3.18** • ESD format.

zero) and the length is the length of the csect. The attribute byte contains flags identifying whether the csect uses 24- or 31-bit program addressing and whether it needs to be loaded into a 24- or a 31-bit address space. PC is a csect with a blank name; names of csects must be unique within a program but there can be multiple unnamed PC sections.

▪ LD (label definition). The base is the label's offset within its csect; the len field is the ESID of the csect. There are no attribute bits.

▪ CM (common). Len is the length of the common block; other fields are ignored.

```
char flag = 0x2;        // 1
char rtype[3] = "TXT";  // 2-4 three-letter type
char pad;
char loc[3];            // 6-8 csect relative origin of the text
char pad[2];
short nbytes;           // 11-12 number of bytes of info
char pad[2];
short esid;             // 15-16 ESID of this csect
char text[56];          // 17-72 data
```

FIGURE 3.19 • TXT format.

- ER (external reference) and WX (weak external). These symbols are defined elsewhere in the program. The linker reports an error if an ER symbol isn't defined elsewhere in the program; an undefined WX is not an error.

- PR (pseudo-register). This is a small area of storage defined at link time but allocated at run time. Attribute bits give the required alignment (1 to 8 bytes) and len is the size of the area.

TXT Records

Next come text records (Figure 3.19) that contain the program code and data. Each text record defines up to 56 contiguous bytes within a single csect.

RLD Records

After the text records come RLD records (Figure 3.20), each of which contains a sequence of relocation entries. Each entry has the ESIDs of the target and the pointer, a flag byte, and the csect-relative address of the pointer. The flag byte has bits giving the type of reference (code, data, PR, or cumulative external dummy—the total size of all pseudo-registers—also referred to as CXD); the length (1, 2, 3, or 4 bytes); a sign bit indicating whether to add or subtract the

```
char flag = 0x2;        // 1
char rtype[3] = "RLD"; // 2-4 three-letter type
char pad[6];
short nbytes;           // 11-12 number of bytes of info
char pad[4];
{                       // 17-72 four or eight-byte relocation entries
  short t_esid;         // target, ESID of referenced csect or symbol
                        // or zero for CXD (total size of PR defs)
  short p_esid;         // pointer, ESID of csect with reference
  char flags;           // type and size of ref,
  char addr[3];         // csect-relative ref address
}
```

FIGURE **3.20** • RLD format.

relocation; and a "same" bit. If the "same" bit is set, the next entry omits the two ESIDs and uses the same ESIDs as the current entry.

END RECORD

The end record (Figure 3.21) gives the starting address for the program, which is either an address within a csect or the ESID of an external symbol.

IBM 360 OBJECT FORMAT SUMMARY

Although the 80-column records are quite dated, the IBM object format is still surprisingly simple and flexible. Extremely small linkers and loaders can handle this format; on one model of 360, I used an absolute loader that fit on a single 80-column punch card and could load a program, interpreting TXT and END records and ignoring the rest.

Disk-based systems either store object files as card images or use a variant version of the format with the same record types but much longer records without sequence numbers. The linkers for DOS (IBM's lightweight operating system for the 360) produce a simplified output format with in effect one csect and a stripped-down RLD without ESIDs.

```
char flag = 0x2;        // 1
char rtype[3] = "END";  // 2-4 three-letter type
char pad;
char loc[3];            // 6-8 csect relative start address or zero
char pad[6];
short esid;             // 15-16 ESID of csect or symbol
```

FIGURE 3.21 • END format.

Within object files, the individual named csects permit a programmer or linker to arrange the modules in a program as desired, putting all the code csects together, for example. The main places this format shows its age are the eight-character maximum symbol length and the lack of type information about individual csects. Recently, OS/390 has defined an extended format with long symbols and features to support C++ and shared libraries.

3.9 MICROSOFT PORTABLE EXECUTABLE FORMAT

Microsoft's Windows NT has extremely mixed heritage, including earlier versions of DOS and MS Windows, Digital's VAX VMS (on which many of the programmers had worked), and UNIX System V (on which many of the rest of the programmers had worked). Windows NT's format is adapted from COFF, a file format that UNIX versions used after a.out but before ELF. We'll take a look at PE and, where it differs from PE, Microsoft's version of COFF.

MS Windows developed in an underpowered environment with slow processors, limited RAM, and originally without hardware paging, so there was always an emphasis on shared libraries to save memory and ad hoc tricks to improve performance, some of which are apparent in the PE/COFF design. Most MS Windows executables contain *resources*, a general term that refers to objects such as cursors, icons, bitmaps, menus, and fonts that are shared between the program and the GUI. A PE file can contain a resource directory for all of the resources the program code in that file uses.

PE executable files are intended for a paged environment, so pages from a PE file are usually mapped directly into memory and run much like an ELF executable. PEs can be either EXE programs or dynamic-link shared libraries

(DLLs). The format of the two is the same, with a status bit identifying a PE as one or the other. Each can contain a list of exported functions and data that can be used by other PE files loaded into the same address space and a list of imported functions and data that need to be resolved from other PEs at load time. Each file contains a set of blocks analogous to ELF segments that have variously been called sections, segments, and objects. We call them sections here (the term that Microsoft now uses).

A PE file (Figure 3.22) starts with a small DOS EXE file that prints out a statement such as "This program needs Microsoft Windows." (Microsoft's dedication to certain kinds of backward compatibility is impressive.) A previously unused field at the end of the EXE header points to the PE signature, which is followed by the file header, which consists of a COFF section and the "optional" header (which, despite its name, appears in all PE files) and a list of section headers. The section headers describe the various sections of the file. A COFF object file starts with the COFF header and omits the optional header.

Figure 3.23 shows the PE, COFF, and optional headers. The COFF header describes the contents of the file, with the most important values being the number of entries in the section table. The optional header contains pointers to the most commonly used file sections. Addresses are all kept as offsets from the place in memory that the program is loaded, also called relative virtual addresses (RVAs).

Each PE file is created in a way that makes it straightforward for the system loader to map it into memory. Each section is physically aligned on a disk block boundary or greater (the FileAlignment value) and logically aligned on a memory page boundary (4096 on the x86). The linker creates a PE file for a specific target address at which the file will be mapped (ImageBase). If a block of address space at that address is available, as it almost always is, no load-time fixups are needed. In a few cases—such as the old win32s compatibility system—target addresses aren't available, so the loader has to map the file somewhere else, in which case the file must contain relocation fixups in the .reloc section that tell the loader what to change. Shared DLL libraries are also subject to relocation, because the address at which a DLL is mapped depends on what's already occupying the address space.

Following the PE header is the section table, an array of entries as shown in Figure 3.24. Each section has both a file address and size (PointerToRawData and SizeOfRawData) and a memory address and size (VirtualAddress and VirtualSize); these aren't necessarily the same. The CPU's page size is often

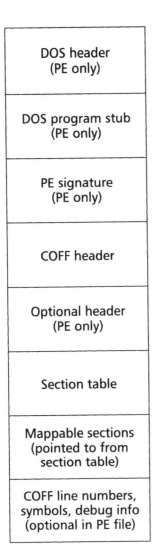

FIGURE **3.22** • Microsoft PE and COFF file.

larger than the disk's block size—typically 4KB pages and 512-byte disk blocks—and a section that ends in the middle of a page need not have blocks for the rest of the page allocated, saving small amounts of disk space. Each section is marked with the hardware permissions appropriate for the pages (e.g., read+execute for code and read+write for data).

text continues on page 81

PE signature

```
char signature[4] = "PE\0\0";          // magic number, also shows byte order
```

COFF header

```
unsigned short  Machine;               // required CPU, 0x14C for 80386, etc.
unsigned short  NumberOfSections;      // creation time or zero
unsigned long   TimeDateStamp;         // creation time or zero
unsigned long   PointerToSymbolTable;  // file offset of symbol table in
                                          COFF or zero
unsigned long   NumberOfSymbols;       // # entries in COFF symbol table
                                          or zero
unsigned short  SizeOfOptionalHeader;  // size of the following optional
                                          header
unsigned short  Characteristics;       // 02 = executable, 0x200 =
                                          nonrelocatable,
                                       // 0x2000 = DLL rather than EXE
```

Optional header that follows PE header; not present in COFF objects

```
// COFF fields
unsigned short  Magic;                 // octal 413, from a.out ZMAGIC
unsigned char   MajorLinkerVersion;
unsigned char   MinorLinkerVersion;
unsigned long   SizeOfCode;            // .text size
unsigned long   SizeOfInitializedData;    // .data size
unsigned long   SizeOfUninitializedData;  // .bss size
unsigned long   AddressOfEntryPoint;   // RVA of entry point
unsigned long   BaseOfCode;            // RVA of .text
unsigned long   BaseOfData;            // RVA of .data

// additional fields.

unsigned long   ImageBase;       // virtual address to map beginning of file
```

FIGURE 3.23 • PE and COFF header.

```
unsigned long   SectionAlignment; // section alignment, typically 4096,
                                  // or 64KB
unsigned long   FileAlignment;    // file page alignment, typically 512
unsigned short  MajorOperatingSystemVersion;
unsigned short  MinorOperatingSystemVersion;
unsigned short  MajorImageVersion;
unsigned short  MinorImageVersion;
unsigned short  MajorSubsystemVersion;
unsigned short  MinorSubsystemVersion;
unsigned long   Reserved1;
unsigned long   SizeOfImage;        // total size of mappable image,
                                    // rounded to SectionAlignment
unsigned long   SizeOfHeaders;      // total size of headers up through
                                    // section table
unsigned long   CheckSum;           // often zero
unsigned short  Subsystem;          // required subsystem: 1 = native,
                                    // 2 = Windows GUI,
                                    // 3 = Windows non-GUI, 5 = OS/2,
                                    // 7 = POSIX
unsigned short  DllCharacteristics; // when to call initialization routine
                                    // (obsolescent)
                                    // 1 = process start, 2 = process end,
                                    // 4 = thread start, 8 = thread end
unsigned long   SizeOfStackReserve; // size to reserve for stack
unsigned long   SizeOfStackCommit;  // size to allocate initially for stack
unsigned long   SizeOfHeapReserve;  // size to reserve for heap
unsigned long   SizeOfHeapCommit;   // size to allocate initially for heap
unsigned long   LoaderFlags;        // obsolete
unsigned long   NumberOfRvaAndSizes; // number of entries in following image
                                     // data directory
// following pair is repeated once for each directory
{
  unsigned long   VirtualAddress;   // relative virtual address of directory
  unsigned long   Size;
}
```

FIGURE 3.23 • Continued

Directories are, in order:

1. Export Directory

2. Import Directory

3. Resource Directory

4. Exception Directory

5. Security Directory

6. Base Relocation Table

7. Debug Directory

8. Image Description String

9. Machine-Specific Data

10. Thread Local Storage Directory

11. Load Configuration Directory

FIGURE **3.23** • Continued

```
// array of entries
unsigned char   Name[8];          // section name in ASCII
unsigned long   VirtualSize;      // size mapped into memory
unsigned long   VirtualAddress;   // memory address relative to image base
unsigned long   SizeOfRawData;    // physical size, multiple of file alignment
unsigned long   PointerToRawData; // file offset
// next four entries present in COFF, present or 0 in PE
unsigned long   PointerToRelocations; // offset of relocation entries
unsigned long   PointerToLinenumbers; // offset of line number entries
unsigned short  NumberOfRelocations;  // number of relocation entries
unsigned short  NumberOfLinenumbers;  // number of line number entries
unsigned long   Characteristics;      // 0x20 = text, 0x40 = data,
                                      // 0x80 = bss, 0x200 = no-load,
  // 0x800 = don't link, 0x10000000 = shared,
  // 0x20000000 = execute, 0x40000000 = read, 0x80000000 = write
```

FIGURE **3.24** • Section table.

PE SPECIAL SECTIONS

A PE file includes text, data, and sometimes bss sections similar to a UNIX executable (usually under those names, in fact) as well as a lot of MS Windows-specific sections, including the following:

- *Exports:* This is a list of the symbols defined in this module and visible to other modules. EXE files typically export no symbols, or maybe they export one or two for debugging. DLLs export symbols for the routines and data that they provide. In keeping with MS Windows space-saving tradition, exported symbols can be referenced by means of small integers called export ordinals as well as by names. The exports section contains an array of the RVAs of the exported symbols. It also contains two parallel arrays of the name of the symbol (as the RVA of an ASCII string) and the export ordinal for the symbol, sorted by string name. To look up a symbol by name, the loader performs a binary search in the string name table, then finds the entry in the ordinal table in the position corresponding to the found name and uses that ordinal to index the array of RVAs. (This is arguably faster than iterating over an array of three-word entries.) Exports can also be "forwarders," in which case the RVA points to a string naming the actual symbol, which is found in another library.

- *Imports:* The imports table lists all of the symbols that need to be resolved at load time from DLLs. The linker predetermines which symbols will be found in which DLLs, so the imports table starts with an import directory, which consists of one entry per referenced DLL. Each directory entry contains the name of the DLL and parallel arrays, one of which identifies the required symbols and the other identifies the place in the image to store the symbol value. The entries in the first value can be either an ordinal (if the high bit is set) or a pointer to a name string preceded by a guess at the ordinal (to speed up the search). The second array contains the place to store the symbol's value: If the symbol is a procedure, the linker will already have adjusted all calls to the symbol to call indirectly through that location; if the symbol is data, references in the importing module are made using that location as a pointer to the actual data. (Some compilers provide the indirect reference automatically; others require explicit program code.)

- *Resources:* The resource table is organized as a tree. The structure supports arbitrarily deep trees, but in practice the tree is three levels—resource type, name, and language. (In this usage, language means a natural language, which permits customizing executables for speakers of languages other than English.) Each resource can have either a name and/or numbers. A typical resource might be type DIALOG (Dialog box), name ABOUT (the About This Program box), language English. Unlike symbols, which have ASCII names, resources have Unicode names to support languages other than English. The actual resources are blocks of binary data, with the format of the resource depending on the resource type.

- *Thread local storage:* MS Windows supports multiple threads of execution per process. Each thread can have its own private storage TLS (thread local storage). This section points to a block of the image that is used to initialize TLS when a thread starts, and it also contains pointers to initialization routines to call when each thread starts. It is usually present in EXE but not DLL files, because MS Windows doesn't allocate TLS storage when a program dynamically links to a DLL. (See Chapter 10.)

- *Fixups:* If the executable is moved, it is moved as a unit so that all fixups have the same value—the difference between the actual load address and the target address. The fixup table, if present, contains an array of fixup blocks, each containing the fixups for one 4KB page of the mapped executable. (Executables with no fixup table can only be loaded at the linked target address.) Each fixup block contains the base RVA of the page, the number of fixups, and an array of 16-bit fixup entries. Each entry contains in the low 12 bits the offset in the block that needs to be relocated and in the high 4 bits the fixup type—for example, for the MIPS architecture, add 32-bit value and adjust high 16 bits or low 16 bits. This block-by-block scheme saves considerable space in the relocation table, because each entry can be squeezed to 2 bytes rather than the 8 or 12 bytes the ELF equivalent takes.

RUNNING A PE EXECUTABLE

Starting a PE executable process is a relatively straightforward procedure.

1. Read in the first page of the file with the DOS header, the PE header, and the section headers.

2. Determine whether the target area of the address space is available; if it is not, allocate another area.

3. Using the information in the section headers, map all of the sections of the file to the appropriate place in the allocated address space.

4. If the file is not loaded into its target address, apply fixups.

5. Go through the list of DLLs in the imports section and load any that aren't already loaded. (This process may be recursive.)

6. Resolve all the imported symbols in the imports section.

7. Create the initial stack and heap using values from the PE header.

8. Create the initial thread and start the process.

PE AND COFF

An MS Windows COFF relocatable object file has the same COFF file header and section headers as a PE, but the structure is more similar to that of a relocatable ELF file. COFF files don't have the DOS header or the optional header following the PE header. Each code or data section also carries along relocation and line number information. (The line numbers in an EXE file, if any, are collected in a debug section that is not handled by the system loader.) COFF objects have section-relative relocations, similar to ELF files, rather than RVA-relative relocations, and they invariably contain a symbol table with the symbols needed. COFF files from language compilers typically do not contain any resources; rather, the resources are in a separate object file created by a specialized resource compiler.

COFF files can also have several other section types that are not used in PE files. The most notable is the .drective section, which contains text command strings for the linker. Compilers usually use .drective to tell the linker to search the appropriate language-specific libraries. Some compilers, including MSVC, also include linker directives to export code and data symbols when creating a DLL. (This mixture of commands and object code goes way back; IBM linkers accepted mixed-card decks of commands and object files in the early 1960s.)

PE SUMMARY

The PE file format is a competent format for a linearly addressed operating system with virtual memory. It has only small amounts of historical baggage from its DOS heritage. It includes some extra features such as ordinal imports and exports, intended to speed up program loading on small systems but of debatable effectiveness on modern 32-bit systems. The earlier NE format for 16-bit segmented executables was far more complicated, and PE is a definite improvement.

3.10 INTEL/MICROSOFT OMF FILES

The final format we look at in this chapter is one of the oldest formats still in use, the Intel Object Module Format (OMF). Intel originally defined OMF in the late 1970s for the 8086. Over the years, a variety of vendors—including Microsoft, IBM, and Phar Lap (who wrote a very widely used set of 32-bit extension tools for DOS)—defined their own extensions. The current Intel OMF is the union of the original specification and most of the extensions, minus a few extensions that either collided with other extensions or were never used.

All of the formats we've seen so far are intended for environments with random access disks and enough RAM to do compiler and linker processing in straightforward ways. OMF dates from the early days of microprocessor development when memories were tiny and storage was often punched paper tapes. As a result, OMF divides the object file into a series of short records (Figure 3.25). Each record contains a type byte, a 2-byte length, the contents, and a checksum byte that makes the bytewise sum of the entire record zero. (Paper tape equipment had no built-in error detection, and errors due to dust or sticky parts were not rare.) OMF files are designed so that a linker on a machine without mass storage can do its job with a minimum number of passes over the files. Usually $1\frac{1}{2}$ passes do the trick: a partial pass to find the symbol names, which are placed near the front of each file, and then a full pass to do the linking and produce the output.

OMF is greatly complicated by the need to deal with the 8086 segmented architecture. One of the major goals of an OMF linker is to pack code and data into a minimum number of segments and segment groups. Every piece of

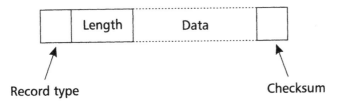

FIGURE 3.25 • OMF record format.

code or data in an OMF object is assigned to a segment, and each segment in turn can be assigned to a segment group or segment class. (A group must be small enough to be addressed by a single segment value, whereas a class can be of any size; hence groups are used for both addressing and storage management, while classes are just for storage management.) Code can reference segments and groups by name and can also reference code within a segment relative to the base of the segment or the base of the group. OMF also contains some support for overlay linking, although no OMF linker I know of has ever supported it (the linkers take their overlay instructions instead from a separate directive file).

OMF RECORDS

OMF currently defines at least 40 record types, too many to enumerate here, so we'll look at a simple representative OMF file. (The complete specification is in the Intel TIS documents.)

OMF uses several coding techniques to make records as short as possible. All name strings are of variable length, stored as a length byte followed by characters. A null name (valid in some contexts) is a single zero byte. Rather than refer to segments, symbols, groups, and so on by name, an OMF module lists each name once in an LNAMES record and subsequently uses an index into the list of names to define the names of segments, groups, and symbols. The first name is 1, the second 2, and so forth through the entire set of names, no matter how many LNAMES records they might have taken. (This saves a small amount of space in the not-uncommon case that a segment and an external symbol have the same name, because the definitions can refer to the same string.) Indexes in the range 0 through 0x7f are stored as 1 byte. Indexes from 0x80 through 0x7fff are stored as 2 bytes, with the high bit in the first byte indicating a 2-byte sequence. Oddly, the low 7 bits of the first byte are the high

7 bits of the value and the second byte is the low 8 bits of the value—the opposite of the native Intel order. Segments, groups, and external symbols are also referred to by index, with separate index sequences for each. For example, assume that a module lists the names DGROUP, CODE, and DATA, defining the name indexes as 1, 2, and 3. Then assume the module defines two segments called CODE and DATA, referring to names 2 and 3. Since CODE is the first segment defined, it will be segment index 1 and DATA will be segment index 2.

The original OMF format was defined for the 16-bit Intel architecture. For 32-bit programs, there are new OMF types defined for the record types where the address size matters. All of the 16-bit record types happened to have even numerical codes, so the corresponding 32-bit record types have the odd code one greater than the 16-bit type.

DETAILS OF AN OMF FILE

Figure 3.26 lists the records in a simple OMF file. The file starts with a THEADR record that marks the start of the module and gives the name of the module's source file as a string. (If this module were part of a library, it would start with a similar LHEADR record.)

The second record is a poorly named COMENT record that contains configuration information for the linker. Each COMENT record contains some flag bits indicating whether to keep the comment when linked, a type byte, and the comment text. Some comment types are indeed comments (e.g., the compiler version number or a copyright notice) but several of them give essential linker information such as the memory model to use (tiny through large), the name of a library to search after processing this file, definitions of weak external symbols, and a grab bag of other types of data that vendors shoehorned into the OMF format.

Next comes a series of LNAMES records that list all of the names used in this module for segments, groups, classes, and overlays. As noted above, all the names in all LNAMES are logically considered an array with the index of the first name being 1.

After the LNAMES record come SEGDEF records, one for each segment defined in the module. The SEGDEF includes an index for the name of the segment and the class and overlay (if any) it belongs to. Also given are the

THEADR program name

COMENT flags and options

LNAMES list of segment, group, and class names

SEGDEF segment (one record per segment)

GRPDEF group (one record per group)

PUBDEF global symbols

EXTDEF undefined external symbols (one per symbol)

COMDEF common blocks

COMENT end of pass 1 information

LEDATA chunk of code or data (multiple)

LIDATA chunk of repeated data (multiple)

FIXUPP relocations and external reference fixups, each following the
LEDATA or LIDATA to which it refers

MODEND end of module

FIGURE **3.26** • Typical OMF record sequence.

segment's attributes, including its alignment requirements, rules for combining it with same-name segments in other modules, and its length.

Next come GRPDEF records, if any, defining the groups in the module. Each GRPDEF has the index for the group name and the indices for the segments in the group.

PUBDEF records define public symbols visible to other modules. Each PUBDEF defines one or more symbols within a single group or segment. The record includes the index of the segment or group and, for each symbol, the symbol's offset within the segment or group, its name, and a 1-byte compiler-specific type field.

EXTDEF records define undefined external symbols. Each record contains the name of one symbol and a byte or two of debugger symbol type. COMDEF records define common blocks and are similar to EXTDEF records except that they also define a minimum size for the symbol. All of the EXTDEF and COMDEF symbols in the module are logically an array, so fixups can refer to them by index.

Next comes an optional specialized COMENT record that marks the end of pass 1 data. It tells the linker that it can skip the rest of the file in the first pass of the linking process.

The rest of the file consists of the actual code and data of the program, intermixed with fixup records containing relocation and external reference information. There are two kinds of data records, LEDATA (enumerated) and LIDATA (iterated). LEDATA simply has the segment index and starting offset followed by the data to store there. LIDATA also starts with the segment and starting offset, but then it has a possibly nested set of repeated blocks of data. LIDATA efficiently handles code generated for statements such as this Fortran code:

```
INTEGER A(20,20) /400*42/
```

A single LIDATA can have a 2- or 4-byte block containing 42 and repeat it 400 times.

Each LEDATA or LIDATA that needs a fixup must be immediately followed by the FIXUPP records. FIXUPP is by far the most complicated record type. Each fixup requires three items: first, the target, which is the address being referenced; second, the frame, which is the position in a segment or group relative to which the address is being calculated; and third, the location to be fixed up. Since it's very common to refer to a single frame in many fixups and somewhat common to refer to a single target in many fixups, OMF defines fixup *threads*, 2-bit codes used as shorthand for frames or targets, so that at any point there can be up to four frames and four targets with thread numbers defined. Each thread number can be redefined as often as needed. For example, if a module includes a data group, that group is usually used as the frame for nearly every data reference in the module, so defining a thread number for the base address of that group saves a great deal of space. In practice, a GRPDEF record is almost invariably followed by a FIXUPP record defining a frame thread for that group.

Each FIXUPP record is a sequence of subrecords, with each subrecord defining either a thread or a fixup. A thread definition subrecord has flag bits indicating whether it's defining a frame or a target thread. A target thread definition contains the thread number; the kind of reference (segment relative, group relative, or external relative); the index of the base segment, group, or symbol; and, optionally, a base offset. A frame thread definition includes the thread number and the kind of reference (segment relative, group relative, or external relative, plus two common special cases, same segment as the location and same segment as the target).

Once the threads are defined, a fixup subrecord is relatively simple. It contains the location to fix up, a code specifying the type of fixup (16-bit offset, 16-bit segment, full segment:offset, 8-bit relative, and so on), and the frame and target. The frame and target can either refer to previously defined threads or be specified in place.

After the LEDATA, LIDATA, and FIXUPP records, the end of the module is marked by a MODEND record. This record can optionally specify the entry point if the module is the main routine in a program.

A real OMF file would contain more record types for local symbols, line numbers, and other debugger information, and in an MS Windows environment it would also contain information to create the imports and exports sections in a target NE file (the segmented 16-bit predecessor of PE), but the structure of the module doesn't change. The order of records is quite flexible, particularly if there's no end of pass 1 COMENT marker. The only hard-and-fast rules are that THEADR and MODEND must come first and last, FIXUPPs must immediately follow the LEDATA and LIDATA to which they refer, and no intramodule forward references are allowed. In particular, it's permissible to generate records for symbols, segments, and groups as they're defined, so long as they precede other records that refer to them.

SUMMARY OF OMF

The OMF format is quite complicated compared to the other formats we've seen. Part of the complication occurs as a result of tricks to compress the data, part results from the division of each module into many small records, part results from incremental features added over the years, and part results from the inherent complexity of segmented program addressing. The consistent record format with typed records is a strong point, because it both permits extension in a straightforward way and permits programs that process OMF files to skip records they don't understand.

Nonetheless, now that even small desktop computers have megabytes of RAM and large disks, the OMF division of the object into many small records has become more trouble than it's worth. The small-record type of object module was very common up through the 1970s but is now obsolete.

3.11   COMPARISON OF OBJECT FORMATS

We've seen seven different object and executable formats in this chapter, ranging from the trivial (COM) to the sophisticated (ELF and PE) to the rococo (OMF). Modern object formats such as ELF try to group all of the data of a single type together to make it easier for linkers to process. They also lay out the file with virtual memory considerations in mind, so that the system loader can map the file into the program's address space with as little extra work as possible.

Each object format shows the style of the system for which it was defined. UNIX systems have historically kept their internal interfaces simple and well defined, and the a.out and ELF formats reflect that in their relative simplicity and lack of special-case features. MS Windows has gone in the other direction, with process management and user interface intertwined.

EXERCISES

EXERCISE • 3.1

After studying the project section following, consider whether such a text object format would be practical. (*Hint:* See Fraser and Hanson's paper, "A Machine-Independent Linker," in the references.)

PROJECT

Here we define the simple object format used in the project assignments through the rest of this book. Unlike nearly every other object format, this one consists entirely of lines of ASCII text. This makes it possible to create sample object files in a text editor, as well as making it easier to check the output files from the project linker. Figure 3.27 sketches the format. The segment, symbol, and relocation entries are represented as lines of text with fields separated by spaces. Each line may have extra fields at the end that programs should be prepared to ignore. Numbers are all hexadecimal.

```
LINK
nsegs nsyms nrels
- segments -
-  symbols -
-  rels -
-  data -
```

Figure 3.27 • Project object format.

The first line is the "magic number," the word LINK. The second line contains at least three decimal numbers—the number of segments in the file, the number of symbol table entries, and the number of relocation entries. There may be other information after the three numbers for extended versions of the linker. If there are no symbols or relocations given, the respective number is zero.

Next come the segment definitions. Each segment definition contains the segment name, the address where the segment logically starts, the length of the segment in bytes, and a string of code letters describing the segment. Code letters include R for readable, W for writable, and P for present in the object file. (Other letters may be present as well.) A typical set of segments for an a.out-like file would be

```
.text 1000 2500 RP
.data 4000 C00 RWP
.bss  5000 1900 RW
```

Segments are numbered in the order their definitions appear, with the first segment being number 1.

Next comes the symbol table. Each entry is of the following form:

```
name value seg type
```

The name is the symbol name. The value is the hexadecimal value of the symbol. seg is the segment number relative to which the symbol is defined (0 for absolute or undefined symbols). The type is a string of letters that includes D for defined or U for undefined. Symbols are also numbered in the order they're listed, starting at 1.

Next come the relocations, one to a line:

```
loc seg ref type ...
```

loc is the location to be relocated, seg is the segment within which the location is found, ref is the segment or symbol number to be relocated there, and type is an architecture-dependent relocation type. Common types are A4 for a 4-byte absolute address or R4 for a 4-byte relative address. Some relocation types may have extra fields after the type.

Following the relocations come the object data. The data for each segment are a single long hexadecimal string followed by a newline. (This makes it easy to read and write section data in perl.) Each pair of hexadecimal digits represents 1 byte. The segment data strings are in the same order as the segment table, and there must be segment data for each segment that is identified as being present. The length of the hexadecimal string is determined by the defined length of the segment; if the segment is 100 bytes long, the line of segment data is 200 characters, not counting the newline at the end.

PROJECT • 3.1

Write a perl program that reads an object file in this format and stores the contents in a suitable form in perl tables and arrays, then writes the file back out. The output file need not be identical to the input, although it should be semantically equivalent. (For example, the symbols need not be written in the same order they were read, although if they're reordered, the relocation entries must be adjusted to reflect the new order of the symbol table.)

STORAGE
ALLOCATION

A linker's or loader's first major task is storage allocation. Once storage is allocated, the linker can proceed to subsequent phases of symbol binding and code fixups. Most of the symbols defined in a linkable object file are defined relative to storage areas within the file, so the symbols cannot be resolved until the addresses of the areas are known.

As is the case with most other aspects of linking, the basic issues in storage allocation are straightforward, but the details to handle peculiarities of computer architecture and programming language semantics (and the interactions between the two) can get complicated. Most of the job of storage allocation can be handled in an elegant and relatively architecture-independent way, but there are invariably a few details that require ad hoc machine-specific hackery.

4.1 SEGMENTS AND ADDRESSES

Every object or executable file uses a model of the target address space. Usually the target is the target computer's application address space, but there are cases where it's something else, such as a shared library. The fundamental issue in a relocating linker or loader is to ensure that all the segments in a program are defined and have addresses, but that addresses don't overlap where they're not supposed to.

Each of the linker's input files contains a set of segments of various types. Different kinds of segments are treated in different ways. Most commonly, all segments of a particular type—such as executable code—are concatenated into a single segment in the output file. Sometimes segments are merged one on top of another, as for Fortran common blocks, and, in an increasing number of cases, for shared libraries and C++ special features, the linker itself needs to create some segments and lay them out.

Storage layout is a two-pass process, because the location of each segment can't be assigned until the sizes of all segments that logically precede it are known.

4.2 SIMPLE STORAGE LAYOUT

In a simple but not unrealistic situation, the input to a linker consists of a set of modules M_1 through M_n, each of which consists of a single segment starting at location 0 of length L_1 through L_n, with the target address space also starting at zero (Figure 4.1).

The linker or loader examines each module in turn, allocating storage sequentially. The starting address of M_i is the sum of L_1 through L_{i-1}, and the length of the linked program is the sum of L_1 through L_n.

Most architectures require that data be aligned on word boundaries, or at least they run faster if the data are aligned, so linkers generally round each L_i up to a multiple of the most stringent alignment that the architecture requires, typically 4 or 8 bytes.

EXAMPLE • 4.1

Assume that a main program called main that allocates venture capital geographically is to be linked with three subroutines called calif, mass, and newyork. The hexadecimal sizes of each routine are

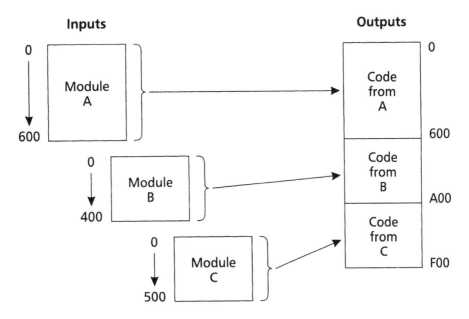

FIGURE **4.1** • Single-segment storage allocation.

Name	Size
main	1017
calif	920
mass	615
newyork	1390

Assume that storage allocation starts at location hex 1000 and that the alignment is 4 bytes. Then the allocations might be

Name	Location
main	1000–2016
calif	2018–2937
mass	2938–2f4c
newyork	2f50–42df

Because of required alignment, 1 byte at 2017 and 3 bytes at 2f4d are wasted—not enough to worry about.

4.3 MULTIPLE-SEGMENT TYPES

In all but the simplest object formats, there are several kinds of segments, and the linker needs to group corresponding segments from all of the input modules together. On a UNIX system with text and data segments, the linked file needs to have all of the text collected together, followed by all of the data, followed logically by the bss. (Even though the bss doesn't take space in the output file, it needs to have space allocated to resolve bss symbols and to indicate the size of bss to allocate when the output file is loaded.) This requires a two-level storage allocation strategy.

Now each module M_i has text size T_i, data size D_i, and bss size B_i (Figure 4.2). As it reads each input module, the linker allocates space for each of T_i, D_i, and B_i as though each segment were separately allocated at zero. After reading all of the input files, the linker now knows the total size of each of the three segments, T_{tot}, D_{tot}, and B_{tot}. Because the data segment follows the text segment, the linker adds T_{tot} to the address assigned for each of the data segments; because the bss segment follows both the text and data segments, the linker adds the sum of T_{tot} and D_{tot} to the allocated bss segments. (Also, once again the linker usually needs to round up each allocated size.)

4.4 SEGMENT AND PAGE ALIGNMENT

If the text and data segments are loaded into separate memory pages, as is generally the case, the size of the text segment has to be rounded up to a full page and the data and bss segment locations correspondingly adjusted. Many UNIX systems use a trick that saves file space by starting the data immediately after the text in the object file and mapping that page in the file into virtual memory twice, once read-only for the text and once copy-on-write for the data. In that case, the data addresses logically start exactly one page beyond the end of the text, so rather than rounding up, the data addresses start exactly 4KB—or whatever the page size is—beyond the end of the text.

EXAMPLE • 4.2

This example expands Example 4.1 so that each routine has a text, data, and bss segment. The word alignment remains 4 bytes, but the page size is 0x1000 bytes. All numbers are hexadecimal.

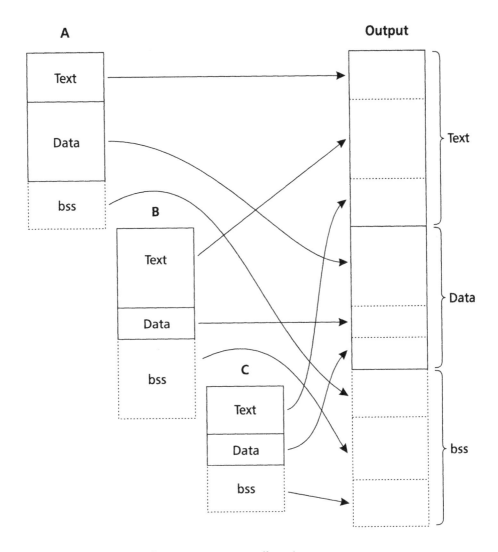

FIGURE 4.2 • Multiple-segment storage allocation.

Name	Text	Data	bss
main	1017	320	50
calif	920	217	100
mass	615	300	840
newyork	1390	1213	1400

The linker first lays out the text, then the data, then the bss. Note that the data section starts on a page boundary at 0x5000, but the bss starts immediately after the data, because at run time data and bss are logically one segment.

Name	Text	Data	bss
main	1000–2016	5000–531f	695c–69ab
calif	2018–2937	5320–5446	69ac–6aab
mass	2938–2f4c	5448–5747	6aac–72eb
newyork	2f50–42df	5748–695a	72ec–86eb

Thus there is wasted space at the end of the page between 42e0 and 5000. The bss segment ends in mid-page at 86eb, but programs allocate heap space starting immediately after that.

4.5   COMMON BLOCKS AND OTHER SPECIAL SEGMENTS

The straightforward segment allocation scheme above works nicely for about 80% of the storage that linkers deal with. The rest is handled with special-case hacks. Here we look at some of the more popular ones.

COMMON

Common storage is a feature dating back to Fortran I in the 1950s. In the original Fortran system, each subprogram (main program, function, or subroutine) had its own statically declared and allocated scalar and array variables. There was also a common area with scalars and arrays that all subprograms could use. Common storage proved very useful, and in subsequent versions of Fortran it was generalized from a single common block—now known as "blank" common, indicating a name consisting of blanks—to multiple named common blocks, with each subprogram declaring the blocks that it uses.

For the first 40 years of its existence, Fortran didn't support dynamic storage allocation, and common blocks were the primary tool that Fortran programmers used to circumvent that restriction. Standard Fortran permits blank common to be declared with different sizes in different routines, with the largest size taking precedence. Fortran systems universally extend this to allow all common blocks to be declared with different sizes, again with the largest size taking precedence.

Large Fortran programs often bump up against the memory limits of the systems in which they run, so in the absence of dynamic memory allocation, programmers frequently rebuild a package, tweaking the sizes to fit whatever problem a package is working on. All but one of the subprograms in such a package declare each common block as a one-element array. One of the subprograms declares the actual size of all the common blocks, and at startup time it puts the sizes in variables (in yet another common block) that the rest of the package can use. This makes it possible to adjust the size of the blocks by changing and recompiling a single routine that defines them and then relinking.

As an added complication, starting in the 1960s Fortran added BLOCK DATA to specify static initial data values for all or part of any common block (except for blank common, a restriction rarely enforced). Usually the size of the common block in the BLOCK DATA that initializes a block is taken to be the block's actual size at link time.

To handle common blocks, the linker treats the declaration of a common block in an input file as a segment but overlays all of the blocks with the same name rather than concatenating these segments. It uses the largest declared size as the segment's size, unless one of the input files has an initialized version of the segment. In some systems, initialized common is a separate segment type, while in others it's just part of the data segment.

UNIX linkers have always supported common blocks, because even the earliest versions of UNIX had a Fortran subset compiler, and UNIX versions of C have traditionally treated uninitialized global variables much like common blocks. But the pre-ELF versions of UNIX object files only had the text, data, and bss segments with no direct way to declare a common block. As a special-case hack, linkers treated a symbol that was flagged as undefined but that nonetheless had a nonzero value as a common block, with the value being the size of the block. The linker took the largest value encountered for such symbols as the size of the common block. For each block, it defined the symbol in the bss segment of the output file, allocating the required amount of space after each symbol (Figure 4.3).

C++ Duplicate Removal

In some compilation systems, C++ compilers produce a great deal of duplicate code as a result of virtual function tables, templates, and extern inline

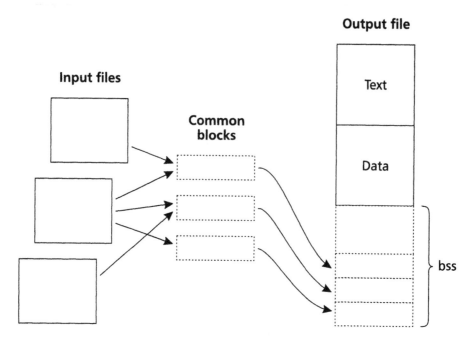

FIGURE 4.3 • UNIX common blocks.

functions. The design of those features implicitly expects an environment in which all of the pieces of a program are processed simultaneously. A virtual function table (usually abbreviated vtbl) contains the addresses of all the virtual functions (routines that can be overridden in a subclass) for a C++ class. Each class with any virtual functions needs a vtbl. Templates are essentially macros with arguments that are datatypes and that expand into distinct routines for every distinct set of type arguments. Whereas it is the programmer's job to ensure that if there is a reference to normal routines called, say, hash(int) and hash(char *), there's exactly one definition of each kind of hash, a template version of hash(T) automatically creates versions of hash for each data type that is used anywhere in the program as an argument to hash.

In an environment in which each source file is separately compiled, a straightforward technique is to place in each object file all of the vtbls, expanded template routines, and extern inlines used in that file, although that results in a great deal of duplicated code. The simplest approach at link time is to live with the duplication. The resulting program works correctly, but the code bloat can bulk up the object program to three times or more of the size that it should be.

```
IMAGE_COMDAT_SELECT_NODUPLICATES        1 Warn if multiple identically
                                            named sections occur.

IMAGE_COMDAT_SELECT_ANY                  2 Link one identically named
                                          section, discard the rest.

IMAGE_COMDAT_SELECT_SAME_SIZE            3 Link one identically named
                                          section, discard the rest.
                       Warn if a discarded section isn't the same size.

IMAGE_COMDAT_SELECT_EXACT_MATCH          4 Link one identically named
                                          section, discard the rest.
                        Warn if a discarded section isn't identical
                            in size and contents. (Not implemented.)

IMAGE_COMDAT_SELECT_ASSOCIATIVE          5 Link this section if another
                                        specified section is also linked.
```

FIGURE 4.4 • MS Windows COMDAT flag.

In systems stuck with simple-minded linkers, some C++ systems have used other approaches: an iterative linking approach, separate databases of what's expanded where, or added pragmas (source code hints to the compiler) that feed back enough information to the compiler to generate just the code that's needed. We cover these techniques in Chapter 11.

Many recent C++ systems have addressed the problem head-on, either by making the linker smarter or by integrating the linker with other parts of the program development system. (We also touch on the latter approach in Chapter 11.) The linker approach has the compiler generate all of the possibly duplicate code in each object file, with the linker identifying and discarding duplicates.

MS Windows linkers define a COMDAT flag for code sections that tells the linker to discard all but one of several identically named sections. The compiler gives the section the name of the template, suitably mangled to include the argument types (Figure 4.4).

The GNU linker deals with the template problem by defining a link-once type of section similar to common blocks. If the linker sees segments with names of the form .gnu.linkonce.*name*, it throws away all but the first such

segment with identical names. Again, compilers expand a template to a
.gnu.linkonce section with a name that includes the mangled template name.

This scheme works pretty well, but it's not a panacea. For one thing, it
doesn't protect against the case in which vtbls and expanded templates are
not actually functionally identical. Some linkers attempt to check that the discarded segments are byte-for-byte identical to the one that's kept. This is very
conservative, but it can produce false errors if two files were compiled with
different optimization options or with different versions of the compiler. For
another, it doesn't discard nearly as much duplicated code as it could. In most
C++ systems, all pointers have the same internal representation. This means
that a template instantiated with, say, a pointer to int type and the same template instantiated with a pointer to float will often generate identical code
even though the C++ types are different. Some linkers may attempt to discard
link-once sections that contain code identical to another section even when
the names don't quite match perfectly, but this issue remains unsatisfactorily
resolved.

Although we've been discussing templates up to this point, exactly the
same issues apply to extern inline functions and default constructor, copy,
and assignment routines, which can be handled the same way.

INITIALIZERS AND FINALIZERS

Another problem not unique to C++ but exacerbated by it is initializers and
finalizers. Frequently, it's easier to write libraries if they can arrange to run an
initializing routine when the program starts and a finalizing routine when the
program is about to exit. C++ allows static variables. If a variable's class has a
constructor, a static variable's constructor needs to be called at startup time to
initialize a static variable, and if it has a destructor, the destructor needs to be
called at exit time. There are various ways to finesse this without linker support, which we discuss in Chapter 11, but modern linkers generally do support
this directly.

The usual approach is for each object file to put any startup code into an
anonymous routine and to put a pointer to that routine into a segment called
.init or something similar. The linker concatenates all the .init segments
together, thereby creating a list of pointers to all the startup routines. The

program's startup stub need only run down the list and call all the routines. Exit time code can be handled in much the same way, with a segment called .fini.

It turns out that this approach is not altogether satisfactory, because some startup code needs to be run earlier than other code. The definition of C++ states that application-level constructors are run in an unpredictable order, but the I/O and other system library constructors need to be run before constructors in C++ applications are called. The "perfect" approach would be for each .init routine to list its dependencies explicitly and to do a topological sort. The BeOS dynamic linker does approximately that, using library reference dependencies. (If library A depends on library B, library B's initializers probably need to run first.)

A much simpler approximation is to have two initialization segments, .init and .ctor; the startup stub first calls the .init routines for library-level initialization and then the .ctor routines for C++ constructors. The same problem occurs at the end of the program, with the corresponding segments being .dtor and .fini. One system goes so far as to allow the programmer to assign priority numbers, 0 to 127 for user code and 128 to 255 for system library code, with the linker sorting the initializer and finalizer routines by priority before combining them so that highest-priority initializers run first. This is still not altogether satisfactory, since constructors can have order dependencies on each other that cause hard-to-find bugs, but at this point C++ makes it the programmer's responsibility to prevent those dependencies.

A variant of this scheme puts the actual initialization code in the .init segments. When the linker combined them, the segment would be inline code to do all of the initializations. A few systems have tried that, but it's hard to make it work on computers without direct addressing, since the block of code from each object file needs to be able to address the data for its own file, usually needing registers that point to tables of address data. The anonymous routines set up their addressing the same way any other routine does, reducing the addressing problem to one that's already solved.

IBM PSEUDO-REGISTERS

IBM mainframe linkers provide an interesting feature called *pseudo-registers* or *external dummy* sections. The 360 was one of the earlier mainframe architectures without direct addressing, which meant that small shared-data areas were expensive to implement. Each routine that refers to a global object needs its own 4-byte pointer to the object, which is a lot of overhead if the object is only 4 bytes to start with. PL/I programs need a 4-byte pointer to each open file and other global object, for example. (PL/I was the only high-level language to use pseudo-registers, although it didn't provide application programmers with access to them. It used them for pointers to control blocks for open files so that application code could include inline calls to the I/O system.)

A related problem is that OS/360 didn't provide any support for what's now called per-process or task local storage, and it provided very limited support for shared libraries. If two jobs ran the same program, either the program was marked reentrant (in which case they shared the entire program, code, and data) or not reentrant (in which case they shared nothing). All programs were loaded into the same address space, so multiple instances of the same program had to make their arrangements for instance-specific data. (System 360s didn't have hardware memory relocation, and although 370s did, it wasn't until after several revisions of the OS/VS operating system that the system provided per-process address spaces.)

Pseudo-registers help solve both of these problems (Figure 4.5). Each input file can declare pseudo-registers. (The alternate name, external dummy sections, comes from the 360 assembler in which a dummy section is analogous to a structure declaration.) Each pseudo-register has a name, length, and alignment. At link time, the linker collects all of the pseudo-registers into one logical segment, taking the largest size and most restrictive alignment for each, and assigns them all non-overlapping offsets in this logical segment.

But the linker doesn't allocate space for the pseudo-register segment. It merely calculates the size of the segment and stores it in the program's data at a location marked by a special cumulative external dummy (CXD) relocation item. To refer to a particular pseudo-register, program code uses yet another special external dummy (XD) relocation type to indicate where to place the offset in the logical segment of one of the pseudo-registers.

The program's initialization code dynamically allocates space for the pseudo-registers, using a CXD to know how much space is needed, and conventionally places the address of that region in register 12, which remains unchanged for the duration of the program. Any part of the program can get the address of a pseudo-register by adding the contents of register 12 to an XD item for that register. The usual way to do this is with a load or store instruction, using register 12 as the index register and an XD item embedded as the

Object file

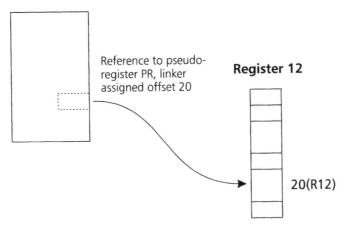

Reference to pseudo-register PR, linker assigned offset 20

Register 12

20(R12)

FIGURE 4.5 • Pseudo-registers.

address displacement field in the instruction. (The displacement field is only 12 bits, but the XD item leaves the high 4 bits of the 16-bit halfword as zero, meaning base register zero, which produces the correct result.)

The result of all this is that all parts of the program have direct access to all the pseudo-registers using load, store, and other RX format instructions. If multiple instances of a program are active, each instance allocates a separate space with a different register 12 value.

Although the original motivation for pseudo-registers is now largely obsolete, the idea of providing linker support for efficient access to thread local data is a good one and has appeared in various forms in more modern systems, notably Win32. Also, modern RISC machines share the 360's limited addressing range and require tables of memory pointers to address arbitrary memory locations. On many RISC UNIX systems, a compiler creates two data segments in each module, one for regular data and one for "small" data static objects below some threshold size. The linker collects all of the small data segments together and arranges for program startup code to put the address of the combined small data segment in a reserved register. This permits direct references to small data using based addressing relative to that register. Note that unlike pseudo-registers, the small data storage is both laid out and allocated by the linker, and there's only one copy of the small data per process. Some UNIX systems support threads, but per-thread storage is handled by explicit program code without any special help from the linker.

SPECIAL TABLES

The last source of linker-allocated storage is the linker itself. Particularly when a program uses shared libraries or overlays, the linker creates segments with pointers, symbols, and whatever other data are needed at run time to support the libraries or overlays. Once these segments are created, the linker allocates storage for them the same way it does for any other segments.

X86 SEGMENTED STORAGE ALLOCATION

The peculiar requirements of 8086 and 286 sort-of-segmented memory addressing led to a few specialized facilities. x86 OMF object files give each segment a name and optionally a class. All segments with the same name are, depending on some flag bits set by the compiler or assembler, combined into one big segment, and all the segments in a class are allocated contiguously in a block. Compilers and assemblers use class names to mark types of segments such as code and static data, so the linker can allocate all the segments of a given class together. So long as all of the segments in a class are less than 64KB total, they can be treated as a single addressing "group" using a single segment register, which saves considerable time and space.

Figure 4.6 shows a program linked from three input files, main, able, and baker. Main contains segments MAINCODE and MAINDATA, able contains ABLECODE and ABLEDATA, and baker contains BAKERCODE, BAKERDATA, and BAKERLDATA. Each of the CODE sections are in the CODE class and the DATA sections are in the DATA class, but the BAKERLDATA (large data) section is not assigned to a class. In the linked program, assuming that the CODE sections are a total of 64KB or less, they can be treated as a single segment at run time, using short rather than long call and jump instructions and a single unchanging CS code segment register. Likewise, if all the DATA fit in 64KB they can be treated as a single segment using short memory reference instructions and a single unchanging DS data segment register. The BAKERLDATA segment is handled at run time as a separate segment, with code loading a segment register (usually the ES) to refer to it.

Real-mode and 286 protected mode programs are linked almost identically. The primary difference is that once the linker creates the linked segments in a protected mode program, the linker is done with its work, leaving the actual assignment of memory locations and segment numbers until the

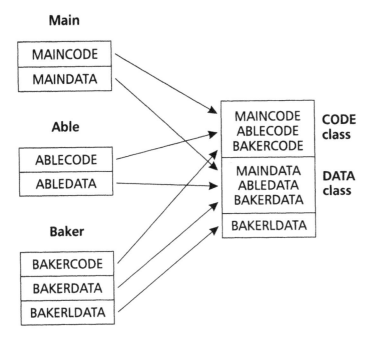

FIGURE 4.6 • x86 segmented storage allocation.

program is loaded. In real mode, the linker has an extra step that allocates the segments to linear addresses and assigns paragraph numbers to the segments relative to the beginning of the program. Then at load time the program loader has to fix up all of the paragraph numbers (in a real-mode program) or segment numbers (in a protected mode program) to refer to the actual location where the program is loaded.

4.6 LINKER CONTROL SCRIPTS

Traditionally, linkers offered the user limited control over the arrangement of output data. As linkers started to target environments with messy memory organizations—such as embedded microprocessors—and multiple target environments, it became necessary to provide finer-grained control over the arrangement of data both in the target address space and in the output file. Simple linkers with a fixed set of segments generally have switches to specify the base address of each segment, to allow programs to be loaded into something other than the standard application environment. (Operating system kernels are the usual application for these switches.) Some linkers have huge numbers of command line switches, often with provision to continue the command line logically in a file because of system limits on the length of the actual command line. For example, the Microsoft linker has about 50 command line switches that can set the characteristics of each section in the file, the base address of the output, and a variety of other output details.

Other linkers have defined a script language to control the linker's output. The GNU linker, which also has a long list of command line switches, defines such a language. Figure 4.7 shows a simple linker script that produces COFF executables for System V Release 3.2 systems such as SCO UNIX.

The first few lines describe the output format, which must be present in a table of formats compiled into the linker; the place to look for object code libraries; and the name of the default entry point, _start in this case. Then it lists the sections in the output file. An optional value after the section name indicates where the section starts (hence the .text section starts immediately after the file headers). The .text section in the output file contains the .init sections from all of the input files, the .text sections, and the .fini sections. The linker defines the symbol etext to be the address after the .fini sections. Then the script sets the origin of the .data section to start on a 4KB page boundary roughly hex 400000 beyond the end of the text, and the section includes the .data sections from all the input files with the symbol edata defined after them. Then the .bss section starts right after the data and includes the input .bss sections as well as any common blocks, with end marking the end of the bss. (COMMON is a keyword in the script language.) After that are two sections for symbol table entries collected from the corresponding parts of the input files but not loaded at run time (because only a debugger looks at those symbols). The linker script language is considerably more flexible than this simple example shows and is adequate to describe everything from simple DOS executables to MS Windows PE executables to complex overlaid arrangements.

4.7 STORAGE ALLOCATION IN PRACTICE

We end this chapter by walking through the storage allocation for various popular linkers—UNIX a.out, ELF, and MS Windows.

```
OUTPUT_FORMAT("coff-i386")
 SEARCH_DIR(/usr/local/lib);
ENTRY(_start)
SECTIONS
{
  .text  SIZEOF_HEADERS : {
    *(.init)
   *(.text)
    *(.fini)
    etext  =  .;
  }
  .data  0x400000 + (. & 0xffc00fff) : {
   *(.data)
    edata  =  .;
  }
  .bss  SIZEOF(.data) + ADDR(.data) :
  {
   *(.bss)
   *(COMMON)
    end = .;
  }
  .stab  0 (NOLOAD) :
  {
   [ .stab ]
  }
  .stabstr  0 (NOLOAD) :
  {
   [ .stabstr ]
  }
}
```

FIGURE **4.7** • GNU linker control script for COFF executable.

STORAGE ALLOCATION IN UNIX A.OUT LINKERS

Allocation in pre-ELF UNIX linkers is only slightly more complex than the idealized example at the beginning of the chapter, because the set of segments is

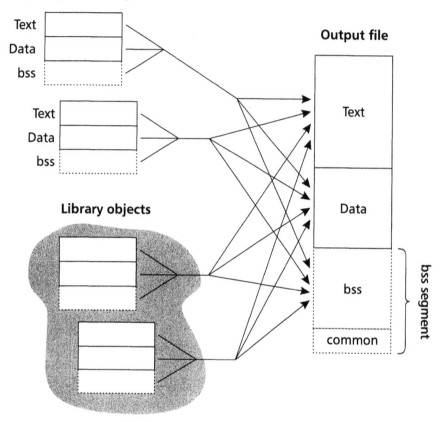

Explicitly linked objects

Text
Data
bss

Text
Data
bss

Library objects

Output file

Text

Data

bss

common

bss segment

FIGURE 4.8 • a.out linking.

known in advance (Figure 4.8). Each input file has text, data, and bss segments and perhaps common blocks disguised as external symbols. The linker collects the sizes of the text, data, and bss from each of the input files as well as from any objects taken from libraries. After reading all of the objects, any unresolved external symbols with nonzero values are taken to be common blocks and are allocated at the end of the bss.

At this point, the linker can assign addresses to all of the segments. The text segment starts at a fixed location that depends on the variety of a.out being created, either location zero (the oldest formats), one page past location zero (NMAGIC formats), or one page past location zero plus the size of the a.out header (QMAGIC). The data segment starts right after the text segment in old unshared a.out, on the next page boundary after the text segment in

NMAGIC, and exactly one page past the end of the text in QMAGIC. In every format, bss starts immediately after the data segment. Within each segment, the linker allocates the segments from each input file starting at the next word boundary after the previous segment.

STORAGE ALLOCATION IN ELF

ELF linking is somewhat more complex than a.out, because the set of input segments can be arbitrarily large and the linker has to turn the input segments (*sections* in ELF terminology) into loadable segments (*segments* in ELF terminology). The linker also has to create the program header table needed for the program loader and some special sections needed for dynamic linking (Figure 4.9).

ELF objects have the traditional text, data, and bss sections, now called .text, .data, and .bss. They also often contain .init and .fini, for startup and exit time code, as well as various odds and ends. The optional .rodata and .data1 sections are used in some compilers for read-only data and out-of-line data literals. (Some also have .rodata1 for out-of-line read-only data.) On RISC systems such as MIPS that have limited-sized address offsets, .sbss and .scommon are small bss and common blocks to help group small objects into one directly addressable area, as we noted above in the discussion of pseudo-registers. On GNU C++ systems, there may also be link-once sections to be included into .text, .rodata, and .data segments.

Despite the profusion of section types, the linking process remains about the same. The linker collects each type of section from the input files together, along with sections from library objects. The linker also notes which symbols will be resolved at run time from shared libraries and creates .interp, .got, .plt, and symbol table sections to support run-time linking. (We defer discussion of the details until Chapter 9.) Once all that is done, the linker allocates space in a conventional order. Unlike a.out, ELF objects are not loaded anywhere near address zero; instead, they are loaded in about the middle of the address space so the stack can grow down below the text segment and the heap can grow up from the end of the data, keeping the total address space in use relatively compact. On 386 systems, the text base address is 0x08048000, which permits a reasonably large stack below the text while still staying above address 0x08000000, thus permitting most programs to use a single second-level page table. (Recall that on the 386, each second-level table maps

Input files

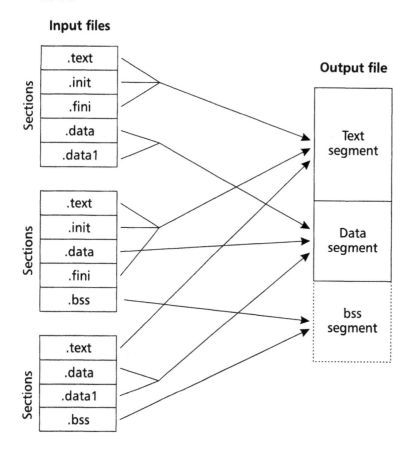

FIGURE 4.9 • ELF linking.

0x00400000 addresses.) ELF uses the QMAGIC trick of including the header in the text segment, so the actual text segment starts after the ELF header and program header table, typically at file offset 0x100. Then it allocates into the text segment .interp (the logical link to the dynamic linker, which needs to run first), the dynamic linker symbol table sections, .init, the .text and link-once text, and the read-only data.

Next comes the data segment, which logically starts one page past the end of the text segment, because at run time the page is mapped in as both the last page of text and the first page of data. The linker allocates the various .data and link-once data, the .got section, and, on platforms that use it, the .sdata small data and the .got global offset table. Finally come the bss sections, logically right after the data, starting with .sbss (if any, to put it next to .sdata and .got), the bss segments, and common blocks.

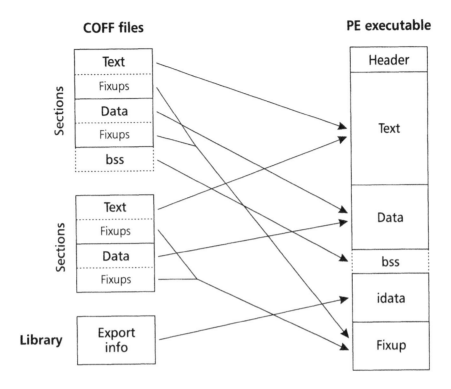

FIGURE **4.10** • PE storage allocation.

STORAGE ALLOCATION
IN MS WINDOWS LINKERS

Storage allocation for MS Windows PE files is somewhat simpler than for ELF files, because the dynamic linking model for PE involves less support from the linker at the cost of requiring more support from the compiler (Figure 4.10).

PE executable files are conventionally loaded at 0x400000, which is where the text starts. The text section includes text from the input files as well as initialize and finalize sections. Next come the data sections, aligned on a logical disk block boundary. (Disk blocks are usually smaller than memory pages on MS Windows machines, 512 bytes or 1KB rather than 4KB.) Following that are bss and common, .rdata relocation fixups (for DLL libraries that often can't be loaded at the expected target address), import and export tables for dynamic linking, and other sections such as MS Windows resources.

An unusual section type is .tls, thread local storage. An MS Windows process can and usually does have multiple threads of control simultaneously active. The .tls data in a PE file is allocated for each thread. It includes both a block of data to initialize and an array of functions to call on thread startup and shutdown.

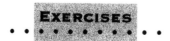

EXERCISE • 4.1

Why does a linker shuffle around segments to put segments of the same type next to each other? Wouldn't it be easier to leave them in the original order?

EXERCISE • 4.2

When, if ever, does it matter in what order a linker allocates storage for routines? In our example, what difference would it make if the linker allocated newyork, mass, calif, main rather than main, calif, mass, newyork? (We'll ask this question again later when we discuss overlays and dynamic linking, so you can disregard those considerations here.)

EXERCISE • 4.3

In most cases, a linker allocates similar sections sequentially, for example, the text of calif, mass, and newyork one after another. But it allocates all common sections with the same name on top of each other. Why?

EXERCISE • 4.4

Is it a good idea to permit common blocks to be declared in different input files with the same name but different sizes? Why or why not?

EXERCISE • 4.5

In Example 4.1, assume that the programmer has rewritten the calif routine so that the object code is now hex 1333 long. Recompute the assigned segment locations. In Example 4.2, further assume that the data and bss sizes for the rewritten calif routine are 975 and 120. Recompute the assigned segment locations.

PROJECT • 4.1

Extend the linker skeleton from Project 3.1 to do simple UNIX-style storage allocation. Assume that the only interesting segments are .text, .data, and .bss. In the output file, text starts at hex 1000, the data start at the next multiple of 1000 after the text, and bss starts on a 4-byte boundary after the data. Your linker needs to write out a partial object file with the segment definitions for the output file. (You need not generate symbols, relocations, or data at this point.) Within your linker, be sure you have a data structure that will let you determine what address each segment in each input file has been assigned, because you'll need that to continue the project in subsequent chapters. Use the sample routines in Example 4.2 to test your allocator.

PROJECT • 4.2

Implement UNIX-style common blocks, that is, scan the symbol table for undefined symbols with nonzero values and add space of appropriate size to the .bss segment. Don't worry about adjusting the symbol table entries (that comes in Chapter 5).

PROJECT • 4.3

Extend the allocator developed in Project 4.1 to handle arbitrary segments in input files, combining all segments with identical names. A reasonable allocation strategy would be to put at location 1000 the segments with RP attributes, then starting at the next 1000 boundary those with RWP attributes, then on a 4-byte boundary those with RW attributes. Allocate common blocks in .bss with attribute RW.

SYMBOL MANAGEMENT

Symbol management is a linker's key function. Without some way to refer from one module to another, there wouldn't be much use for a linker's other facilities.

5.1 BINDING AND NAME RESOLUTION

Linkers handle a variety of kinds of symbols. All linkers handle symbolic references from one module to another. Each input module includes a symbol table. The symbols include the following:

- Global symbols defined and perhaps referenced in the module.
- Global symbols referenced but not defined in the module (generally called externals).
- Segment names, which are usually also considered to be global symbols defined to be at the beginning of the segment.

- Nonglobal symbols, usually for debuggers and crash dump analysis (optional). These aren't really symbols needed for the linking process, but sometimes they are mixed in with global symbols so the linker has to at least skip over them. In other cases they may be in a separate table in the file or in a separate debug information file.

- Line number information, to tell source language debuggers the correspondence between source lines and object code (optional).

The linker reads all of the symbol tables in the input module and extracts the useful information, which is sometimes all of the incoming information but frequently just what's needed to link. Then it builds the link-time symbol tables and uses those to guide the linking process. Depending on the output file format, the linker may place some or all of the symbol information in the output file.

Some formats have multiple symbol tables per file. For example, ELF shared libraries can have one symbol table with just the information needed for the dynamic linker and a separate, larger table useful for debugging and relinking. This isn't necessarily a bad design; the dynamic linker table is usually much smaller than the full table and making it separate can speed up the dynamic linking process, which is performed far more often than a library is debugged or relinked.

5.2 SYMBOL TABLE FORMATS

Linker symbol tables are similar to those in compilers, although usually simpler because the kinds of symbols a linker needs to keep are usually less complex than those in a compiler. Within the linker, there's one symbol table that lists the input files and library modules, keeping the per-file information. A second symbol table handles global symbols, the ones that the linker has to resolve among input files. A third table may handle intramodule debugging symbols, although more often than not the linker need not create a full-fledged symbol table for debug symbols (it only needs to pass the debugging symbols through from the input to the output file).

Within the linker itself, a symbol table is often kept as an array of table entries, using a hash function to locate entries, or as an array of pointers

Hash headers

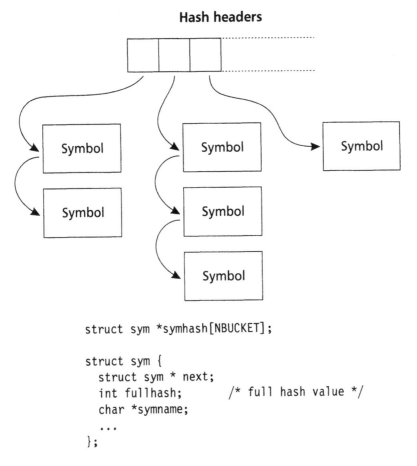

```
struct sym *symhash[NBUCKET];

struct sym {
  struct sym * next;
  int fullhash;          /* full hash value */
  char *symname;
  ...
};
```

FIGURE **5.1** • Symbol table.

indexed by a hash function, with all of the entries that hash together chained from each header (Figure 5.1). To locate a symbol in the table, the linker computes a hash of the symbol name, uses that hash value modulo the number of buckets to select one of the hash buckets (symhash[h%NBUCKET] in Figure 5.1, where h is the hash), and then runs down the chain of symbols looking for the symbol.

Traditionally, linkers only supported short names—ranging from eight characters on IBM mainframes and early UNIX systems, six on most DEC systems, to as few as two on some (justly) obscure minicomputers. Modern linkers support much longer names, both because programmers use longer names than they used to (or, in the case of COBOL, are no longer willing to twist the names around to make them unique in the first eight characters) and because compilers mangle names by adding extra characters to encode type information.

Older linkers with limited name lengths did a string comparison of each symbol name in the lookup hash chain until they found a match or ran out of symbols. These days, a program can easily contain many long symbols that are identical up to the last few characters, as is often the case with C++ mangled names; this makes the string comparisons expensive. An easy fix is to store the full hash value in the symbol table and to do the string comparison only when the hashes match. Depending on the context, if a symbol is not found, the linker may either add it to the chain or report an error.

MODULE TABLES

The linker needs to track every input module seen during a linking run, both modules linked explicitly and those extracted from libraries. Figure 5.2 shows the structure of a simplified version of the module table for a GNU linker that produces a.out object files. Because most of the key information for each a.out file is in the file header, the table just stores a copy of the header.

The table also contains pointers to in-memory copies of the symbol table string table (because in an a.out file, the symbol name strings are in a separate table from the symbol table itself) and relocation tables, along with the computed offsets of the text, data, and bss segments in the output. If the file is a library, each library member that is linked has its own module table entry. (These details are not shown in Figure 5.2.)

During the first pass, the linker reads in the symbol table from each file, generally just copying it verbatim into an in-memory buffer. In symbol formats that put the symbol names in a separate string table, the linker also reads in the symbol names and, for ease of subsequent processing, runs down the symbol table and turns each name string offset into a pointer to the in-memory version of the string.

GLOBAL SYMBOL TABLE

The linker keeps a global symbol table with an entry for every symbol referenced or defined in *any* input file (Figure 5.3). Each time the linker reads an

```
/* Name of this file.  */
char *filename;
/* Name to use for the symbol giving address of text start */
char *local_sym_name;

/* Describe the layout of the contents of the file */
/* The file's a.out header.  */
struct exec header;
/* Offset in file of debug symbol segment, or 0 if there is none.  */
int symseg_offset;

/* Describe data from the file loaded into core */

/* Symbol table of the file.  */
struct nlist *symbols;
/* Size in bytes of string table.  */
int string_size;
/* Pointer to the string table. */
char *strings;

/* Next two used only if 'relocatable_output' or if needed for */
/* output of undefined reference line numbers. */

/* Text and data relocation info  */
struct relocation_info *textrel;
struct relocation_info *datarel;

/* Relation of this file's segments to the output file */

/* Start of this file's text seg in the output file core image.  */
int text_start_address;
/* Start of this file's data seg in the output file core image.  */
int data_start_address;
/* Start of this file's bss seg in the output file core image.  */
int bss_start_address;
/* Offset in bytes in the output file symbol table
   of the first local symbol for this file.  */
int local_syms_offset;
```

FIGURE **5.2** • Module table.

```
/* abstracted from gnu ld a.out */
  struct glosym
    {
      /* Pointer to next symbol in this symbol's hash bucket. */
      struct glosym *link;
      /* Name of this symbol. */
      char *name;
      /* Value of this symbol as a global symbol. */
      long value;
      /* Chain of external 'nlist's in files for this symbol, both defs
         and refs. */
      struct nlist *refs;
      /* Nonzero means definitions of this symbol as common have been seen,
         and the value here is the largest size specified by any of them. */
      int max_common_size;
      /* Nonzero means a definition of this global symbol is known to exist.
         Library members should not be loaded on its account. */
      char defined;
      /* Nonzero means a reference to this global symbol has been seen
         in a file that is surely being loaded.
         A value higher than 1 is the n_type code for the symbol's
         definition. */
      char referenced;
      /* 1 means that this symbol has multiple definitions. 2 means
         that it has multiple definitions, and some of them are set
         elements, one of which has been printed out already. */
      unsigned char multiply_defined;
    }
```

FIGURE **5.3** • Global symbol table.

input file, it adds all of the file's global symbols to the symbol table, keeping a chain of the places where the symbol is defined or referenced. When the first pass is done, every global symbol should have exactly one definition and zero or more references. (This is a minor oversimplification, because UNIX object files disguise common blocks as undefined symbols with nonzero values, but that's a straightforward special case for the linker to handle.)

As the symbols in each file are added to the global symbol table, the linker links each entry from the file to its corresponding global symbol table entry

Module   **Linker symbol table**

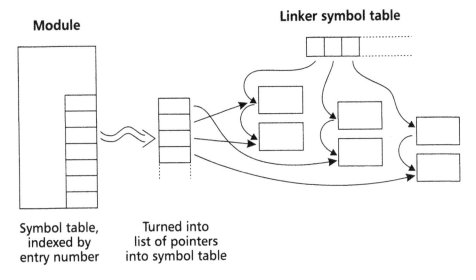

Symbol table,   Turned into
indexed by   list of pointers
entry number   into symbol table

FIGURE **5.4** • Resolving a symbol from a file to the global symbol table.

(Figure 5.4). Relocation items generally refer to symbols by index in the module's own symbol table, so for each external reference, the linker has to be able to tell that, for example, symbol 15 in module A is named fruit while symbol 12 in module B is also named fruit (that is, it's the same symbol). Each module has its own set of indices and needs its own vector of pointers.

SYMBOL RESOLUTION

During the second pass of linking, the linker resolves symbol references as it creates the output file. The details of resolution interact with relocation (see Chapter 7) because in most object formats, relocation entries identify the program references to the symbol. In the simplest case, in which the linker is creating an output file with absolute addresses (such as data references in UNIX linkers), the address of the symbol simply replaces the symbol reference. For example, if the symbol is resolved to address 20486, the linker replaces the reference with 20486.

Real situations are more complex. For one thing, there are many ways that a symbol might be referred to: in a data pointer, in an instruction, or even synthesized from multiple instructions. For another, the output of the linker is itself frequently relocatable. This means that if, say, a symbol is resolved to offset 426 in the data section, the output file has to contain a relocatable reference to data+426 where the symbol reference was.

The output file will usually have a symbol table of its own, so the linker needs to create a new set of indices of the symbols to be used in the output file; then it must map symbol numbers in outgoing relocation entries to those new indices.

SPECIAL SYMBOLS

Many systems use a few special symbols defined by the linker itself. UNIX systems all require that the linker define etext, edata, and end as the end of the text, data, and bss segments, respectively. The system routine sbrk() uses end as the address of the beginning of the run-time heap, so it can be allocated contiguously with the existing data and bss.

For programs with constructor and destructor routines, many linkers create tables of pointers to the routines from each input file, with a linker-created symbol like __CTOR_LIST__ that the language startup stub uses to find the list and call all the routines.

5.3 NAME MANGLING

The names used in object file symbol tables and in linking are often not the same names that are used in the source programs from which the object files were compiled. There are three reasons for this: avoiding name collisions, name overloading, and type checking. The process of turning the source program names into the object file names is called *name mangling*. This section discusses mangling typically done to names in C, Fortran, and C++ programs.

SIMPLE C AND FORTRAN NAME MANGLING

In older object formats (before approximately 1970), compilers used names from the source program directly as the names in the object file, perhaps truncating long names to a name length limit. This worked reasonably well, but problems occurred as a result of collisions with names reserved by compilers and libraries. For example, Fortran programs that do formatted I/O implicitly call routines in the library to do their reads and writes. Other routines handle arithmetic errors, complex arithmetic, and everything else in a programming language that's too complicated to be generated as inline code.

The names of all of these routines are in effect reserved names, and part of the programming folklore was to know which names not to use. As a particularly egregious example, for many years this Fortran program would crash an OS/360 system:

```
CALL MAIN
END
```

Why? The OS/360 programming convention is that every routine including the main program has a name, and the name of the main program is MAIN. When a Fortran main program starts, it calls the operating system to catch a variety of arithmetic error traps, and each trap catch call allocates some space in a system table. But this program calls itself recursively over and over again (each time establishing another nested set of trap calls), the system table runs out of space, and the system crashes. OS/390 is a lot more robust than its predecessors were 30 years ago, but the reserved name problem remains. It's even worse in mixed-language programs, since code in all languages has to avoid using any name used by any of the language run-time libraries in use.

One approach to the reserved name problem was to use something other than procedure calls to call the run-time library. On the PDP-6 and -10, for example, the interface to the Fortran I/O package was through a system call instruction that trapped back to the program rather than to the operating system. This was a clever trick, but it was quite specific to the PDP-6/10 architecture and didn't scale well, because there was no way for mixed-language code to share the trap, nor was it practical to link the minimum necessary part of the I/O package because there was no easy way to tell which traps the input modules in a program used.

The approach taken on UNIX systems was to mangle the names of C and Fortran procedures so they wouldn't inadvertently collide with names of libraries and other routines. C procedure names were modified with a leading underscore, so that main became _main. Fortran names were further mangled with both a leading and trailing underscore so that calc became _calc_. (This particular approach made it possible to call C routines whose names ended with an underscore from Fortran, which made it possible to write Fortran libraries in C.) The only significant disadvantage of this scheme is that it shrank the C name space from the eight characters permitted by the object format to seven characters for C and six characters for Fortran. At the time, the Fortran-66 standard only required six character names, so it wasn't much of an imposition.

On other systems, compiler designers took an opposite tack. Most assemblers and linkers permit characters in symbols that are forbidden in C and C++, identifiers such as . and $. Rather than mangling names from C or Fortran programs, the run-time libraries use names with forbidden characters that can't collide with application program names. The choice of name mangling vs. collision-proof library names is one of developer convenience. At the time UNIX was rewritten in C in about 1974, its authors already had extensive assembler language libraries, and it was easier to mangle the names of new C and C-compatible routines than to go back and fix all the existing code. Now, 20 years later, the assembler code has all been rewritten five times and UNIX C compilers, particularly ones that create COFF and ELF object files, no longer prepend the underscore.

C++ Type Encoding: Types and Scopes

Another use for mangled names is to encode scope and type information, which makes it possible to use existing linkers to link programs in C++, Ada, and other languages that have more complex naming rules than do C, COBOL, or Fortran.

In a C++ program, the programmer can define many functions and variables with the same name but different scopes and, for functions, different argument types. A single program may have a global variable V and a static member of a class C::V. C++ permits function name overloading, with several functions having the same name but different arguments, such as f(int x) and f(float x). Class definitions can include functions (including overloaded names) and even functions that redefine built-in operators; that is, a class can contain a function whose name is in effect >> or any other built-in operator.

C++ was initially implemented as a translator called cfront that produced C code and used an existing linker, so its author used name mangling to produce names that can sneak through the C compiler into the linker. All the linker had to do with them was its usual job of matching identically named defined and undefined global names. Since then, nearly all C++ compilers generate object code or at least assembler code directly, but name mangling remains the standard way to handle overloaded names. Modern linkers now know enough about name mangling to demangle names that are reported in error messages; otherwise they leave mangled names alone. Ellis and Stroustrup's influential *Annotated C++ Reference Manual,* cited in the references, describes the name mangling scheme that cfront used. With minor variations, this scheme has become a de facto standard and we describe it here.

Data variable names outside of C++ classes don't get mangled at all. An array called foo has a mangled name of foo. Function names not associated with classes are mangled to encode the types of the arguments by appending __F and a string of letters that represent the argument types and type modifiers listed in Figure 5.5. For example, a function func(float, int, unsigned char) becomes func__FfiUc. Class names are considered types and are encoded as the length of the class name followed by the name, such as 4Pair. Classes can contain names of internal classes to multiple levels; these "qualified" names are encoded as Q, followed by a digit indicating the number of levels, followed by the encoded class names; the name First::Second ::Third thus becomes Q35First6Second5Third. This means that a function that takes two class arguments f(Pair, First::Second::Third) becomes f__F4PairQ35First6Second5Third.

Class member functions are encoded as the function name, two underscores, the encoded class name, then F and the arguments, so cl::fn(void) becomes fn__2clFv. All of the operators have four or five character-encoded names as well, such as __ml for * and __aor for |=. Special functions including constructor, destructor, new, and delete have encodings as well: __ct, __dt, __nw, and __dl, respectively. A constructor for class Pair that takes two character pointer arguments Pair(char*,char*) becomes __ct__4PairFPcPc.

Finally, since mangled names can be so long, there are two shortcut encodings for functions with multiple arguments of the same type. The code Tn means "same type as the *n*th argument" and Nnm means "*n* arguments of the same type as the *m*th argument." A function segment(Pair, Pair) would be segment__F4PairT1 and a function trapezoid(Pair, Pair, Pair, Pair) would be trapezoid__F4PairN31.

Name mangling does the job of giving unique names to every possible C++ object at the cost of generating tremendously long and (lacking linker and debugger support) unreadable names in error messages and listings. Nonetheless, C++ has an intrinsic problem in that it has a potentially huge name space. Any scheme for representing the names of C++ objects has to be nearly

Type	Letter
void	v
char	c
short	s
int	i
long	l
float	f
double	d
long double	r
varargs	e
unsigned	U
const	C
volatile	V
signed	S
pointer	P
reference	R
array of length n	An_
function	F
pointer to nth member	MnS

FIGURE 5.5 • Type letters in C++ mangled names.

as verbose as name mangling, and mangled names do have the advantage of being readable by at least some humans.

Early users of mangled names often found that although linkers in theory supported long names, in practice the long names didn't work very well, and performance was dreadful when the programs to be linked contained many long names that were identical up to the last few characters. Fortunately, symbol table algorithms are a well-understood subject, and now we can expect linkers to handle long names without trouble.

LINK-TIME TYPE CHECKING

Although mangled names only became popular with the advent of C++, the idea of linker type checking has been around for a long time. (I first encountered it in the Dartmouth PL/I linker in about 1974.) The idea of linker type checking is quite straightforward. Most languages have procedures with declared argument types, and if the caller doesn't pass the number and type of arguments that the callee expects, it's an error (often a hard-to-diagnose error if the caller and callee are in separately compiled files). For linker type checking, each defined or undefined global symbol has associated with it a string representing the argument and return types, similar to the mangled C++ argument types. When the linker resolves a symbol, it compares the type strings for the reference and definition of the symbol and reports an error if they don't match. A nice property of this scheme is that the linker need not understand the type encoding at all—just whether the strings are the same or not.

Even in an environment with C++ mangled names, this type checking would still be useful, because not all C++ type information is encoded into a mangled name. The types that functions return and the types of global data could profitably be checked by a scheme such as this one.

5.4 WEAK EXTERNAL AND OTHER KINDS OF SYMBOLS

Up to this point, we've considered all linker global symbols to work the same way, and we have regarded each mention of a name as being either a definition or a reference to a symbol. Many object formats can qualify a reference as weak or strong. A strong reference must be resolved; a weak reference may be resolved if there's a definition, but it's not an error if it's not defined. Linker processing of weak symbols is much like that for strong symbols, except that at the end of the first pass an undefined reference to a weak symbol isn't an error. Generally, the linker defines undefined weak symbols to be zero, a value that application code can check. Weak symbols are primarily useful in connection with libraries, so we revisit them in Chapter 6.

5.5 MAINTAINING DEBUGGING INFORMATION

Modern compilers all support source language debugging. That means that the programmer can debug the object code by referring to source program function and variable names and can set breakpoints and single-step the program. Compilers support this by putting information in the object file that provides a mapping from source file line numbers to object code addresses as well as information that describes all of the functions, variables, types, and structures used in the source program.

UNIX compilers have two somewhat different debug information formats: stab (short for symbol table), used primarily in a.out, COFF, and non–System V ELF files; and DWARF, which was defined for System V ELF files. Microsoft has defined its own formats for its Codeview debugger, with CV4 being the most recent.

LINE NUMBER INFORMATION

All symbolic debuggers need to be able to map between program addresses and source line numbers. This lets the user set breakpoints by line number with the debugger placing the breakpoint at the appropriate place in the code, and it also lets the debugger relate the program addresses in call stack tracebacks and error reports back to source lines. Line number information is simple except with optimizing compilers that can move code around so that the sequence of code in the object file doesn't match the sequence of source lines.

For each line in the source file for which the compiler generated any code, the compiler generates a line number entry giving the line number and the beginning address of the corresponding object code. If a program address lies between two line number entries, the debugger reports it as being the lower of the two line numbers. The line numbers need to be scoped by file name, both source file name and include file name. Some formats do this by creating a list of files and putting a file index in each line number entry. Others intersperse "begin include" and "end include" items in the list of line numbers, implicitly maintaining a stack of filenames.

When compiler optimization makes the generated code from a single statement discontiguous, some object formats (notably DWARF) let the compiler map each byte of object code back to a source line (using a lot of space in the process) while others just specify approximate locations.

SYMBOL AND VARIABLE INFORMATION

Compilers also have to generate the names, types, and locations of each program variable. The debug symbol information is somewhat more complex than mangled names are, because it needs to encode not just the type names, but for structure types it needs to encode the definitions of the types so that the debugger can correctly format all of the subfields in a structure.

The symbol information is an implicit or explicit tree. Defined at the top level in each file is a list of types, variables, and functions, and within each of those are the fields of structures, variables defined within functions, and so forth. Within functions, the tree includes "begin block" and "end block" markers referring to line numbers, to allow the debugger to identify what variables are in scope at each point in the program.

The trickiest part of the symbol information is the location information. The location of a static variable doesn't change, but a local variable within a routine may be static, on the stack, in a register, or in optimized code, moved from place to place in different parts of the routine. On most architectures, the standard calling sequence for routines maintains a chain of saved stack and frame pointers for each nested routine, with the local stack variables in each routine allocated at known offsets from the frame pointer. In leaf routines or routines that allocate no local stack variables, a common optimization is to skip setting the frame pointer. The debugger needs to know about this in order both to interpret call stack tracebacks correctly and to find local variables in a routine with no frame pointer. Microsoft's Codeview does this with a specific list of routines with no frame pointer.

PRACTICAL ISSUES

For the most part, the linker just passes debug information through uninterpreted, perhaps relocating segment-relative addresses on the way through. One thing that linkers are starting to do is to detect and remove duplicate debug information. In C and particularly in C++, programs usually have a set of header files that define types and declare functions, and each source file includes the headers that define all of the types and functions that that file might use.

Compilers pass through the debug information for everything in all of the header files that each source file includes. This means that if a particular header file is included by 20 source files that are compiled and linked together, the linker will receive 20 copies of the debug information for that file. Although debuggers have never had any trouble disregarding the duplicated information, header files—particularly in C++—can be large, which means that the amount of duplicated header information can be substantial. Linkers can safely discard the duplicated material, and increasingly do so, both to speed the linker and debugger and to save space. In some cases, compilers put the debug information directly into files or databases to be read by the debugger, bypassing the linker, so the linker need only add or update information about the relative locations of the segments contributed by each source file and any data such as jump tables created by the linker itself.

When the debug information is stored in an object file, sometimes the debug information is intermixed with the linker symbols in one big symbol table, while sometimes the two are separate. UNIX systems added debug information to the compilers a little at a time over the years, so it all ended up in one huge symbol table. Other formats such as Microsoft's ECOFF tend to separate linker symbols from debug symbols and to separate both from line numbers.

Sometimes the resulting debug information goes into the output file, sometimes into a separate debug file, or sometimes into both. The advantage of putting all of the debug information into the output file is simplicity in the build process, because all of the information used to debug the program is present in one place. (The most obvious disadvantage is that it makes the executable file enormous.) On the other hand, if the debug information is separated out, it's easy to build a final version of a program, then to ship the executable but not the debug files. This keeps the size of the shipped program down and discourages casual reverse engineering, while the developers still have the debug files if needed to debug errors found in the shipping project. UNIX systems have a "strip" command that removes the debugging symbols from an object file without changing the code at all. The developers keep the unstripped file and ship the stripped version. Even though the two files are different, the running code is the same and the debugger can use the symbols from the unstripped file to debug a core dump made from the stripped version.

EXERCISE • 5.1

Write a C++ program with a lot of functions whose mangled names differ only in the last few characters. See how long they take to compile. Change them so the mangled names differ in the first few characters. Time a compile and link again. Do you need a new linker?

EXERCISE • 5.2

Investigate the debug symbol format that your favorite linker uses. (Some on-line resources are listed in the references.) Write a program to dump the debugging symbols from an object file and see how much of the source program you can reconstruct from it.

PROJECT

PROJECT • 5.1

Extend the linker to handle symbol name resolution. Make the linker read the symbol tables from each file and create a global symbol table that subsequent parts of the linker can use. Each symbol in the global symbol table needs to include, along with the name, whether the symbol is defined and which module defines it. Be sure to check for undefined and multiply defined symbols.

PROJECT • 5.2

Add symbol value resolution to the linker. Because most symbols are defined relative to segments in linker input files, the value of each symbol has to be adjusted to account for the address to which each segment is relocated. For example, if a symbol is defined as location 42 within a file's text segment and the segment is relocated to 3710, the symbol becomes 3752.

PROJECT • 5.3

Finish the work from Project 4.2; make the linker handle UNIX-style common blocks. Assign location values to each common block.

LIBRARIES

Libraries are collections of object files that are included as needed in a linked program. Every modern linker handles libraries. In this chapter we cover traditional statically linked libraries, leaving the more complex shared libraries to Chapters 9 and 10.

6.1 PURPOSE OF LIBRARIES

In the 1940s and early 1950s, programming shops had actual code libraries containing reels of tape (or later, decks of cards) that a programmer would visit and select routines from to load with his program. Once loaders and linkers started to resolve symbolic references, it became possible to automate the process by selecting routines from the library that resolve otherwise undefined symbols.

A library file is fundamentally no more than a collection of object files, usually with some added directory information to make it faster to search. As always, the details are more complicated than the basic idea, so we work them out in this chapter. We use the term *file* to refer to a separate object file and *module* to refer to an object file included in a library.

6.2 LIBRARY FORMATS

The simplest library formats are just sequences of object modules. On sequential media like magnetic or paper tape, there's little point in adding a directory because the linker has to read through the whole library anyway, and skipping over library members is no faster than reading them in. On disks, however, a directory can speed up library searching considerably and is now a standard facility.

USING THE OPERATING SYSTEM

OS/360 and its descendants including MVS provide *partitioned data sets* (PDSs) that contain named members, each of which can be treated as a sequential file. The system provides features for giving multiple aliases to a single member, for treating multiple PDSs as a single logical PDS for the duration of a program, for enumerating the names in a logical PDS, and of course for reading or writing the members. Member names are eight characters, which probably not coincidentally is the length of an external symbol in the linker. (MVS introduced an extended PDS [PDSE], which has some support for names up to 1024 characters, for the benefit of C, C++, and COBOL programmers.)

A linker library is merely a PDS where each member is an object file named by its entry point. Object files that define multiple global symbols have an alias for each global symbol that is manually created when the library is built. The linker searches the logical PDS specified as the library for members whose names match undefined symbols. An advantage of this scheme is that there's no object library update program needed, because the standard file maintenance utilities for PDS suffice.

Although I've never seen a linker do so, a linker on a UNIX-like system could handle libraries the same way; the library would be a directory, the members would be object files within the directory, and each file name would be a global symbol defined in the file. (UNIX permits multiple names for a single file.)

UNIX AND MS WINDOWS ARCHIVE FILES

UNIX linker libraries use an archive format, which can be used for collections of any type of files although in practice it's rarely used for anything else.

Libraries consist of an archive header followed by alternating file headers and object files. The earliest archives had no symbol directories, just a set of object files, but later versions had various sorts of directories, which finally settled down to one used for about a decade in BSD versions (text archive headers and a directory called __.SYMDEF) and the current version used with COFF or ELF libraries (text archive headers with an extension for long file names and a directory called /) in System V.4, later versions of BSD, and Linux. MS Windows ECOFF libraries use the same archive format as COFF libraries, but the directory—although also called /—has a different format.

All modern UNIX systems use minor variations of the same archive format (Figure 6.1). The format uses only text characters in the archive headers, which means that an archive of text files is itself a text file (a quality that has turned out in practice to be useless). Each archive starts with the magic eight-character string !<arch>\n, where \n is a newline. Each archive member is preceded by a 60-byte header containing the following:

- The name of the member, padded to 16 characters as described below.

- The modification time, as a decimal number of seconds since January 1, 1970.

- The user and group IDs as decimal numbers.

- The UNIX file mode as an octal number.

- The size of the file in bytes as a decimal number. If the file size is odd, the file's contents are padded with a newline character to make the total length even, although the padding character isn't counted in the size field.

- The two characters reverse quote and newline, to make the header a line of text and to provide a simple check that the header is indeed a header.

Each member header contains the modification time, user and group IDs, and file mode, although linkers ignore them.

Member names that are 15 characters or less are followed by enough spaces to pad the name to 16 characters, or in COFF or ELF archives, a slash followed by enough spaces to pad the total to 16 characters. (UNIX and MS Windows both use slashes to separate components in file names.) The version of this archive format used with a.out files didn't support member names

File header:

```
!<arch>\n
```

Member header:

```
char name[16];    /* member name */
char modtime[12]; /* modification time */
char uid[6];      /* user ID */
char gid[6];      /* group ID */
char mode[8];     /* octal file mode */
char size[10];    /* member size */
char eol[2];      /* reverse quote, newline */
```

FIGURE **6.1** • UNIX archive format.

longer than 16 characters, reflecting the pre-BSD UNIX file system that limited file names to 14 characters per component. (Some BSD archives actually
did have a provision for longer file names, but because linkers didn't handle
the longer names correctly, nobody used them.) COFF, ELF, and MS Windows
archives store names longer than 16 characters in an archive member called
//. This member contains the long names separated by a slash and newline
pair on UNIX or a null character on MS Windows. The name field of the
header for members with a long name contains a slash followed by the decimal offset in the // member of the name string. In MS Windows archives, the
// member must be the third member of the archive. In UNIX archives, the
member need not exist if there are no long names, but it follows the symbol
directory if it does. Although the symbol directory formats have varied somewhat, they are all functionally the same, mapping names to member positions
so that linkers can directly move to and read the members they need to use.

The a.out archives store the directory in a member called __.SYMDEF,
which has to be the first member in the archive (Figure 6.2). This member
starts with a word containing the size in bytes of the symbol table that follows
it, so the number of entries in the table is 1/8 of the value in that word. Following the symbol table is a word containing the size of the string table, and the
string table, each string followed by a null byte. Each symbol table entry

```
int tablesize;   /* size in bytes of following table */
struct symtable {
   int symbol;    /* offset in string table */
   int member;    /* member pointer */
} symtable [];
int stringsize;  /* size of string table */
char strings[];  /* null-terminated strings */
```

FIGURE **6.2** • SYMDEF directory format.

```
int nsymbols;    /* number of symbols */
int member[];    /* member offsets */
char strings[];  /* null-terminated strings */
```

FIGURE **6.3** • COFF and ELF directory format.

contains a zero-based offset into the string table of the symbol's name and the file position of the header of the member that defines the symbol. The symbol table entries are conventionally in the order of the members in the file.

COFF and ELF archives use the otherwise impossible name / for the symbol directory rather than __.SYMDEF and use a somewhat simpler format (Figure 6.3). The first 4-byte value is the number of symbols. Following that is an array of file offsets of archive members and a set of null-terminated strings. The first offset points to the member that defines the symbol named by the first string, and so forth. COFF archives usually use a big-endian byte order for the symbol table regardless of the native byte order of the architecture.

Microsoft ECOFF archives add a second symbol directory member (Figure 6.4), confusingly also called /, that follows the first one. The ECOFF directory consists of a count of member offsets followed by an array of member offsets, one per archive member. Following that is a count of symbols, an array of 2-byte member offset pointers, followed by the null-terminated symbols in alphabetical order. The member offset pointers contain the one-based index in the member offset table of the member that defines the corresponding symbol. For example, to locate the member corresponding to the fifth symbol, consult the fifth entry in the pointer array, which contains the index in the

```
int nmembers;      /* count of member offsets */
int members[];     /* member offsets */
int nsymbols;      /* number of symbols */
ushort symndx[];   /* pointers to member offsets */
char strings[];    /* symbol names, in alphabetical order */
```

FIGURE **6.4** • ECOFF second symbol directory.

members array of the offset of the defining member. In theory the sorted symbols allow faster searching, but in practice the speedup is not likely to be large, because linkers typically scan the entire table anyway looking for symbols to load.

EXTENSION TO 64 BITS

Even if an archive contains objects for a 64-bit architecture, there's no need to change the archive format for ELF or ECOFF unless the archive grows to be larger than 4GB. Nonetheless, some 64-bit architectures have a different symbol directory format with a different member name such as /SYM64/.

INTEL OMF LIBRARIES

The final library format we look at is that used for Intel OMF libraries. Again, a library is a set of object files with a directory of symbols. Unlike the UNIX libraries, the directory is at the end of the file (Figure 6.5). Although this format is a little clunky, it contains the necessary information and does the job.

The library starts with a LIBHED record that contains the file offset of the LIBNAM record in a (block,offset) format used by Intel's ISIS operating system. The LIBNAM simply contains a list of module names, each name preceded by a count byte indicating the length of the name. The LIBLOC record contains a parallel list of (block,offset) file locations where each module starts. The LIBDIC contains a list of groups of counted strings with the names defined in each module, with each group followed by a null byte to separate it from the subsequent group.

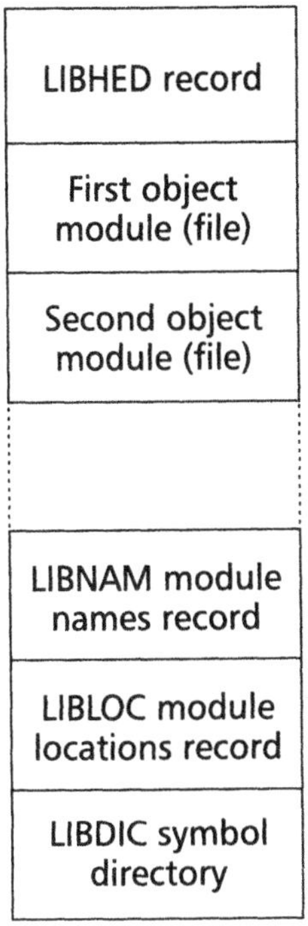

FIGURE **6.5** • OMF libraries.

6.3 CREATING LIBRARIES

Each archive format has its own technique for creating libraries. Depending
on how much support the operating system provides for the archive format,
library creation can involve anything from standard system file management
programs to library-specific tools.

At one end of the spectrum, IBM MVS libraries are created by the standard
IEBCOPY utility that creates partitioned data sets. In the middle, UNIX libraries are created by the ar command that combines files into archives. (For a.out
archives, a separate program called ranlib added the symbol directory, reading the symbols from each member, creating the __.SYMDEF member, and
splicing it into the file. In principle ranlib could have created the symbol directory as a real file, then called ar to insert it in the archive, but in practice ranlib
manipulated the archive directly. For COFF and ELF archives, the function of

ranlib has moved into ar, which creates the symbol directory if any of the members appear to be object modules, although ar still can create archives of non-objects.) At the other end of the spectrum, OMF archives and MS Windows ECOFF archives are created by specialized librarian programs, because those formats have never been used for anything other than object code libraries.

One minor issue for library creation is the order of object files, particularly for the ancient formats that didn't have a symbol directory. Pre-ranlib UNIX systems contained a pair of programs called lorder and tsort to help create archives. Although the symbol directories in modern libraries allow the linking process to work regardless of the order of the objects within a library, most libraries are still created with lorder and tsort to speed up the linking process. The program lorder takes as its input a set of object files (not libraries) and produces a dependency list of what files refer to symbols in what other files. (This is not hard to do; lorder was and still is typically implemented as a shell script that extracts the symbols using a symbol listing utility, does a little text processing on the symbols, then uses standard sort and join utilities to create its output.) The program tsort does a topological sort on the output of lorder, producing a sorted list of files so that each symbol is defined after all the references to it, which allows a single sequential pass over the files to resolve all undefined references. The output of lorder is used to control ar.

6.4 SEARCHING LIBRARIES

After a library is created, the linker has to be able to search it. Library search generally happens during the first linker pass, after all of the individual input files have been read. If the library or libraries have symbol directories, the linker reads in the directory and checks each symbol in turn against the linker's symbol table. If the symbol is used but undefined, the linker includes that symbol's file from the library. It's not enough to mark the file for later loading; the linker has to process the symbols in the segments in the library file just like those in an explicitly linked file. The segments go in the segment table, and the symbols, both defined and undefined, are entered into the global symbol table. It's quite common for one library routine to refer to symbols in another library routine—for example, a higher-level I/O routine like printf might refer to a lower-level putc or write routine.

Library symbol resolution is an iterative process. After the linker has made a pass over the symbols in the directory, if the linker included any files from the library during that pass, it should make another pass to resolve any symbols required by the newly included files, until eventually it makes a complete pass over the directory and finds nothing else to include. Not all linkers do this; many just make a single sequential pass over the directory and miss any backward dependencies from a file to another file earlier in the library. Tools like tsort and lorder can minimize the difficulty of using single-pass linkers, but it's not uncommon for programmers to explicitly list the same library several times on the linker command line to force multiple passes and thus finally resolve all the symbols.

UNIX linkers and many MS Windows linkers take an intermixed list of object files and libraries on the command line or in a control file and process each in order, so the programmer can control the order in which objects are loaded and libraries are searched. Although in principle this offers a great deal of flexibility and the ability to interpose private versions of library routines by listing the private versions before the library versions, in practice the ordered search provides little extra utility. Programmers invariably list all of their object files; then any application-specific libraries; then system libraries for math functions, network facilities, and the like; and finally the standard system libraries.

When programmers use multiple libraries, it's often necessary to list libraries more than once when there are circular dependencies among libraries. That is, if a routine in library A depends on a routine in library B, but another routine in library B depends on a routine in library A, neither searching A followed by B nor B followed by A will find all of the required routines. The problem becomes even worse when the dependencies involve three or more libraries. Directing the linker to search A B A or B A B or sometimes even A B C D A B C D is inelegant but solves the problem. Because there are rarely any duplicated symbols among the libraries, if the linker simply searched them all as a group (as IBM's mainframe linkers and AIX linker do) programmers would be well served.

The primary exception to this rule is that applications sometimes define private versions of a few routines—notably malloc and free for heap storage management—and they want to use them rather than the standard system versions. For such a case, a linker flag specifically saying "don't look for these symbols in the library" would in most cases be preferable to getting the effect by putting the private malloc in the search order in front of the public one.

6.5 PERFORMANCE ISSUES

The primary performance issue related to libraries used to be the time spent scanning libraries sequentially. Once symbol directories became standard, reading an input file from a library became insignificantly slower than reading a separate input file, and so long as libraries are topologically sorted, the linker rarely needs to make more than one pass over the symbol directory.

Library searches can still be slow if a library has a lot of tiny members. A typical UNIX system library has over 600 members. Particularly in the now-common case that all of the library members are combined at run time into a single shared library anyway, it'd probably be faster to create a single object file that defines all of the symbols in the library and to link using that rather than by searching a library. We examine this in more detail in Chapter 9.

6.6 WEAK EXTERNAL SYMBOLS

The simple definition-reference model used for symbol resolution and library member selection turns out to be insufficiently flexible for many applications. For example, most C programs call routines in the printf family to format data for output. printf can format all sorts of data, including floating point, which means that any program that uses printf will get the floating-point libraries linked in even if the program doesn't actually use floating point.

For many years, PDP-11 UNIX programs had to trick the linker to avoid linking the floating-point libraries in integer-only programs. The C compiler generated a reference to the special symbol fltused in any routine that used floating-point code. The C library was arranged as in Figure 6.6, taking advantage of the fact that the linker searched the library sequentially. If the program used floating point, the reference to fltused would cause the real floating-point routines to be linked, including the real version of fcvt, the floating-point output routine. Then when the I/O module was linked to define printf, there was already a version of fcvt that satisfied the reference in the I/O module. In programs that didn't use floating point, the real floating-point routines wouldn't be loaded, because there wouldn't be any undefined symbols they resolved and the reference to fcvt in the I/O module would be resolved by the stub floating-point routines that follow the I/O routines in the library. While this trick works, using it for more than one or two symbols would rapidly

...

Real floating-point module, define `fltused` and `fcvt`

I/O module, defines printf, refers to `fcvt`

Stub floating-point routines, define stub `fcvt`

...

FIGURE **6.6** • UNIX classic C library.

become unwieldy, and its correct operation critically depends on the order of the modules in the library, something that's easy to get wrong when the library is rebuilt.

The solution to this dilemma is *weak external symbols*, external symbols that do not cause library members to be loaded. Using this technique, if a definition for the symbol is available, either in an explicitly linked file or when a normal external causes a library member to be linked, a weak external is resolved like a normal external reference. But if no definition is available, the weak external is left undefined and in effect is resolved to zero, which is not considered to be an error. In the case discussed above, the I/O module would make a weak reference to `fcvt`, the real floating-point module would follow the I/O module in the library, and no stub routines would be necessary. If there's a reference to `fltused`, the floating-point routines are linked and define `fcvt`; if not, the reference to `fcvt` remains unresolved. This no longer is dependent on library order and will work even if the library makes multiple resolution passes over the library.

ELF adds yet another kind of weak symbol: a weak definition in addition to the weak reference. A weak definition defines a global symbol if no normal definition is available; if a normal definition is available, the weak definition is ignored. Weak definitions are infrequently used but can be useful to define error stubs without putting the stubs in separate modules.

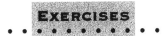

EXERCISES

EXERCISE • **6.1**

What should a linker do if two modules in different libraries define the same symbol? Is it an error?

EXERCISE • 6.2

Library symbol directories generally include only defined global symbols. Would it be useful to include undefined global symbols as well?

EXERCISE • 6.3

When sorting object files using lorder and tsort, it's possible that tsort won't be able to come up with a total order for the files. When will this happen, and is it a problem?

EXERCISE • 6.4

Some library formats put the directory at the front of the library while others put it at the end. What practical difference does it make?

EXERCISE • 6.5

Describe some other situations where weak externals and weak definitions are useful.

This part of the project adds library searching to the linker. We'll experiment with two different library formats. The first is the IBM-like directory format suggested early in the chapter. A library is a directory, each member is a file in the directory, and each file has names for each of the exported symbols in the directory. If you're using a system that doesn't support UNIX-style multiple names, fake it: Give each file a single name (choose one of the exported symbols). Then make a file named MAP that contains lines of the form

```
name sym sym sym ...
```

where name is the file's name and sym are the rest of the exported symbols.

The second library format is a single file. The library starts with a single line

```
LIBRARY nnnn pppppp
```

where nnnn is the number of modules in the library and pppppp is the offset in the file where the library directory starts. Following that line are the library members, one after another. At the end of the file, starting at offset pppppp, is the library directory, which consists of lines, one per module, in the format

```
pppppp 111111 sym1 sym2 sym3 ...
```

where pppppp is the position in the file where the module starts, 111111 is the length of the module, and the sym*n* are the symbols defined in this module.

PROJECT • 6.1

Write a librarian that creates a directory format library from a set of object files. Be sure to do something reasonable with duplicate symbols. Optionally, extend the librarian so that it can take an existing library and add, replace, or delete modules in place.

PROJECT • 6.2

Extend the linker to handle directory format libraries. When the linker encounters a library in its list of input files, search the library and include each module in the library that defines an undefined symbol. Be sure you correctly handle library modules that depend on symbols defined in other library members.

PROJECT • 6.3

Write a librarian that creates a file format library from a set of object files. Note that you can't correctly write the LIBRARY line at the front of the file until you know the sizes of all of the modules. Reasonable approaches include writing a dummy library line, then seeking back and rewriting the line in place with the correct values; collecting the sizes of the input files and computing the size; or buffering the entire file in main memory. Optionally, extend the librarian to update an existing library (note that it's a lot harder than updating a directory format library).

PROJECT • **6.4**

Extend the linker to handle file format libraries. When the linker encounters a library in its list of input files, search the library and include each module in the library that defines an undefined symbol. You'll have to modify your routines that read object files so that they can read an object module from the middle of a library.

RELOCATION

Once a linker has scanned all of the input files to determine segment sizes and symbol definitions and symbol references, figured out which library modules to include, and decided where in the output address space all of the segments will go, the next stage is the heart of the linking process: relocation. We use the term *relocation* to refer both to the process of adjusting program addresses to account for nonzero segment origins and to the process of resolving references to external symbols, because the two are frequently handled together.

The linker's first pass lays out the positions of the various segments and collects the segment-relative values of all global symbols in the program. Once the linker determines the position of each segment, it potentially needs to fix up all storage addresses to reflect the new locations of the segments. On most architectures, addresses in data are absolute, while those embedded in instructions may be absolute or relative. The linker needs to fix them up accordingly, as we'll discuss in Section 7.4.

The first pass also creates the global symbol table, as described in Chapter 5. The linker also resolves stored references to global symbols to the symbol addresses.

7.1 HARDWARE AND SOFTWARE RELOCATION

Because nearly all modern computers have hardware relocation, you might wonder why a linker or loader still does software relocation. (This question confused me when programming a PDP-6 in the late 1960s, and the situation has only gotten more complicated since then.) The answer has partly to do with performance and partly with binding time.

Hardware relocation allows an operating system to give each process a separate address space that starts at a fixed known address, which makes program loading easier and prevents buggy programs in one address space from damaging programs in other address spaces. Software linker or loader relocation combines input files into one large file that's ready to be loaded into the address space provided by hardware relocation, frequently with no load-time fixing up at all.

On a machine like a 286 or a 386 with several thousand segments, it would indeed be possible to load one routine or global datum per segment, completely doing away with software relocation. Each routine or datum would start at location zero in its segment, and all global references would be handled as intersegment references to be looked up in the system's segment tables and bound at run time. Unfortunately, x86 segment lookups are very slow, and a program that did a segment lookup for every intermodule call or global data reference would be far slower than one linked conventionally.

Equally importantly, although run-time binding can be useful (a topic we cover in Chapter 10), most programs are better off avoiding it. For reliability reasons, program files are best bound together and addresses fixed at link time, so they hold still during debugging and remain consistent after shipping. Library "bit creep" is a chronic and very-hard-to-debug source of program errors when a program is run using different versions of libraries than its authors anticipated. (MS Windows applications are prone to this problem as a result of the large number of shared libraries they use, with different versions of libraries often shipped with various applications, all loaded on the same computer.) Even without the overhead of 286-style segments, dynamic linking tends to be far slower than static linking, and there's no point in paying for it where it's not needed.

7.2 LINK-TIME AND LOAD-TIME RELOCATION

Many systems perform both link-time and load-time relocation. A linker combines a set of input files into a single output file that is ready to be loaded at a specific address. If, when the program is loaded, storage at that address isn't available, the loader has to relocate the loaded program to reflect the actual load address. On some systems (including DOS and MVS), every program is linked as though it would be loaded at location zero. The actual address is chosen from available storage and the program is always relocated as it's loaded. On others, notably MS Windows, programs are linked to be loaded at a fixed address that is generally available, and no load-time relocation is needed except in the unusual case that the standard address is already in use by something else. (In practice, current versions of MS Windows never do load-time relocation of executable programs, although they do relocate DLL shared libraries. Similarly, UNIX systems never relocate ELF programs although they do relocate ELF shared libraries.)

Load-time relocation is quite simple compared to link-time relocation. At link time, different addresses need to be relocated by different amounts, depending on the size and locations of the segments. At load time, on the other hand, the entire program is invariably treated as a single big segment for relocation purposes, and the loader need only adjust program addresses by the difference between the nominal and actual load addresses.

7.3 SYMBOL AND SEGMENT RELOCATION

The linker's first pass lays out the positions of the various segments and collects the segment-relative values of all global symbols in the program. Once the linker determines the position of each segment, it needs to adjust the stored addresses. This involves several main tasks.

- Data addresses and absolute program address references within a segment need to be adjusted. For example, if a pointer refers to location 100 but the segment base is relocated to 1000, the pointer needs to be adjusted to location 1100.

- Intersegment program references need to be adjusted as well. Absolute address references need to be adjusted to reflect the new position of the target address's segment, while relative addresses need to reflect the positions of both the target segment and the segment in which the reference lies.

- References to global symbols have to be resolved. If an instruction calls a routine detonate, and detonate is at offset 500 in a segment that starts at 1000, the address in that instruction has to be adjusted to refer to location 1500.

The requirements of relocation and symbol resolution are slightly different. For relocation, the number of base values is fairly small—the number of segments in an input file—but the object format has to permit relocation of references to any address in any segment. For symbol resolution, the number of symbols is far greater, but in most cases the only action the linker needs to take with the symbol is to plug the symbol's value into a word in the program.

Many linkers unify segment and symbol relocation by treating each segment as a pseudo-symbol whose value is the base of the segment. This makes segment-relative relocations a special case of symbol-relative relocations. Even in linkers that unify the two kinds of relocation, there is still one important difference between the two kinds: A symbol reference involves two addends, the base address of the segment in which the symbol resides and the offset of the symbol within that segment. Some linkers precompute all the symbol addresses before starting the relocation phase, adding the segment base to the symbol value in the symbol table. Others look up the segment base and do the addition as each item is relocated. In most cases, there's no compelling reason to do it one way or the other. In a few linkers, notably those for real-mode x86 code, a single location can be addressed relative to several different segments, so the linker can only determine the address to use for a symbol in the context of an individual reference using a specified segment.

Symbol Lookups

Object formats invariably treat each file's set of symbols as an array and internally refer to the symbols using a small integer (the index in that array). This causes minor complications for the linker, as mentioned in Chapter 5, because each input file will have different indexes, as will the output if the output is relinkable. The most straightforward way to handle this is to keep an array of pointers for each input file that points to entries in the global symbol table.

7.4 BASIC RELOCATION TECHNIQUES

Each relocatable object file contains a relocation table, which is a list of places in each segment in the file that need to be relocated. The linker reads in the contents of the segment, applies the relocation items, then disposes of the segment, usually by writing it to the output file. Usually—but not always—relocation is a one-time operation and the resulting file can't be relocated again. Some object formats, notably the IBM 360 and AIX, are relinkable and keep all the relocation data in the output file. (In the case of the 360, the output file needs to be relocated when loaded, so it has to keep all the relocation information anyway.) With UNIX linkers, a linker option makes the output relinkable, and in some cases (notably shared libraries) the output always has relocation information because libraries need to be relocated when loaded as well.

In the simplest case, the relocation information for a segment is just a list of places in the segment that need to be relocated (Figure 7.1). As the linker processes the segment, it adds the base position of the segment to the value at each location identified by a relocation entry. This handles direct addressing and pointer values in memory for a single segment.

Real programs on modern computers are somewhat more complicated because of multiple segments and addressing modes. The classic UNIX a.out format is about the simplest that handles these issues (Figure 7.2).

Each object file has two sets of relocation entries, one for the text segment and one for the data segment. (The bss segment is defined to be all zero, so there's nothing to relocate there.) Each relocation entry contains a bit r_extern that specifies whether this is a segment-relative or symbol-relative entry. If the bit is clear, it's segment relative and r_symbolnum is actually a code for the segment: N_TEXT (4), N_DATA (6), or N_BSS (8). The r_pcrel bit specifies whether the reference is absolute or relative to the current location (program counter).

The exact details of each relocation depend on the type and segments involved. In the discussion below, TR, DR, and BR are the relocated bases of the text, data, and bss segments, respectively.

address | address | address | . . .

FIGURE **7.1** • Simple relocation entry.

```
int address      /* offset in text or data segment */
unsigned int r_symbolnum : 24,  /* ordinal number of add symbol */
r_pcrel : 1,   /* 1 if value should be pc-relative */
r_length : 2,  /* log base 2 of value's width */
r_extern :  1,  /* 1 if need to add symbol to value */
```

FIGURE **7.2** • a.out relocation entry.

For a pointer or direct address within the same segment, the linker adds TR or DR to the stored value already in the segment. For a pointer or direct address from one segment to another, the linker adds the relocated base of the target segment (TR, DR, or BR) to the stored value. Since a.out input files already have the target addresses in each segment relocated to the tentative segment positions in the new file, this is all that's necessary. For example, assume that in the input file, the text starts at 0 and data starts at 2000, and a pointer in the text segment points to offset 200 in the data segment. In the input file, the stored pointer will have the value 2200. If the final relocated address of the data segment in the output turns out to be 15000, then DR will be 13000, and the linker will add 13000 to the existing 2200 to yield a final stored value of 15200.

Some architectures have different sizes of addresses. Both the IBM 360 and the Intel 386 have both 16- and 32-bit addresses, and linkers have generally supported relocation items of both sizes. In both cases, it's up to the programmer who uses 16-bit addresses to make sure that the addresses will fit in the 16-bit fields; the linker doesn't do any more than verify that the address fits in each specified field.

INSTRUCTION RELOCATION

Relocating addresses in instructions is somewhat trickier than relocating pointers in data because of the profusion of quirky instruction formats. The a.out format described above has only two relocation formats, absolute and pc-relative, which were adequate on the PDP-11 and VAX, but most computer architectures require a longer list of relocation formats to handle all the instruction formats.

x86 Instruction Relocation

Despite the complex instruction encodings on the x86, from the linker's point of view the architecture is easy to handle because there are only two kinds of addresses the linker has to handle, direct and pc-relative. (We ignore segmentation here, as do most 32-bit linkers.) Data reference instructions can contain the 32-bit address of the target, which the linker can relocate the same as any other 32-bit data address, by adding the relocated base of the segment in which the target resides.

Call and jump instructions use relative addressing, so the value in the instruction is the difference between the target address and the address of the byte following the instruction itself. For calls and jumps within the same segment, no relocation is required because the relative positions of addresses within a single segment never change. For intersegment jumps, the linker needs to add the relocation for the target segment and then to subtract that of the instruction's segment. For a jump from the text to the data segment, for example, the relocation value to apply would be DR – TR.

SPARC Instruction Relocation

In contrast to the linker-friendly instruction encodings of the x86 architecture, the SPARC has no direct addressing, four different branch formats, and some specialized instructions used to synthesize a 32-bit address, with individual instructions only containing part of an address. The linker needs to handle all of this.

Unlike the x86, none of the SPARC instruction formats have room for a 32-bit address in the instruction itself. This means that in the input files, the target address of an instruction with a relocatable memory reference can't be stored in the instruction itself. Instead, SPARC relocation entries (Figure 7.3) have an extra field r_addend that contains the 32-bit value to which the reference is made. Because SPARC relocation can't be described as simply as that of the x86, the various type bits are replaced by a field r_type that contains a code that describes the format of the relocation. Also, rather than dedicate a bit to distinguish between segment and symbol relocations, each input file defines

```
int r_address;    /* offset of data to relocate */
int r_index:24,   /* symbol table index of symbol */
    r_type:8;     /* relocation type */
int r_addend;     /* datum addend */
```

FIGURE 7.3 • SPARC relocation entry.

symbols .text, .data, and .bss as the beginnings of their respective segments, and segment relocations refer to those symbols.

The SPARC relocations fall into three categories: absolute addresses for pointers in data, relative addresses of various sizes for branches and calls, and the special SETHI absolute address hack. Absolute addresses are relocated almost the same as on the x86—the linker adds TR, DR, or BR to the stored value. In this case, the addend in the relocation entry isn't really needed because there's room for a full address in the stored value, but the linker adds the addend to the stored value anyway for consistency.

For branches, the stored offset value is generally zero, with the addend being the offset to the target (the difference between the target address and the address of the stored value). The linker adds the appropriate relocation value to the addend to get the relocated relative address. Then it shifts the relative address right 2 bits (because SPARC relative addresses are stored without the low bits); checks to make sure that the shifted value will fit in the number of bits available (16, 19, 22, or 30 depending on format); masks the shifted address to that number of bits; and adds it into the instruction. The 16-bit format stores 14 low bits in the low bits of the word, but the 15th and 16th bits are in bit positions 20 and 21. The linker does the appropriate shifting and masking to store those bits without modifying the intervening bits.

The special SETHI hack synthesizes a 32-bit address with a SETHI instruction, which takes a 22-bit value from the instruction and places it in the 22 high bits of a register, followed by an OR-immediate to the same register that provides the low 10 bits of the address. The linker handles this with two specialized relocation modes: One mode puts the 22 high bits of the relocated address (the addend plus the appropriate relocated segment base) in the low 22 bits of the stored value, and the other mode puts the low 10 bits of the relocated address in the low 10 bits of the stored value. Unlike the branch modes described above, these relocation modes *do not* check that each value fits in the stored bits, because in both cases the stored bits don't represent the entire value.

```
int address;   /* offset of data to relocate */
int index;     /* symbol index */
short type;    /* relocation type */
```

FIGURE **7.4** • MS ECOFF relocation entry.

Instruction relocation on other architectures uses variations on the SPARC techniques, with a different relocation type for each instruction format that can address memory.

ECOFF SEGMENT RELOCATION

Microsoft's ECOFF object format is an extended version of COFF, which is descended from a.out, so it's not surprising that Win32 relocation bears a lot of similarities to a.out relocation. Each section in an ECOFF object file can have a list of relocation entries similar to a.out entries (Figure 7.4). A peculiarity of ECOFF relocation entries is that even on 32-bit machines, they're 10 bytes long, which means that on machines that require aligned data, the linker can't just load the entire relocation table into a memory array with a single read, but rather has to read and unpack entries one at a time. (COFF is old enough that saving 2 bytes per entry probably appeared worthwhile when it was originally developed.) In each entry, the address is the relative virtual address (RVA) of the stored data, the index is the segment or symbol index, and the type is a machine-specific relocation type. For each section of the input file, the symbol table contains an entry with a name like .text, so segment relocations use the index of the symbol corresponding to the target section.

On the x86, ECOFF relocations work much like they do in a.out. An IMAGE_REL_I386_DIR32 is a 32-bit direct address or stored pointer, an IMAGE_REL_I386_DIR32NB is a 32-bit direct address or stored pointer relative to the base of the program, and an IMAGE_REL_I386_REL32 is a pc-relative 32-bit address. A few other relocation types support special MS Windows features, mentioned in the subsection titled Special Segments in Section 7.6.

ECOFF supports several RISC processors including MIPS, the Alpha, and the PowerPC. These processors all present the same relocation issues that SPARC does, using branches with limited addressing and multi-instruction sequences to synthesize a direct address. ECOFF has relocation types to handle each of those situations, along with the conventional full-word relocations.

MIPS, for example, has a jump instruction that contains a 26-bit address that is shifted 2 bits to the left and placed in the 28 low bits of the program counter, leaving the high 4 bits unchanged. The relocation type IMAGE_ REL_MIPS_JMPADDR relocates a branch target address. Because there's no place in the relocation item for the target address, the stored instruction already contains the unrelocated target address. To do the relocation, the linker has to reconstruct the unrelocated target address by extracting the low 26 bits of the stored instruction (by shifting and masking); then has to add the relocated segment base for the target segment; then has to undo the shifting and masking to reconstruct the instruction. In the process, the linker also has to check that the target address is reachable from the instruction.

MIPS also has an equivalent of the SETHI trick. MIPS instructions can contain 16-bit literal values. To load an arbitrary 32-bit value, you would use a load upper immediate (LUI) instruction to place the high half of an immediate value in the high 16 bits of a register, followed by an OR-immediate (ORI) to place the low 16 bits in the register. The relocation types IMAGE_REL_MIPS_ REFHI and IMAGE_REL_MIPS_REFLO support this trick, telling the linker to relocate the high or low half, respectively, of the target value in the relocated instruction. REFHI presents a problem, however. Imagine that the target address before relocation is hex 00123456, so the stored instruction will contain 0012, the high half of the unrelocated value. Now imagine that the relocation value is 1E000. The final value will be 123456 plus 1E000, which is 141456, so the stored value will be 0014. But wait—to do this calculation, the linker needs the full value 00123456, but only the 0012 is stored in the instruction. Where does it find the low half with the value 3456? ECOFF's answer is that the next relocation item after the REFHI is IMAGE_REL_MIPS_PAIR, in which the index contains the low half of the target for a preceding REFHI. This is arguably a better approach than using an extra addend field in each relocation item, because the PAIR item only occurs after REFHI, rather than wasting space in every item. The disadvantage is that the order of relocation items now becomes important, while it wasn't before.

ELF RELOCATION

ELF relocation is similar to a.out and ECOFF relocation. ELF does rationalize the use of relocation items with addends and those without, having two kinds of relocation sections: SHT_REL (without) and SHT_RELA (with). In practice, all of the relocation sections in a single file are of the same type, depending on the target architecture. If the architecture has room for all the addends in the object code, as the x86 does, it uses REL; if not, the architecture uses RELA. But in principle a compiler could save some space on architectures that need addends by putting all the relocations with zero addends (e.g., procedure references) in an SHT_REL section and the rest in an SHT_RELA.

ELF also adds some extra relocation types to handle dynamic linking and position-independent code. We discuss these in Chapters 8 and 10.

OMF RELOCATION

OMF relocation is conceptually the same as the schemes we've already looked at, although the details are quite complex. Since OMF was originally designed for use on microcomputers with limited memory and storage, the format permits relocation to take place without having to load an entire segment into memory. OMF intermixes LIDATA or LEDATA data records with FIXUPP relocation records, with each FIXUPP referring to the preceding data. Hence, the linker can read and buffer a data record, then read a following FIXUPP, apply the relocations, and write out the relocated data. FIXUPPs refer to relocation threads, 2-bit codes that indirectly refer to a frame (an OMF relocation base). The linker has to track the four active frames, updating them as FIXUPP records redefine them and using them as FIXUPP records refer to them.

7.5 RELINKABLE AND RELOCATABLE OUTPUT FORMATS

A few formats are *relinkable*, which means that the output file has a symbol table and relocation information so that it can be used as an input file in a subsequent link. Many formats are *relocatable*, which means that the output file has relocation information for load-time relocation.

For relinkable files, the linker needs to create a table of output relocation entries from the input relocation entries. Some entries can be passed through verbatim, some modified, and some discarded. Entries for segment-relative fixups in formats that don't combine segments can generally be passed through unmodified other than adjusting the segment index, because the final link will handle the relocation. In formats that do combine segments, the item's offset needs to be adjusted. For example, in a linked a.out file, an incoming text segment has a segment-relative relocation at offset 400, but that segment is combined with other text segments so the code from that segment is at location 3500. Then the relocation item is modified to refer to location 3900 rather than 400.

Entries for symbol resolution can be passed through unmodified, changed to segment relocations, or discarded. If an external symbol remains undefined, the linker passes through the relocation item, possibly adjusting the offset and symbol index to reflect combined segments and the order of symbols in the output file's symbol table. If the symbol is resolved, what the linker does depends on the details of the symbol reference. If the reference is a pc-relative one within the same segment, the linker can discard the relocation entry because the relative positions of the reference and the target won't move. If the reference is absolute or intersegment, the relocation item turns into a segment-relative one. For output formats that are relocatable but not relinkable, the linker discards all relocation items other than segment-relative fixups.

7.6 OTHER RELOCATION FORMATS

Although the most common format for relocation items is an array of fixups, there are a few other possibilities, including chained references and bitmaps. Most formats also have segments that need to be treated specially by the linker.

CHAINED REFERENCES

For external symbol references, one surprisingly effective format is a linked list of references, with the links in the object code itself. The symbol table entry points to one reference, the word at that location points to a subsequent reference, and so forth to the final reference, which has a stop value such as zero or –1. This works on architectures where address references are a full word or at least enough bits to cover the maximum size of an object file segment. (SPARC branches, for example, have a 22-bit offset that—because instructions are aligned on 4-byte boundaries—is enough to cover a 2^{24}-byte section; this is a reasonable limit on a single file segment.)

This trick does not handle symbol references with offsets. This is usually an acceptable limitation for code references but a problem for data. In C, for example, you can write static initializers that point into the middle of arrays:

```
extern int a[];
static int *ap = &a[3];
```

On a 32-bit machine, the contents of ap are a plus 12. A way around this problem is either to use this technique just for code pointers, or else to use the link list for the common case of references with no offset and something else for references with offsets.

BITMAPS

On architectures such as the PDP-11, the Z8000, and some digital signal processors (DSPs) that use absolute addressing, code segments can end up with a lot of segment relocations because most memory reference instructions contain an address that needs to be relocated. Rather than making a list of locations to fix up, it can be more efficient to store fixups as a bitmap, with one bit for every word in a segment, the bit being set if the location needs to be fixed up. On 16-bit architectures, a bitmap saves space if more than 1/16 of the words in a segment need relocation; on a 32-bit architecture, a bitmap is useful if more than 1/32 of the words need relocation.

SPECIAL SEGMENTS

Many object formats define special segment formats that require special relocation processing. MS Windows objects have thread local storage (TLS), a special segment (containing global variables) that is replicated for each thread started within a process. IBM 360 objects have pseudo-registers, similar to thread local storage, which provide an area with named subchunks referred to from different input files. Many RISC architectures define "small" segments that are collected together into one area, with a register being set at program startup to point to that area, allowing direct addressing from anywhere in the program. In each of these cases, the linker needs a special relocation type or two to handle special segments.

For MS Windows thread local storage, the details of the relocation type(s) vary by architecture. For the x86, IMAGE_REL_I386_SECREL fixups store the target symbol's offset from the beginning of its segment. This fixup is generally an instruction with an index register that is set at run time to point to the current thread's TLS, so the SECREL provides the offset within the TLS. For the MIPS and other RISC processors, there are both SECREL fixups to store a 32-bit value as well as SECRELLO and SECRELHI (the latter followed by a PAIR, as with REFHI) to generate section-relative addresses.

For IBM pseudo-registers, the object format adds two relocation types. One is a PR pseudo-register reference, which stores the offset of the pseudo-register typically into 2 bytes in a load or store instruction. The other is CXD, the total size of the pseudo-registers used in a program. This value is used by run-time startup code to determine how much storage to allocate for a set of pseudo-registers.

For small data segments, object formats define a relocation type such as GPREL (global pointer relocation) for MIPS or LITERAL for Alpha that stores the offset of the target data in the small data area. The linker defines a symbol like _GP as the base of the small data area, so that run-time startup code can load a pointer to the area into a fixed register.

7.7 RELOCATION SPECIAL CASES

Many object formats have weak external symbols, which are treated as normal global symbols if some input file happens to define them or zero otherwise. (See Chapter 5 for details.) These usually require no special effort in the relocation process, because the symbol is either a normal defined global or else it's zero. Either way, references are resolved like any other symbol.

Some older object formats permitted much more complex relocation than the formats we've discussed here. In the IBM 360 format, for example, each relocation item can either add or subtract the address to which it refers, and multiple relocation items can modify the same location, permitting references like A – B where either or both of A and B are external symbols.

Some older linkers permitted arbitrarily complex relocations, with elaborate reverse polish strings representing link-time expressions to be resolved and stored into program memory. Although these schemes had great expressive power, it turned out to be power that wasn't very useful, and modern linkers have retreated to references with optional offsets.

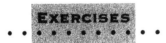

EXERCISE • 7.1

Why does a SPARC linker check for address overflow when relocating branch addresses but not when doing the high and low parts of the addresses in a SETHI sequence?

EXERCISE • 7.2

In the MIPS example, a REFHI relocation item needs a following PAIR item, but a REFLO doesn't. Why not?

EXERCISE • 7.3

References to symbols that are pseudo-registers and thread local storage are resolved as offsets from the start of the segment, while normal symbol references are resolved as absolute addresses. Why?

EXERCISE • 7.4

We said that a.out and ECOFF relocation doesn't handle references like A – B where A and B are both global symbols. Can you come up with a way to fake it?

Recall that relocations are of the format

```
loc seg ref type ...
```

where `loc` is the location to be relocated, `seg` is the segment it's in, `ref` is the segment or symbol to which the relocation refers, and `type` is the relocation type. For concreteness, we define these relocation types as follows:

- **A4** Absolute reference. The 4 bytes at `loc` are an absolute reference to segment `ref`.

- **R4** Relative reference. The 4 bytes at `loc` are a relative reference to segment `ref`, that is, the bytes at `loc` contain the difference between the address after `loc` (`loc+4`) and the target address. (This is the x86 relative jump instruction format.)

- **AS4** Absolute symbol reference. The 4 bytes at `loc` are an absolute reference to symbol `ref`, with the addend being the value already stored at `loc`. (The addend is usually zero.)

- **RS4** Relative symbol reference. The 4 bytes at `loc` are a relative reference to symbol `ref`, with the addend being the value already stored at `loc`. (The addend is usually zero.)

- **U2** Upper half reference. The 2 bytes at `loc` are the most significant 2 bytes of a reference to symbol `ref`.

- **L2** Lower half reference. The 2 bytes at `loc` are the least significant 2 bytes of a reference to symbol `ref`.

PROJECT • 7.1

Make the linker handle these relocation types. After the linker has created its symbol table and assigned the addresses of all of the segments and symbols, process the relocation items in each input file. Keep in mind that the relocations are defined to affect the actual byte values of the object data, not the hexadecimal representation. If you're writing your linker in perl, it's probably easiest to convert each segment of object data to a binary string using the perl pack function, to do the relocations, then to convert back to hexadecimal format using unpack.

PROJECT • 7.2

Which endianness did you assume when you handled your relocations in Project 7.1? Modify your linker to assume the other endianness instead.

LOADING AND OVERLAYS

Loading is the process of bringing a program into main memory so it can run. In this chapter we look at the loading process, concentrating on loading programs that have already been linked. Many systems used to have linking loaders that combined the linking and loading process, but those have now practically disappeared; the only ones I know of on current hardware are on MVS and the dynamic linkers we'll cover in Chapter 10. Linking loaders weren't all that different from plain linkers, with the primary and obvious difference being that the output was left in memory rather than placed in a file.

8.1 BASIC LOADING

We touched on most of the basics of loading in Chapter 3 in the context of object file design. Loading is a little different depending on whether a program is loaded by mapping into a process address space by means of the virtual memory system or just read in using normal I/O calls.

On most modern systems, each program is loaded into a fresh address space, which means that all programs are loaded at a known fixed address and can be linked for that address. In that case, loading is pretty simple and requires the following steps:

1. Read enough header information from the object file to find out how much address space is needed.

2. Allocate that address space, in separate segments if the object format has separate segments.

3. Read the program into the segments in the address space.

4. Zero out any bss space at the end of the program if the virtual memory system doesn't do so automatically.

5. Create a stack segment if the architecture needs one.

6. Set up any run-time information such as program arguments or environment variables.

7. Start the program.

If the program isn't mapped through the virtual memory system, reading in the object file just means reading in the file with normal read system calls. On systems that support shared read-only code segments, the system needs to check whether there's already a copy of the code segment loaded in and uses that rather than making another copy.

On systems that do memory mapping, the process is slightly more complicated. The system loader has to create the segments and then arrange to map the file pages into the segments with appropriate permissions, either read-only (RO) or copy-on-write (COW). In some cases, the same page is double mapped at the end of one segment and the beginning of the next as RO in one and COW in the other (in formats like compact UNIX a.out). The data segment is generally contiguous with the bss segment, so the loader has to zero out the part of the last page after the end of the data (because the disk version usually has symbols or something else there) and allocate enough zero pages following the data to cover the bss segment.

8.2 BASIC LOADING, WITH RELOCATION

A few systems still do load-time relocation for executables, and many do load-time relocation of shared libraries. Some, like DOS, lack usable hardware relocation. Others, like MVS, have hardware relocation but are descended from systems that didn't have it. Some systems have hardware relocation but can load multiple executable programs and shared libraries into the same address space, so linkers can't count on having specific addresses available.

As discussed in Chapter 7, load-time relocation is far simpler than link-time relocation, because the entire program is relocated as a unit. If, for example, the program is linked as though it would be loaded at location zero but is in fact loaded at location 15000, all of the places in the program that require fixups will get 15000 added. After reading the program into memory, the loader consults the relocation items in the object file and fixes up the memory locations to which the items point.

Load-time relocation can present a performance problem, because code loaded at different virtual addresses can't usually be shared between address spaces (the fixups for each address space are different). One approach, used by MVS and to some extent by MS Windows and AIX, is to create a shared-memory area that is present in multiple address spaces and to load often-used programs into that. (MVS calls this the link pack area.) This has the problem that different processes don't get separate copies of writable data, so the application has to be written to allocate all of its writable storage explicitly.

8.3 POSITION-INDEPENDENT CODE

One popular solution to the dilemma of loading the same program at different addresses is *position-independent code* (PIC). The idea is simple: separate the code from the data and generate code that won't change regardless of the address at which it's loaded. That way the code can be shared among all processes, with only data pages being private to each process.

This is a surprisingly old idea. TSS/360 used it in 1966, and I don't believe it was original there. (TSS was notoriously buggy, but I can report from personal experience that the PIC features really worked.)

On modern architectures, it's not difficult to generate PIC-executable code. Jumps and branches are generally either pc-relative or relative to a base register set at run time, so no load-time relocation is required for them. The problem is with data addressing. The code can't contain any direct data addresses, because those would be relocatable and wouldn't be PIC. The usual solution is to create a table of data addresses in a data page and to keep a pointer to that table in a register, so the code can use indexed addressing

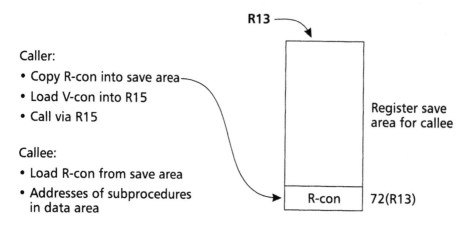

R13

Caller:
- Copy R-con into save area
- Load V-con into R15
- Call via R15

Callee:
- Load R-con from save area
- Addresses of subprocedures in data area

Register save area for callee

R-con   72(R13)

FIGURE **8.1** • TSS-style two-address procedure call.

relative to that register to pick up the data addresses. This works at the cost of an extra indirection for each data reference, but there's still the question of how to get the initial data address into the register.

TSS/360 POSITION-INDEPENDENT CODE

TSS took a brute-force approach. Every routine had two addresses: the address of the code, known as the V-con (short for V-style address constant, which even non-PIC code needed), and the address of the data, known as the R-con. The standard OS/360 calling sequence requires that the caller provide an 18-word register save area pointed to by register 13. TSS extended the save area to 19 words and required that the caller place the callee's R-con into that 19th word at 72(R13) before making the call (Figure 8.1). Each routine had in its data segment the V-cons and R-cons for all of the routines that it called and stored the appropriate R-con into the outgoing save area before each call. The main routine in a program received a save area from the operating system that provided the initial R-con.

This scheme worked, but it is poorly suited for modern systems. For one thing, copying the R-cons made the calling sequence bulky. For another, it made procedure pointers two words, which didn't matter in the 1960s but is an issue now because in programs written in C, all pointers have to be the same size. (The C standard doesn't mandate it, but far too much existing C code assumes it to do anything else.)

Caller:

- Load pointer table address into RP
- Load code address from 0(RP) into RC
- Call via RC

Callee:

- RP points to pointer table
- Table has addresses of pointer tables for subprocedures

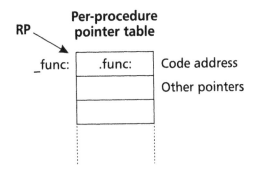

FIGURE **8.2** • Accessing code by means of data pointers.

PER-ROUTINE POINTER TABLES

A simple modification used in some UNIX systems is to treat the address of a procedure's data as the address of the procedure and to place a pointer to the procedure's code at that address (Figure 8.2). To call a procedure, the caller loads the data address into an agreed data pointer register, then it loads the code address from the location pointed to by the data pointer into a scratch register and calls the routine. This is easy to implement and has adequate if not fabulous performance.

TABLE OF CONTENTS

IBM's AIX uses a more sophisticated version of this scheme. AIX programs group routines into *modules,* with a module typically being the object code generated from a single C or C++ source file or a group of related source files. The data segment of each module contains a table of contents (TOC), which contains the combined pointer tables for all of the routines in the module as well as some of the small static data for the routines. Register 2 always contains the address of the TOC for the current module, permitting direct access to the static data in the TOC and indirect addressing of code and data to which the TOC contains pointers. Calls within a single module are a single call instruction, since the caller and callee share the same TOC. Intermodule calls have to switch TOCs before the call and switch back afterward.

Compilers generate each call as a call instruction, followed by a place-holder no-op instruction, which is correct for intramodule calls. When the linker encounters an intermodule call, it generates a routine called a global linkage or glink at the end of the module's text segment. The glink saves the caller's TOC on the stack, loads the callee's TOC and address from pointers in the caller's TOC, then jumps to the routine. The linker redirects each intermodule call to the glink for the called routine and patches the following no-op to a load instruction that restores the TOC from the stack. Procedure pointers are pointers to a TOC/code pair, and calls through a pointer use a generic glink routine that uses the TOC and the code address that the pointer points to.

This scheme makes intramodule calls as fast as possible. Intermodule calls are slowed down somewhat by the detour through the glink routine, but the slowdown is small compared to some of the alternatives we'll see in the next section.

ELF Position-Independent Code

UNIX System V Release 4 introduced a PIC scheme similar to the TOC scheme for its ELF shared libraries. This scheme is now universally used by systems that use ELF executables. It has the advantage of returning to the normal convention that the address of a procedure is the address of the code for the procedure, regardless of whether you are calling PIC code (found in shared ELF libraries) or non-PIC code (found in regular ELF executables); it works at the cost of somewhat more per-routine overhead than in the TOC scheme.

Its designers noticed that an ELF executable consists of a group of code pages followed by a group of data pages, and regardless of where in the address space the program is loaded, the offset from the code to the data doesn't change. So if the code can load its own address into a register, the data will be at a known distance from that address, and references to data in the program's own data segment can use efficient based addressing with fixed offsets (Figure 8.3).

The linker creates a global offset table (GOT) that contains pointers to all of the global data that the executable file addresses. (Each shared library has its own GOT, and if the main program is compiled with PIC—which it normally isn't—it will have a GOT as well.) Because the linker creates the GOT, there is only one pointer per ELF executable for each datum, regardless of how many routines in the executable refer to it.

If a procedure needs to refer to global or static data, it's up to the procedure itself to load up the address of the GOT. The details vary by architecture, but the following 386 code is typical:

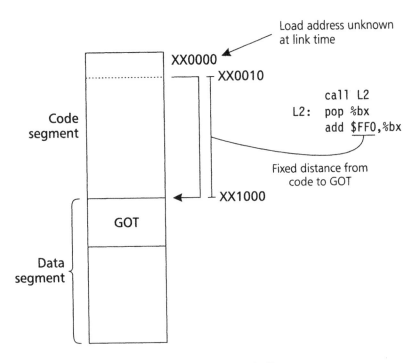

FIGURE **8.3** • PIC code and data with fixed offsets.

```
  call .L2   ;; push PC in on the stack
.L2:
  popl %ebx  ;; PC into register EBX
  addl $_GLOBAL_OFFSET_TABLE_+[.-.L2],%ebx  ;; adjust ebx to GOT address
```

This code consists of a call instruction to the immediately following location—which has the effect of pushing the PC on the stack but not jumping—
then a pop to get the saved PC in a register and an add-immediate of the difference between the address of the GOT and the address of the target of the call.
In an object file generated by a compiler, there's a special R_386_GOTPC relocation item for the operand of the addl instruction. This item tells the linker to
substitute in the offset from the current instruction to the base address of the
GOT, and it also serves as a flag to the linker to build a GOT in the output file. In
the output file, there's no relocation needed for the instruction because the
distance from the addl to the GOT is fixed.

Once the GOT register is loaded, code can reference local static data using
the GOT register as a base register, because the distance from a static datum in
the program's data segment to the GOT is fixed at link time. Addresses of

global data aren't bound until the program is loaded (see Chapter 10), so to reference global data, code has to load a pointer to the data from the GOT and then dereference the pointer. This extra memory reference makes programs somewhat slower, although it's a cost that most programmers are willing to pay for the convenience of dynamically linked libraries. Speed-critical code can use static shared libraries (see Chapter 9) or no shared libraries at all.

To support PIC, ELF defines a handful of special relocation types for code that uses the GOT in addition to R_386_GOTPC or its equivalent. The exact types are architecture specific, but the following x86 types are typical:

- R_386_GOT32. This is the relative location of the slot in the GOT where the linker has placed a pointer to the given symbol. It is used for indirectly referenced global data.

- R_386_GOTOFF. This is the distance from the base of the GOT to the given symbol or address. It is used to address static data relative to the GOT.

- R_386_RELATIVE. This is used to mark data addresses in a PIC shared library that need to be relocated at load time.

For example, consider this piece of C code:

```
static int a;  /* static variable */
extern int b;  /* global variable */
...
a = 1; b = 2;
```

Variable a is allocated in the bss segment of the object file, which means that it is at a known fixed distance from the GOT. Object code can reference this variable directly, using the ebx as a base register and a GOT-relative offset:

```
movl $1,a@GOTOFF(%ebx)   ;; R_386_GOTOFF reference to variable "a"
```

Variable b is global, and its location may not be known until run time if it turns out to be in a different ELF library or executable. In this case, the object code references a pointer to b, which the linker creates in the GOT:

```
movl b@GOT(%ebx),%eax   ;; R_386_GOT32 ref to address of "b"
movl $2,(%eax)
```

Note that the compiler only creates the R_386_GOT32 reference, and it's up to the linker to collect all such references and make slots for them in the GOT.

Finally, ELF shared libraries contain R_386_RELATIVE relocation entries that the run-time loader, part of the dynamic linker we examine in Chapter 10, uses to do load-time relocation. Because the text in shared libraries is invariably PIC, there are no relocation entries for the code, but data can't be PIC, so there is a relocation entry for every pointer in the data segment. (Actually, you can build a shared library with non-PIC code, in which case there will be relocation entries for the text as well, although almost nobody does that because it makes the text nonsharable.)

PIC COSTS AND BENEFITS

The advantages of PIC are straightforward; PIC makes it possible to load code without having to do load-time relocation and to share memory pages of code among processes even though they don't all have the same address space allocated. The possible disadvantages are slowdowns at load time, in procedure calls, and in function prologue and epilogue, as well as overall slower code.

At load time, although the code segment of a PIC file need not be relocated, the data segment does need to be relocated. In large libraries, the TOC or GOT can be very large and it can take a long time to resolve all the entries. This is as much a problem with dynamic linking, which we'll address in Chapter 10, as with PIC. Handling R_386_RELATIVE items or the equivalent to relocate GOT pointers to data in the same executable is fairly fast, but the problem is that many GOT entries point to data in other executables and require a symbol table lookup to resolve.

Calls in ELF executables are usually dynamically linked, even calls within the same library, which adds significant overhead. We examine this in Chapter 10.

Function prologues and epilogues in ELF files are quite slow. They have to save and restore the GOT register—ebx in the x86—and the dummy call and pop to get the program counter into a register are quite slow. From a performance viewpoint, the TOC approach used in AIX wins here, because each procedure can assume that its TOC register is already set at procedure entry.

Finally, PIC code is bigger and slower than non-PIC code. The slowdown varies greatly by architecture. On RISC systems with plenty of registers and no direct addressing, the loss of one register as the TOC or GOT pointer isn't significant, and lacking direct addressing they need a constant pool of some sort anyway. The worst case is on the x86: It only has six registers, so losing one of them to be the GOT pointer can make code significantly worse. Since the x86 does have direct addressing, a reference to external data that would be a simple MOV or ADD instruction in non-PIC code turns into a load of the address followed by the MOV or ADD, which both adds an extra memory reference and uses yet another precious register for the temporary pointer.

Particularly on x86 systems, the performance loss in PIC code is significant in speed-critical tasks, enough so that some systems retreat to a sort-of-PIC approach for shared libraries. We'll revisit this issue in Chapters 9 and 10.

8.4 BOOTSTRAP LOADING

Up to this point, the discussions of loading have all presumed that there's already an operating system or at least a program loader resident in the computer to load the program of interest. The chain of programs being loaded by other programs has to start somewhere, so the obvious question is, how is the first program loaded into the computer?

In modern computers, the first program the computer runs after a hardware reset invariably is stored in a ROM area known as the *bootstrap*, or *boot*, *ROM*. When the CPU is powered on or reset, it sets its registers to a known state. On x86 systems, for example, the reset sequence jumps to the address 16 bytes below the top of the system's address space. The bootstrap ROM occupies the top 64KB of the address space; ROM code then starts up the computer. On IBM-compatible x86 systems, the boot ROM code reads the first block of the floppy disk—or if that fails, the first block of the first hard disk—into memory location zero and then jumps to location zero. The program in block zero in turn loads a slightly larger operating system boot program from a known place on the disk into memory, and it jumps to that program, which in turn loads in the operating system and starts it. (There can be even more steps such as a boot manager that decides from which disk partition to read the operating system boot program, but the sequence of increasingly capable loaders remains.)

Why not just load the operating system directly? The answer here is that you can't fit an operating system loader into 512 bytes. The first-level loader typically is only able to load a single-segment program from a file with a fixed name in the top-level directory of the boot disk. The operating system loader contains more sophisticated code that can read and interpret a configuration file, uncompress a compressed operating system executable, and address large amounts of memory. (On an x86 the loader usually runs in real mode, which means that it's tricky to address more than 1MB of memory.) The full operating system can turn on the virtual memory system, load the drivers it needs, and then proceed to run user-level programs.

Many UNIX systems use a similar bootstrap process to get user-mode programs running. The kernel creates a process and then inserts a tiny program, only a few dozen bytes long, into that process. The tiny program executes a system call that runs /etc/init, the user-mode initialization program that in turn runs configuration files and starts the daemons and login programs that a running system needs.

None of this matters much to the application-level programmer, but it becomes more interesting if you want to write programs that run on the bare hardware of the machine, because then you need to arrange to intercept the bootstrap sequence somewhere in order to run your program rather than the usual operating system. Some systems make this quite easy (just stick the name of your program in AUTOEXEC.BAT and reboot Windows 95, for example); others make it nearly impossible. It also presents opportunities for customized systems. For example, a single-application system could be built over a UNIX kernel by naming the application /etc/init.

8.5 TREE-STRUCTURED OVERLAYS

The final topic of this chapter is tree-structured overlays, an approach that was widely used in the days before there was virtual memory to fit a program into a memory area smaller than the program. Overlays are another technique that dates back to before 1960 and are still in use in some memory-constrained environments. Several DOS linkers in the 1980s supported them in a form nearly identical to that used 25 years earlier on mainframe computers. Although overlays are now little used on conventional architectures, the techniques that linkers use to create and manage overlays remain interesting. Also, the intersegment call tricks developed for overlays point the way to dynamic linking. In environments like DSPs that have constrained program address spaces, overlay techniques can be a good way to squeeze programs in, especially because overlay managers tend to be small. The OS/360 overlay

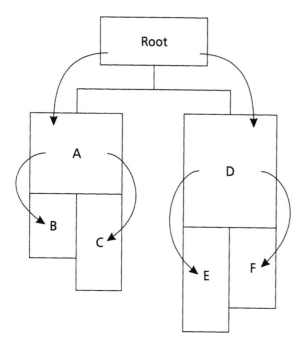

FIGURE 8.4 • Typical overlay tree format.

manager is only about 500 bytes, and I once wrote one for a graphics processor with a 512-word address space that used only a dozen words or so.

Overlay programs divide the code into a tree of segments, such as the one
in Figure 8.4. The programmer manually assigns object files or individual
object code segments to overlay segments. Sibling segments in the overlay
tree share the same memory. In the example in Figure 8.4, segments A and D
share the same memory, B and C share the same memory, and E and F share
the same memory. The sequence of segments that lead to a specific segment is
called a *path,* so the path for E includes the root, D, and E.

When the program starts, the system loads the root segment, which contains the entry point of the program. Each time a routine makes a downward
intersegment call, the overlay manager ensures that the path to the call target
is loaded. For example, if the root calls a routine in segment A, the overlay
manager loads segment A if it's not already loaded. If a routine in A calls a routine in B, the manager has to ensure that B is loaded; if a routine in the root
calls a routine in B, the manager has to ensure that both A and B are loaded.
Upward calls don't require any linker help, because the entire path from the
root is already loaded.

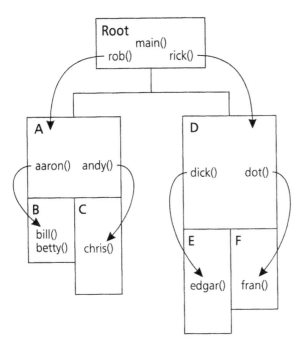

FIGURE **8.5** • Overlay tree example.

Calls across the tree are known as *exclusive calls* and are usually considered to be errors because it's not possible to return. Overlay linkers let the programmer force exclusive calls for situations where the called routine is known
not to return.

DEFINING OVERLAYS

Overlay linkers create overlay executables from ordinary input object files.
The objects don't contain any overlay instructions; instead, the programmer
specifies the overlay structure with a command language that the linker reads
and interprets. Figure 8.5 shows the same overlay structure as before with the
names of the routines loaded into each segment.

   Figure 8.6 shows the linker commands that you might give to the IBM 360
linker to create this structure. Spacing doesn't matter, so we've indented the
commands to show the tree structure. OVERLAY commands define the beginning of each segment; commands with the same overlay name define segments that overlay each other. Hence the first OVERLAY AD defines segment A,

```
INCLUDE ROB
INCLUDE RICK
OVERLAY AD
  INCLUDE AARON, ANDY
  OVERLAY BC
    INCLUDE BILL, BETTY
  OVERLAY BC
    INCLUDE CHRIS
OVERLAY AD
  INCLUDE DICK, DOT
  OVERLAY EF
    INCLUDE EDGAR
  OVERLAY EF
    INCLUDE FRAN
```

FIGURE **8.6** • Linker commands corresponding to overlay tree example
                in Figure 8.5.

and the second defines segment D. Overlay segments are defined in a depth-first left-to-right tree walk. INCLUDE commands name logical files for the linker to read.

It's up to the programmer to lay out overlays to be space efficient. The storage allocated for each segment is the maximum length of any of the segments that occupy the same space. For example, assume that the file lengths in decimal are as follows:

Name	Size	Name	Size
rob	500	chris	3000
rick	1500	dick	3000
aaron	3000	dot	4000
andy	1000	edgar	2000
bill	1000	fran	3000
betty	1000		

The corresponding storage allocation looks like Figure 8.7. Each segment starts immediately after the preceding segment in the path, and the total program size is the length of the longest path. This program is fairly well

```
                                 0 rob
                               500 rick
2000 aaron                              2000 dick
5000 andy                               5000 dot

6000 bill          6000 chris
7000 betty         9000 —             9000 edgar      9000 fran
8000 —                                11000 —         12000 —
```

FIGURE **8.7** • Overlay storage allocation example.

balanced, with the longest path being 12000 and the shortest being 8000. Juggling the overlay structure to find one that is as compact as possible while still being valid (no exclusive calls) and reasonably efficient is a black art requiring considerable trial and error. Since the overlays are defined entirely in the linker, each trial requires a relink but no recompilation.

IMPLEMENTATION OF OVERLAYS

The implementation of overlays is surprisingly simple. Once the linker determines the layout of the segments, it relocates the code in each segment appropriately based on the memory location of the segment. The linker needs to create a segment table that goes in the root segment and, in each segment, glue code (linker-generated code that hooks into the overlay manager) for each routine that is the target of a downward call from that segment. The segment table lists each segment, a flag to note if the segment is loaded, the segment's path, and information needed to load the segment from disk (Figure 8.8).

The linker interposes the glue code in front of each downward call so that the overlay manager can ensure that the required segment(s) are loaded. Segments can use glue code in higher-level but not lower-level routines. For example, if routines in the root call aaron, dick, and betty, the root needs glue code for each of those three symbols. If segment A contains calls to bill, betty, and chris, segment A needs glue code for bill and chris but can use the glue for betty already present in the root. All downward calls (which are to global symbols) are resolved to glue code (Figure 8.9) rather than to the actual routine.

```
struct segtab {
  struct segtab *path;   // preceding segment in path
  boolean ispresent;     // true if this segment is loaded
  int memoffset;         // relative load address
  int diskoffset;        // location in executable
  int size;              // segment size
} segtab[];
```

FIGURE 8.8 • Idealized segment table.

The glue code has to save any registers it changes, because it has to be transparent to the calling and called routine, then it has to jump into the overlay manager, providing the address of the real routine and an indication of which segment that address is in. Here we use a pointer, but an index into the segtab array would work as well.

At run time, the system loads in the root segment and starts it. At each downward call, the glue code calls the overlay manager. The manager checks the target segment's status. If the segment is present, the manager just jumps to the real routine. If the segment is not present, the manager loads the target segment and any unloaded preceding segments in the path, marks any conflicting segments as not present, marks the newly loaded segments as present, and jumps.

OVERLAY FINE POINTS

As always, details make elegant tree-structured overlays messier than they might be.

Data

We've been talking about structuring code overlays, without any consideration of where the data go. Individual routines may have private data loaded into the segments with the routines, but any data that have to be remembered from one call to the next need to be promoted high enough in the tree that they won't get unloaded and reloaded, which would lose any changes made. In practice, this means that most global data usually end up in the root. When

```
glue'betty: call load_overlay
  .long betty      // address of real routine
  .long segtab+N   // address of segment B's segtab
```

FIGURE 8.9 • Idealized glue code for the x86.

Fortran programs are overlaid, overlay linkers can position common blocks appropriately to be used as communication areas. For example, if dick calls edgar and fran, and the latter two both refer to a common block, that block has to reside in segment D to be a communication area.

Duplicated Code

The overall structure of an overlay program frequently can be improved by duplicating code. In our example, imagine that chris and edgar both call a routine called greg that is 500 bytes long. A single copy of greg would have to go in the root, increasing the total loaded size of the program, because placing it anywhere else in the tree would require a forbidden exclusive call from either chris or edgar. On the other hand, if both segments C and E include copies of greg, the overall loaded size of the program doesn't increase, because the end of segment C would grow from 9000 to 9500 and of segment E from 11000 to 11500, both of which are still smaller than the 12000 bytes that F requires.

Multiple Regions

Frequently, a program's calling structure doesn't map very well to a single tree. Overlay systems handle multiple code regions, with a separate overlay tree in each region. Calls between regions, other than to root segments, always go through glue code. The IBM linker supports up to four regions, although in my experience I have never found a use for more than two.

OVERLAY SUMMARY

Even though overlays have been rendered largely obsolete by virtual memory, they remain of historical interest because they were the first significant use of link-time code generation and modification. They required a great deal of manual programmer work to design and specify the overlay structure, generally with a lot of trial-and-error "digital origami," but they were a very effective way to squeeze a large program into limited memory.

Overlays originated the important technique of wrapping call instructions in the linker to turn a simple procedure call into one that does more work (in this case, loading the required overlay). Linkers have used wrapping in a variety of ways. The most important is dynamic linking, which we cover in Chapter 10, where it is used to link to a called routine in a library that may not have been loaded yet. Wrapping is also useful for testing and debugging, in order to insert checking or validation code in front of a suspect routine without changing or recompiling the source file.

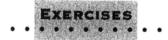

EXERCISE • **8.1**

Compile some small C routines with PIC and non-PIC code. How much slower is the PIC code than the non-PIC code? Is it slower enough to be worth having non-PIC versions of libraries for programmers who are in a hurry?

EXERCISE • **8.2**

In the overlay example, assume that dick and dot each call both edgar and fran, but dick and dot don't call each other. Restructure the overlay so that dick and dot share the same space, and adjust the structure so that the call tree still works. How much space does the overlay program take now?

EXERCISE • **8.3**

In the overlay segment table, there's no explicit marking of conflicting segments. When the overlay manager loads a segment and the segment's path, how does the manager determine what segments to mark as not present?

Exercise • **8.**4

In an overlay program with no exclusive calls, is it possible that a series of calls could end up jumping to unloaded code anyway? In the example in this chapter, what happens if rob calls bill, which calls aaron, which calls chris, and then the routines all return? How hard would it be for the linker or overlay manager to detect or prevent that problem?

Project • **8.1**

Add a feature to the linker to wrap routines. Create a linker switch

```
-w name
```

that wraps the given routine. Change all references to the named routine in the program to be references to wrap_name. (Be sure not to miss internal references within the segment in which the name is defined.) Change the name of the routine to real_name. (This lets the programmer write a wrapper routine called wrap_name that can call the original routine as real_name.)

Project • **8.2**

Starting with the linker skeleton from Chapter 3, write a tool that modifies an object file to wrap a name, that is, that causes references to name to turn into external references to wrap_name and the existing routine to be renamed real_name. Why would we want to use such a program rather than building the feature into the linker? (*Hint:* Consider the case where you're not the author or maintainer of the linker.)

Project • **8.3**

Add support to the linker to produce executables with position-independent code. Add the following new 4-byte relocation types:

```
loc seg ref GA4
loc seg ref GP4
loc seg ref GR4
loc seg ref ER4
```

The types have the following roles:

- GA4 (GOT address). At location `loc`, store the distance to the GOT.

- GP4 (GOT pointer). Put a pointer to symbol `ref` in the GOT, and at location `loc`, store the GOT-relative offset of that pointer.

- GR4 (GOT relative). Location `loc` contains an address in segment `ref`; replace that with the offset from the beginning of the GOT to that address.

- ER4 (Executable relative). Location `loc` contains an address relative to the beginning of the executable. The `ref` field is ignored.

In your linker's first pass, look for GP4 relocation entries, build a GOT segment with all the required pointers, and allocate the GOT segment just before the data and bss segments. In the second pass, handle the GA4, GP4, and GR4 entries. In the output file, create ER4 relocation entries for any data that would have to be relocated if the output file were loaded at other than its nominal address. This would include anything marked by an A4 or AS4 relocation entry in the input. (*Hint:* Don't forget the GOT.)

SHARED LIBRARIES

Program libraries date back to the earliest days of computing, when programmers quickly realized that they could save a lot of time and effort by reusing blocks of program code. With the advent of compilers for languages like Fortran and COBOL, libraries became an integral part of programming. Compiled languages use libraries explictly when a program calls a standard procedure such as sqrt(), and they use libraries implicitly for I/O, conversions, sorting, and many other functions too complex to express as inline code. As languages have gotten more complex, libraries have gotten correspondingly more complex. When I wrote a Fortran-77 compiler 20 years ago, the run-time library was already more work than the compiler itself, and a Fortran-77 library is far simpler than one for C++.

The growth of language libraries means not only that all programs include library code but that most programs include a lot of the same library code. Every C program, for example, uses the system call library, nearly all use the standard I/O library routines such as printf, and many use other popular libraries for math, networking, and other common functions. This means that in a typical UNIX system with a thousand compiled programs, there are close to a thousand copies of printf. If all those programs could share a single copy of the library routines they use, the savings in disk space would be substantial. (On a UNIX system without shared libraries, there are 5–10MB of copies of `printf` alone.) Even more important, if running programs could share a single in-memory copy of the libraries, the main memory savings could be very significant, both in saving memory and in improving paging behavior.

All shared-library schemes work essentially the same way. At link time, the linker searches through libraries as usual to find modules that resolve otherwise undefined external symbols. But rather than copying the contents of the module into the output file, the linker makes a note of what library the module came from and puts a list of the libraries in the executable. When the program is loaded, startup code finds those libraries and maps them into the program's address space before the program starts (Figure 9.1). Standard operating system file-mapping semantics automatically share pages that are mapped read-only or copy-on-write. The startup code that does the mapping may be in the operating system, in the executable, in a special dynamic linker mapped into the process's address space, or in some combination of the three.

In this chapter, we look at statically linked shared libraries, that is, libraries where program and data addresses in libraries are bound to executables at link time. In Chapter 10 we look at the considerably more complex dynamically linked libraries. Although dynamic linking is more flexible and more modern, it's also a lot slower than static linking because a great deal of work that would otherwise have been done once at link time is redone each time a dynamically linked program starts. Also, dynamically linked programs usually use extra glue code to call routines in shared libraries. The glue usually contains several jumps, which can slow down calls considerably. On systems that support both static and dynamic shared libraries, unless programs need the extra flexibility of dynamic linking, they're faster and smaller with statically linked libraries.

9.1 BINDING TIME

Shared libraries raise binding-time issues that don't apply to conventionally linked programs. A program that uses a shared library depends on having that shared library available when the program is run. One kind of error occurs when the required libraries aren't present. There's not much to be done in that case other than printing a cryptic error message and exiting.

mydir/myprog   **/shlib/libc**

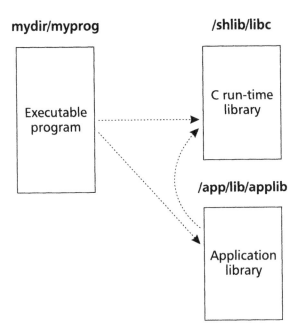

FIGURE **9.1** • Program with shared libraries.

A much more interesting problem occurs when the library is present, but the library has changed since the program was linked. In a conventionally linked program, symbols are bound to addresses and library code is bound to the executable at link time, so the library the program was linked with is the one it uses regardless of subsequent changes to the library. With static shared libraries, symbols are still bound to addresses at link time, but library code isn't bound to the executable until run time. (With dynamic shared libraries, they're both delayed until run time.)

A static shared library can't change very much without breaking the programs that it is bound to. Because the addresses of routines and data in the library are bound into the program, any changes in the addresses to which the program is bound will cause havoc.

A static shared library can sometimes be updated without breaking the programs that use it, if the updates can be made in a way that doesn't move any addresses in the library that programs depend on. This permits minor version updates, typically for small bug fixes. Larger changes unavoidably change program addresses, which means that a system either needs multiple versions of the library or forces programmers to relink all their programs each time the library changes. In practice, the solution is invariably multiple versions, since disk space is cheap and tracking down every executable that might have used a shared library is rarely possible.

9.2 SHARED LIBRARIES IN PRACTICE

In the rest of this chapter we concentrate on the static shared libraries provided in UNIX System V Release 3.2 (COFF format), older Linux systems (a.out format), and the BSD/OS derivative of 4.4BSD (a.out and ELF formats). All three work nearly the same, but some of the differences are instructive. The System V Release 3.2 implementation required changes in the linker to support searching shared libraries and extensive operating system support to do the run-time startup required. The Linux implemention required one small tweak to the linker and added a single system call to assist in library mapping. The BSD/OS implementation made no changes at all to the linker or operating system, using a shell script to provide the necessary arguments to the linker and a modified version of the standard C library startup routine to map in the libraries.

9.3 ADDRESS SPACE MANAGEMENT

The most difficult aspect of static shared libraries is address space management. Each shared library occupies a fixed piece of address space in each program in which it is used. Different libraries have to use non-overlapping addresses if they can be used in the same program. Although it's possible to check mechanically that libraries don't overlap, assigning address space to libraries is a black art. On the one hand, you want to leave some space in between them so that if a new version of one library grows a little, it won't bump into the next library up. On the other hand, you'd like to put your popular libraries as close together as possible to minimize the number of page tables needed. (Recall that on an x86, for example, there's a second-level table for each 4MB block of address space that is active in a process.)

There's invariably a master table of shared-library address space on each system, with libraries starting someplace in the address space far away from applications. Linux's start at hex 60000000, BSD/OS's at a0000000. Commercial vendors subdivide the address space further between vendor-supplied libraries and user and third-party libraries (which start at a0800000 in BSD/OS, for example).

Generally both the code and data addresses for each library are explicitly defined, with the data area starting on a page boundary a page or two after the end of the code. This makes it possible to create minor version updates, because the updates frequently don't change the data layout, but just add or change code.

Each individual shared library exports symbols, both code and data, and usually also imports symbols if the library depends on other libraries. Although it would work if we just linked routines together into a shared library in a haphazard order, real libraries use some discipline in assigning addresses to make it easier—or at least possible—to update a library without changing the addresses of exported symbols. For code addresses, rather than exporting the actual address of each routine, the library contains a table of jump instructions that jump to all of the routines, with the addresses of the jump instructions exported as the addresses of the routines. All jump instructions are the same size, so the addresses in the jump table are easy to compute and won't change from version to version so long as no entries are added or deleted in the middle of the table. One extra jump per routine is an insignificant slowdown, but because the actual routine addresses are not visible, new versions of the library will be compatible even if routines in the new version aren't all the same sizes and addresses as in the old version.

For exported data, the situation is more difficult, because there's no easy way to add a level of indirection like the one for code addresses. In practice, it turns out that exported data tend to be tables of known size that change rarely, such as the array of FILE structures for the C standard I/O library or single word values like errno (the error code from the most recent system call) or tzname (pointers to two strings giving the name of the local time zone). With some manual effort, the programmer who creates the shared library can collect the exported data at the front of the data section to precede any anonymous data that are part of individual routines, making it less likely that exported addresses will change from one version to the next.

9.4 STRUCTURE OF SHARED LIBRARIES

The shared library is an executable-format file that contains all of the library code and data, ready to be mapped in (Figure 9.2). Some shared libraries start with a small bootstrap routine that is used to map in the rest of the library. After that comes the jump table, aligned on a page boundary if it's not the first thing in the library. The exported address of each public routine in the library is the jump table entry. Following the jump table is the rest of the text section (the jump table is considered to be text, because it's executable code), then the exported data and private data. The bss segment logically follows the data, but as in any other executable file, isn't actually present in the file.

9.5 CREATING SHARED LIBRARIES

A UNIX shared library actually consists of two related files, the shared library itself and a stub library for the linker to use. A library creation utility takes as input a normal library in archive format and some files of control information and uses them to create the two files. The stub library contains no code or data at all (other than possibly a tiny bootstrap routine) but contains symbol definitions for programs linked with the library to use.

Creating the shared library involves the following basic steps, which we discuss in greater detail below:

1. Determine at what address the library's code and data will be loaded.

2. Scan through the input library to find all of the exported code symbols. (One of the control files may be a list of some symbols not to export, if they're just used for inter-routine communication within the library.)

3. Make up the jump table with an entry for each exported code symbol.

4. If there's an initialization or loader routine at the beginning of the library, compile or assemble that.

5. Create the shared library: Run the linker and link everything together into one big executable-format file.

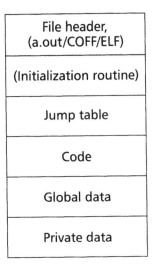

File header, (a.out/COFF/ELF)
(Initialization routine)
Jump table
Code
Global data
Private data

FIGURE **9.2** • Structure of typical shared library.

6. Create the stub library: Extract the necessary symbols from the newly created shared library, reconcile those symbols with the symbols from the input library, create a stub routine for each library routine, then compile or assemble the stubs and combine them into the stub library. (In COFF libraries, there's also a little initialization code placed in the stub library to be linked into each executable.)

CREATING THE JUMP TABLE

The easiest way to create the jump table is to write an assembler source file full of jump instructions (Figure 9.3) and assemble it. Each jump instruction needs to be labeled in a systematic way so that the addresses can later be extracted for the stub library.

A minor complication occurs on architectures such as the x86 that have different sizes of jump instructions. For libraries containing less than 64KB of code, short 3-byte jumps are adequate. For libraries larger than that, longer 5-byte jumps are necessary. Mixed sizes of jumps aren't very satisfactory, both because it makes the table addresses harder to compute and because it makes it far harder to make the jump table compatible in future builds of the library.

... start on a page boundary

```
        .align 8  ; align on 8-byte boundary for variable length insns
JUMP_read: jmp _read
        .align 8
JUMP_write: jmp _write
```

later in library

```
_read: ... code for read()
  ...
_write: ... code for write()
```

FIGURE 9.3 • Jump table.

The simplest solution is to make all of the jumps the largest size. Alternatively, we can make all of the jumps short, and for routines that are too far away for short jumps, we can generate anonymous long jump instructions at the end of the table to which short instructions can jump. (That's usually more trouble than it's worth, because jump tables are rarely more than a few hundred entries in the first place.)

CREATING THE SHARED LIBRARY

Once the jump table and, if needed, the loader routine are created, the creation of the shared library is easy. Just run the linker with suitable switches to make the code and data start at the right places and link together the bootstrap, the jump tables, and all of the routines from the input library. This both assigns addresses to everything in the library and creates the shared-library file.

One minor complication involves interlibrary references. If you're creating, say, a shared math library that uses routines from the shared C library, the references have to be made correctly. Assuming that the library whose routines are needed has already been built when the linker builds the new library, the linker need only search the old library's stub library, just like any normal executable that refers to the old library. This will make all of the references correct. The only remaining issue is that there needs to be some way to ensure that any programs that use the new library also link to the old library. Suitable design of the new stub library can ensure that.

CREATING THE STUB LIBRARY

Creating the stub library is one of the trickier parts of the shared-library process. For each routine in the real library, the stub library needs to contain a corresponding entry that defines both the exported and the imported global symbols.

The global data symbols are wherever the linker puts them in the shared-library image, and the most reasonable way to get their values is to create the shared library with a symbol table and to extract the symbols from that symbol table. For global code symbols, the entry points are all in the jump table, so it's equally easy to extract the symbols from the shared library or to compute the addresses from the base address of the jump table and each symbol's position in the table.

Unlike a normal library module, a module in the stub library contains no code or data, just symbol definitions. The symbols have to be defined as absolute rather than relocatable numbers, because the shared library has already had all of its relocation done. The library creation program extracts each routine from the input library, and from that routine it gets the defined and undefined globals as well as the type (text or data) of each global. It then writes the stub routine—usually as a little assembler program—defining each text global as the address of the jump table entry, each data or bss global as the actual address in the shared library, and each undefined global as undefined. When it has a complete set of stub sources, it assembles them all and combines them into a normal library archive.

COFF stub libraries use a different, more primitive design. They're single object files with two named sections. The `.lib` section contains all of the relocation information pointing at the shared library, and the `.init` section contains initialization code that is linked into each client program, typically to initialize variables in the shared library.

Linux shared libraries are simpler still. They use an a.out file containing the symbol definitions with set vector symbols (described in Section 9.6) for use at program link time.

VERSION NAMING

Shared libraries in UNIX systems are assigned names that are mechanically derived from the original library, adding a version number. If the original library was called /lib/libc.a (the usual name for the C library) and the current library version is 4.0, then the stub library might be /lib/libc_s.4.0.0.a and the shared-library image might be /shlib/libc_s.4.0.0. (The extra zero allows for minor version updates.) Once the libraries are moved into the appropriate directories they're ready to use.

Any shared-library system needs a way to handle multiple versions of libraries. When a library is updated, the new version may or may not be address compatible and call compatible with previous versions. (UNIX systems address this issue with the multinumber version names mentioned above.)

Generally, the first number changes each time a new incompatible version of the library is released. A program linked with a 4.x.x library can't use a 3.x.x or a 5.x.x library. The second number is the minor version. On Sun systems, each executable requires a minor version at least as great as the one with which the executable was linked. If it were linked with 4.2.x, for example, it would run with a 4.3.x library but not a 4.1.x. Other systems treat the second component as an extension of the first component, so an executable linked with a 4.2.x library will only run with a 4.2.x library. The third component is universally treated as a patch level. Executables prefer the highest available patch level, but any patch level will do.

Different systems take slightly different approaches to finding the appropriate libraries at run time. Sun systems have a fairly complex run-time loader that looks at all of the file names in the library directory and picks the best one. Linux systems use symbolic links to avoid the search process. If the latest version of the libc.so library is version 4.2.2, the library's name is libc_s.4.2.2, but the library is also linked to libc_s.4.2, so the loader need only open the shorter name and the correct version is selected.

Most systems permit shared libraries to reside in multiple directories. An environment variable such as LD_LIBRARY_PATH can override the path built into the executable, permitting developers to substitute library versions in their private directories for debugging or performance testing. (Programs that use the "set user ID" feature to run as other than the current user have to ignore LD_LIBRARY_PATH to prevent a malicious user from substituting a Trojan horse library.)

9.6 LINKING WITH SHARED LIBRARIES

Linking with static shared libraries is far simpler than creating the libraries, because the process of creating the stub libraries has already done nearly all the hard work to make the linker resolve program addresses to the appropriate places in the libraries. The only hard part is arranging for the necessary shared libraries to be mapped in when the program starts.

Each format provides a trick to let the linker create a list of libraries that startup code can use to map in the libraries. COFF libraries use a brute-force approach; ad hoc code in the linker creates a section in the COFF file with the names of the libraries. The Linux linker has a somewhat less brute-force approach that creates a special symbol type called a *set vector.* Set vectors are treated like normal global symbols, except that if there are multiple definitions, the definitions are all put in an array named by the symbol. Each shared-library stub defines a set vector symbol ___SHARED_LIBRARIES__ that is the address of a structure containing the name, version, and load address of the library. The linker creates an array of pointers to each of those structures and calls it ___SHARED_LIBRARIES__ so that the run-time startup code can use it.

The BSD/OS shared-library scheme creates the list externally and passes it to the regular linker. The shell script wrapper used to create a shared executable runs down the list of libraries that are passed as arguments to the command or that are used implicitly (the C library), extracts the file names and load addresses for those libraries from a list in a system file, writes a little assembler source file containing an array of structures that contain library names and load addresses, assembles that file, and includes the object file in the list of arguments to the linker.

In each case, the references from the program code to the library addresses are resolved automatically from the addresses in the stub library.

9.7 RUNNING WITH SHARED LIBRARIES

Starting a program that uses shared libraries involves three steps: loading the executable, mapping the libraries, and doing library-specific initialization. In each case, the program executable is loaded into memory by the system in the usual way. After that, the different schemes diverge. The System V.3 kernel had extensions to handle COFF shared-library executables, and the kernel internally looked at the list of libraries and mapped them in before starting the program. The disadvantages of this scheme were "kernel bloat" (adding more code to the nonpageable kernel) and inflexibility, because it didn't permit any flexibility or upgradability in future versions. System V.4 scrapped the whole scheme and went to ELF dynamic shared libraries, which we address in Chapter 10.

Linux adds a single `uselib()` system call that takes the file name and address of a library and maps it into the program address space. The startup routine bound into the executable runs down the list of libraries, doing a `uselib()` on each.

The BSD/OS scheme uses the standard `mmap()` system call that maps pages of a file into the address space and a bootstrap routine that is linked into each shared library as the first thing in the library. The startup routine in the executable runs down the table of shared libraries, and for each one opens the file, maps the first page of the file to the load address, and then calls the bootstrap routine, which is at a fixed location near the beginning of that page following the executable file header. The bootstrap routine then maps the rest of the text segment, maps the data segment, and maps fresh address space for the bss segment, then returns.

Once the segments are all mapped, there's often some library-specific initialization to do (for example, putting a pointer to the system environment strings in the global variable `environ` specified by standard C). The COFF implementation collects the initialization code from the `.init` segments in the program file and runs it from the program startup code. Depending on the library, it may or may not call routines in the shared library. The Linux implementation doesn't do any library initialization and the documentation notes that variables defined in both the program and the library don't work very well.

In the BSD/OS implementation, the bootstrap routine for the C library receives a pointer to the table of shared libraries and maps in all of the other libraries, minimizing the amount of code that has to be linked into individual executables. Recent versions of BSD use ELF format executables. The ELF header has an `interp` section that contains the name of an interpreter program to use when running the file. BSD uses the shared C library as the interpreter, which means that the kernel maps in the shared C library before the program starts, saving the overhead of some system calls. The library boot-strap routine does the same initializations, maps the rest of the libraries and, through a pointer, calls the main routine in the program.

9.8 THE malloc HACK AND OTHER SHARED-LIBRARY PROBLEMS

Although static shared libraries have excellent performance, their long-term maintenance is difficult and error prone. This section gives an anecdote that illustrates this difficulty and also mentions other additional problems that occur in shared libraries.

In a static library, all intralibrary calls are permanently bound, and it's not possible to substitute a private version of a routine by redefining the routine in a program that uses the library. For the most part, that's not a problem because few programs redefine standard library routines like read() or strcmp(), or even if they do it's not a major problem if the program uses a private version of strcmp() while routines in the library call the standard version.

But a lot of programs define their own versions of malloc() and free(), the routines that allocate heap storage, and multiple versions of those routines in a program don't work. The standard strdup() routine, for example, returns a pointer to a string allocated by malloc, which the application can free up when no longer needed. If the library allocated the string with one version of malloc but the application freed that string with a different version of free, chaos would ensue.

To permit applications to provide their own versions of malloc and free, the System V.3 shared C library uses an ugly hack (Figure 9.4). The system's maintainers redefined malloc and free as indirect calls through pointers (which we'll call malloc_ptr and free_ptr) bound into the data part of the shared library:

```
extern void *(*malloc_ptr)(size_t);
extern void (*free_ptr)(void *);
#define malloc(s) (*malloc_ptr)(s)
#define free(s) (*free_ptr)(s)
```

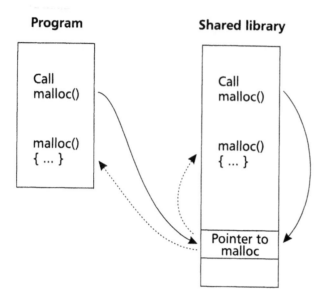

FIGURE **9.4** • The `malloc` hack.

Then they recompiled the entire C library and added these lines (or the assembler equivalent) to the `.init` section of the stub library, so that they are included in every program that uses the shared library:

```
#undef malloc
#undef free
malloc_ptr = &malloc;
free_ptr = &free;
```

Because the stub library is bound into the application, not the shared library, its references to `malloc` and `free` are resolved at the time each program is linked. If there's a private version of `malloc` and `free`, it puts pointers to them in the pointers; otherwise it will use the standard library version. Either way, the library and the application use the same version of `malloc` and `free`.

Although the implementation of this trick made maintenance of the library harder and doesn't scale to more than a few carefully chosen names, the idea that intralibrary calls can be made through pointers that are resolved at program run time is a good one, so long as it's automated and doesn't

```
#include <stdio.h>

/* extern */
int errno;

main()
{
  unlink("/non-existent-file");
  printf("Status was %d\n", errno);
}
```

FIGURE **9.5** • Address conflict example.

require fragile manual source code tweaks. We'll find out how the automated version works in Chapter 10.

Name conflicts in global data remain a problem with static shared libraries. Consider the small program in Figure 9.5. If you compile and link it with any of the shared libraries we describe in this chapter, it will print a status code of zero rather than the correct error code. That's because int errno; defines a new instance of errno that isn't bound to the one in the shared library. If you uncomment the extern, the program works, because now it's an undefined global reference that the linker binds to the errno in the shared library. As we'll see in Chapter 10, dynamic linking solves this problem as well at some cost in performance.

Finally, even the jump table in UNIX shared libraries has been known to cause compatibility problems. From the point of view of routines outside a shared library, the address of each exported routine in the library is the address of the jump table entry. But from the point of view of routines within the library, the address of that routine may be the jump table entry or it may be the real entry point to which the table entry jumps. There have been cases where a library routine examined an address passed as an argument to see if it was one of the other routines in the library, in order to do some special-case processing.

An obvious but less than totally effective solution is to bind the address of the routine to the jump table entry while building the shared library, because that ensures that all symbolic references to routines within the library are resolved to the table entry. But if two routines are within the same object file, the reference in the object file is usually a relative reference to the routine's address in the text segment. (Because it's in the same object file, the routine's address is known; other than this peculiar case, there's no reason to make a symbolic reference back into the same object file.) Although it would be possible to scan relocatable text references for values that match exported symbol addresses, the most practical solution to this problem is "don't do that," don't write code that depends on recognizing the address of a library routine.

MS Windows DLLs have a similar problem, because within each EXE or DLL the addresses of imported routines are considered to be the addresses of the stub routines that make indirect jumps to the real address of the routine. Again, the most practical solution to the problem is "don't do that."

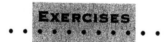

Exercise • 9.1

If you look in a /shlib directory on a UNIX system with shared libraries, you'll usually see three or four versions of each library with names like libc_s.2.0.1 and libc_s.3.0.0. Why not just have the most recent one?

Exercise • 9.2

In a stub library, why is it important to include all of the undefined globals for each routine, even if the undefined global refers to another routine in the shared library?

Exercise • 9.3

What difference does it make whether a stub library is a single large executable with all of the library's symbols (as in COFF or Linux) or an actual library with separate modules?

Now we will extend the linker to support static shared libraries. This involves several subprojects, first to create the shared libraries and then to link executables with the shared libraries.

In our system, a shared library is merely an object file that is linked at a given address. There can be no relocations and no unresolved symbol references, although references to other shared libraries are acceptable. Stub libraries are normal directory format or file format libraries, with each entry in the library containing the exported (absolute) and imported symbols for the corresponding library member but no text or data. Each stub library has to tell the linker the name of the corresponding shared library. If you use directory format stub libraries, a file called LIBRARY NAME contains lines of text. The first line is the name of the corresponding shared library, and the rest of the lines are the names of other shared libraries upon which this one depends. (The space prevents name collisions with symbols.) If you use file format libraries, the initial line of the library has the extra fields

```
LIBRARY nnnn pppppp fffff ggggg hhhhh ...
```

where `fffff` is the name of the shared library and the subsequent fields are the names of any other shared libraries on which it depends.

PROJECT • 9.1

Make the linker produce static shared libraries and stub libraries from regular directory or file format libraries. If you haven't already done so, you'll have to add a linker flag to set the base address at which the linker allocates the segments. The input is a regular library and stub libraries for any other shared libraries on which this one depends. The output is an executable-format shared library containing the segments of all of the members of the input library and a stub library with a stub member corresponding to each member of the input library.

PROJECT • 9.2

Extend the linker to create executables using static shared libraries. Project 9.1 already has most of the work for searching stub libraries for symbol resolution, because the way that an executable refers to symbols in a shared library is the same as the way that one shared library refers to another. The linker needs to put the names of the required libraries in the output file, so that the run-time loader knows what to load. Have the linker create a segment called .lib that contains the names of the shared libraries as strings with a null byte separating the strings and two null bytes at the end. Create a symbol _SHARED_LIBRARIES that refers to the beginning of the .lib section, to which code in the startup routine can refer.

DYNAMIC LINKING
AND LOADING

Dynamic linking defers much of the linking process until a program starts running or sometimes even later. It provides a variety of benefits that are hard to get otherwise:

- Dynamically linked shared libraries are easier to create than statically linked shared libraries.

- Dynamically linked shared libraries are easier to update than statically linked shared libraries.

- The semantics of dynamically linked shared libraries can be much closer to those of unshared libraries.

- Dynamic linking permits a program to load and unload routines at run time, a facility that can otherwise be very difficult to provide.

There are a few disadvantages, of course. The run-time performance costs of dynamic linking are substantial compared to those of static linking, because a large part of the linking process has to be redone every time a program runs. Every dynamically linked symbol used in a program has to be looked up

- in a symbol table and resolved. (MS Windows dynamic-link libraries mitigate
- this cost somewhat, as we describe in Section 10.7.) Dynamic shared libraries
- are also larger than static shared libraries, because the dynamic ones have to
- include symbol tables.

Beyond issues of call compatibility, a chronic source of problems is changes in library semantics. Because dynamic shared libraries are so easy to update compared to unshared or static shared libraries, it's easy to change libraries that are in use by existing programs, which means that the behavior of those programs changes even though "nothing has changed." This is a frequent source of problems on MS Windows, where programs use a lot of shared libraries, libraries go through a lot of versions, and library version control is not very sophisticated. Most programs ship with copies of all of the libraries they use, and installers often will inadvertently install an older version of a shared library on top of a newer one, breaking programs that are expecting features found in the newer one. Well-behaved applications pop up a warning before installing an older library over a newer one, but even so, programs that depend on the semantics of older libraries have been known to break when newer versions replace the older ones.

10.1 ELF DYNAMIC LINKING

The Sun Microsystems SunOS introduced dynamic shared libraries to UNIX in the late 1980s. UNIX System V Release 4, which Sun co-developed, introduced the ELF object format and adapted the Sun scheme to ELF. ELF was clearly an improvement over the previous object formats, and by the late 1990s it had become the standard for UNIX and UNIX-like systems, including Linux and BSD derivatives.

10.2 CONTENTS OF AN ELF FILE

As discussed in Chapter 3, an ELF file can be viewed as a set of *sections*, interpreted by the linker, or a set of *segments*, interpreted by the program loader.

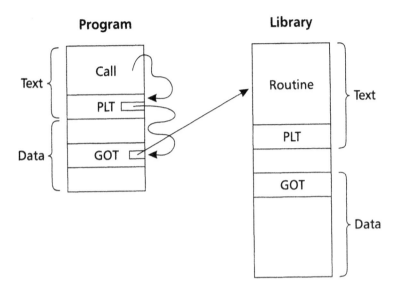

FIGURE **10.1** • PLT and GOT.

ELF programs and shared libraries have the same general structure, but with different sets of segments and sections.

ELF shared libraries can be loaded at any address, so they invariably use position-independent code (PIC) so that the text pages of the file need not be relocated and can be shared among multiple processes. As described in Chapter 8, ELF linkers support PIC code with a global offset table (GOT) in each shared library that contains pointers to all of the static data referenced in the program. The dynamic linker resolves and relocates all of the pointers in the GOT. This can be a performance issue, but in practice the GOT is small except in very large libraries; a commonly used version of the standard C library has only 180 entries in the GOT for over 350KB of code.

Because the GOT is in the same loadable ELF file as the code that references it, and the relative addresses within a file don't change regardless of where the program is loaded, the code can locate the GOT with a relative address, load the address of the GOT into a register, and then load pointers from the GOT whenever it needs to address static data. A library need not have a GOT if it references no static data (but in practice all libraries do).

To support dynamic linking, each ELF shared library and each executable that uses shared libraries has a procedure linkage table, or PLT (Figure 10.1). The PLT adds a level of indirection for function calls analogous to that provided by the GOT for data. The PLT also permits lazy evaluation, that is, not resolving procedure addresses until they're called for the first time. Because the PLT tends to have a lot more entries than the GOT (over 600 in the C library mentioned above), and because most of the routines will never be called in any given program, lazy evaluation can both speed startup and save considerable time overall. The details of the PLT are discussed in Section 10.4.

An ELF dynamically linked file contains all of the linker information that the run-time linker will need to relocate the file and resolve any undefined symbols. The .dynsym section (the dynamic symbol table) contains all of the file's imported and exported symbols. The .dynstr and .hash sections contain the name strings for the symbol and a hash table the run-time linker can use to look up symbols quickly.

The final extra piece of an ELF dynamically linked file is the DYNAMIC segment (also marked as the .dynamic section), which the run-time dynamic linker uses to find the information about the file the linker needs. It's loaded as part of the data segment but is pointed to from the ELF file header so the run-time dynamic linker can find it. The DYNAMIC segment is a list of tagged values and pointers. Some of the following entry types occur just in programs, some just in libraries, some in both:

- NEEDED. This is the name of a library this file needs. (Always in programs, sometimes in libraries when one library is dependent on another; can occur more than once.)

- SONAME (shared-object name). This is the name of the file the linker uses. (Libraries.)

- SYMTAB, STRTAB, HASH, SYMENT, STRSZ. These point to the symbol table, associated string and hash tables, size of a symbol table entry, and size of the string table, respectively. (Both.)

- PLTGOT. This points to the GOT or on some architectures to the PLT. (Both.)

- REL, RELSZ, and RELENT; or RELA, RELASZ, and RELAENT. These give pointer to, number of, and size of relocation entries, respectively. REL entries don't contain addends; RELA entries do. (Both.)

- JMPREL, PLTRELSZ, and PLTREL. These give pointer to, size, and format (REL or RELA) of relocation table, respectively, for data referred to by the PLT. (Both.)

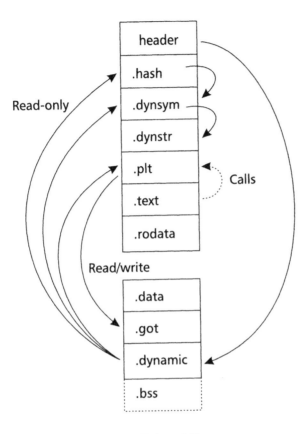

FIGURE **10.2** • An ELF shared library.

- INIT and FINI. These point to initializer and finalizer routines to be called at program startup and finish. (Optional but usually in both.)

There are a few other obscure types that are not often used. An entire ELF shared library might look like Figure 10.2. First come the read-only parts, including the symbol table, the PLT, the text, and read-only data; then the read/write parts, including regular data, the GOT, and the dynamic section. The bss logically follows the last read/write section, but as always isn't present in the file.

An ELF program looks much the same, but in the read-only segment has INIT and FINI routines, and an INTERP section near the front of the file to specify the name of the dynamic linker (usually ld.so). The data segment has no GOT, because program files aren't relocated at run time.

10.3   LOADING A DYNAMICALLY LINKED PROGRAM

Loading a dynamically linked ELF program is a lengthy but straightforward process.

STARTING THE DYNAMIC LINKER

When the operating system runs the program, it maps in the file's pages as normal but notes that there's an INTERPRETER section in the executable. The specified interpreter is the dynamic linker, ld.so, which is itself in ELF shared-library format. Rather than starting the program, the system maps the dynamic linker into a convenient part of the address space as well and starts ld.so, passing on the stack an *auxiliary vector* of information needed by the linker. The vector includes the following elements:

- AT_PHDR, AT_PHENT, and AT_PHNUM. These give the address of the program header for the program file, the size of each entry in the header, and the number of entries, respectively. This structure describes the segments in the loaded file. If the system hasn't mapped the program into memory, there may instead be an AT_EXECFD entry that contains the file descriptor on which the program file is open.

- AT_ENTRY. This gives the starting address of the program, to which the dynamic linker jumps after it has finished initialization.

- AT_BASE. This is the address at which the dynamic linker was loaded.

At this point, bootstrap code at the beginning of ld.so finds its own GOT, the first entry of which points to the dynamic segment in the ld.so file. From the dynamic segment, the linker can find its own relocation entries, relocate pointers in its own data segment, and resolve code references to the routines needed to load everything else. (The Linux ld.so names all of the essential routines with names starting with _dt_ and special-case code looks for symbols that start with the string and resolves them.)

The linker then initializes a chain of symbol tables with pointers to the program's symbol table and the linker's own symbol table. Conceptually, the program file and all of the libraries loaded into a process share a single symbol table. But rather than build a merged symbol table at run time, the linker keeps a linked list of the symbol tables in each file. Each file contains a hash table to speed symbol lookup, with a set of hash headers and a hash chain for each header. The linker can search for a symbol quickly by computing the symbol's hash value once, then running through the appropriate hash chain in each of the symbol tables in the list.

FINDING THE LIBRARIES

Once the linker's own initializations are done, it finds the names of the libraries required by the program. The program's program header has a pointer to the dynamic segment that contains dynamic linking information for the program. That segment contains a pointer DT_STRTAB to the file's string table and entries DT_NEEDED, each of which contains the offset in the string table of the name of a required library.

For each library, the linker finds the library's ELF shared-library file, which is in itself a fairly complex process. The library name in a DT_NEEDED entry is something like libXt.so.6 (the Xt toolkit, version 6). The library file might be in any of several library directories and might not even have the same file name. On my system, the actual name of that library is /usr/X11R6/lib/libXt.so.6.0, with the .0 at the end being a minor version number.

The linker looks in the following places to find the library:

1. If the dynamic segment contains an entry called DT_RPATH, it's a colon-separated list of directories to search for libraries. This entry is added by a command line switch or environment variable to the regular (not dynamic) linker at the time a program is linked. It's mostly used for sub-systems such as databases that load a collection of programs and supporting libraries into a single directory.

2. If there's an environment symbol LD_LIBRARY_PATH, it's treated as a colon-separated list of directories in which the linker looks for the library. This lets a developer build a new version of a library, put it in the LD_LIBRARY_PATH, and use it with existing linked programs either to test the new library or equally well to instrument the behavior of the program. (It skips this step if the program is set-uid, for security reasons.)

3. The linker looks in the library cache file /etc/ld.so.conf, which contains a list of library names and paths. If the library name is present, it uses the

corresponding path. This is the usual way that most libraries are found. (The file name at the end of the path need not be exactly the same as the library name; see Library Versions in Section 10.5.)

4. If all else fails, the linker looks in the default directory /usr/lib; if the library's still not found, it displays an error message and exits.

Once it has found the file containing the library, the dynamic linker opens the file and reads the ELF header to find the program header, which in turn points to the file's segments including the dynamic segment. The linker allocates space for the library's text and data segments and maps them in, along with zeroed pages for the bss. From the library's dynamic segment, it adds the library's symbol table to the chain of symbol tables, and if the library requires further libraries that are not already loaded, it adds any new libraries to the list to be loaded. When this process terminates, all of the libraries have been mapped in, and the loader has a logical global symbol table consisting of the union of all of the symbol tables of the program and the mapped library.

SHARED-LIBRARY INITIALIZATION

Now the loader revisits each library and handles the library's relocation entries, filling in the library's GOT and performing any relocations needed in the library's data segment. Load-time relocations on an x86 include the following:

- R_386_GLOB_DAT, used to initialize a GOT entry to the address of a symbol defined in another library.

- R_386_32, a non-GOT reference to a symbol defined in another library (generally a pointer in static data).

- R_386_RELATIVE, for relocatable data references, typically a pointer to a string or other locally defined static data.

- R_386_JMP_SLOT, used to initialize GOT entries for the PLT (see Section 10.4).

If a library has an .init section, the loader calls it to do library-specific initializations, such as C++ static constructors, and any .fini section is noted to be run at exit time. (It doesn't do the .init for the main program, because that's handled in the program's own startup code.) When this pass is done, all of the libraries are fully loaded and ready to execute, and the loader calls the program's entry point to start the program.

10.4 LAZY PROCEDURE LINKAGE WITH THE PLT

Programs that use shared libraries generally contain calls to a lot of functions. In a single run of the program, many of the functions are never called (in error routines or other parts of the program that aren't used). Furthermore, each shared library also contains calls to functions in other libraries, even fewer of which will be executed in a given program run because many of them are in routines that the program never calls either directly or indirectly.

To speed program startup, dynamically linked ELF programs use lazy binding of procedure addresses; that is, the address of a procedure isn't bound until the first time the procedure is called. This is accomplished by means of a PLT. Each dynamically bound program and shared library has a PLT, with the PLT containing an entry for each nonlocal routine called from the program or library (Figure 10.3). Note that the PLT in PIC code is itself PIC, so it can be part of the read-only text segment.

All calls within the program or library to a particular routine are adjusted (when the program or library is built) to be calls to the routine's entry in the PLT. The first time the program or library calls a routine, the PLT entry calls the run-time linker to resolve the actual address of the routine. After that, the PLT entry jumps directly to the actual address, so after the first call, the cost of using the PLT is a single extra indirect jump at a procedure call and nothing at a return.

The first entry in the PLT, which we call PLT0, is special code to call the dynamic linker. At load time, the dynamic linker automatically places two values in the GOT. At GOT+4 (the second word of the GOT), it puts a code that identifies the particular library. At GOT+8, it puts the address of the dynamic linker's symbol resolution routine.

The rest of the entries in the PLT, which we call PLTn, each start with an indirect jump through a GOT entry. Each PLT entry has a corresponding GOT entry that is initially set to point to the push instruction in the PLT entry that follows the first jmp. (In a PIC file, this requires a load-time relocation but not

Special first entry:

```
PLT0: pushl  GOT+4
   jmp    *GOT+8
```

Regular entries, non-PIC code:

```
PLTn: jmp     *GOT+m
   push    #reloc_offset
   jmp     PLT0
```

Regular entries, PIC code:

```
PLTn: jmp     *GOT+m(%ebx)
   push    #reloc_offset
   jmp     PLT0
```

FIGURE 10.3 • PLT structure in x86 code.

an expensive symbol lookup.) Following the jump is a push instruction that pushes a relocation offset, the offset in the file's relocation table of a special relocation entry of type R_386_JMP_SLOT. The relocation entry's symbol reference points to the symbol in the file's symbol table, and its address points to the GOT entry.

This compact but rather complex arrangement means that the first time the program or library calls a PLT entry, the first jump in the PLT entry in effect does nothing, because the GOT entry through which it jumps points back into the PLT entry. Then the push instruction pushes the offset value, which indirectly identifies both the symbol to resolve and the GOT entry into which to resolve it, and jumps to PLT0. The instructions in PLT0 push another code that identifies which program or library it is, and then jump into stub code in the dynamic linker with the two identifying codes at the top of the stack. Note that this is a jump, rather than a call; above the two identifying words just pushed is the return address back to the routine that called into the PLT.

Now the stub code saves all the registers and calls an internal routine in the dynamic linker to do the resolution. The two identifying words suffice to find the library's symbol table and the routine's entry in that symbol table. The

Main program:

```
extern int token;
```

Routine in shared library:

```
int token = 42;
```

FIGURE **10.4** • Global data initialization.

dynamic linker looks up the symbol value using the concatenated run-time symbol table and stores the routine's address into the GOT entry. Then the stub code restores the registers, pops the two words that the PLT pushed, and jumps off to the routine. With the GOT entry having been updated, subsequent calls to that PLT entry jump directly to the routine itself without entering the dynamic linker.

10.5 OTHER PECULIARITIES OF DYNAMIC LINKING

The ELF linker and the dynamic linker have a lot of obscure code to handle special cases and to try to keep the run-time semantics as similar as possible to those of unshared libraries.

STATIC INITIALIZATIONS

If a program has an external reference to a global variable that is defined in a shared library, the linker has to create in the program a copy of the variable, because program data addresses have to be bound at link time (Figure 10.4). This poses no problem for the code in the shared library, because the code can refer to the variable by means of a GOT pointer that the dynamic linker can fix up, but there is a problem if the library initializes the variable. To deal with this problem, the linker puts an entry in the program's relocation table—which otherwise just contains R_386_JMP_SLOT, R_386_GLOB_DAT, R_386_32, and R_386_RELATIVE entries—of type R_386_COPY that points to the place in the program where the copy of the variable is defined and that tells the dynamic linker to copy the initial value of that word of data from the shared library.

Although this feature is essential for certain kinds of code, it occurs very rarely in practice. This is a band-aid, because it only works for single-word data. The initializers that do occur are always pointers to procedures or other data, so the band-aid suffices.

LIBRARY VERSIONS

Dynamic libraries are generally named with major and minor version numbers such as libc.so.1.1, but programs should be bound only to major version numbers such as libc.so.1 because minor versions are supposed to be upward compatible. To keep program loading reasonably fast, the system manager maintains a cache file containing the full pathname of the most recent version of each library, which is updated by a configuration program whenever a new library is installed.

To support this design, each dynamically linked library can have a "true name" called the SONAME (shared-object name) that is assigned at library creation time. For example, the library called libc.so.1.1 would have a SONAME of libc.so.1. (The SONAME defaults to the library's name.) When the linker builds a program that uses shared libraries, it lists the SONAMEs of the libraries it used rather than the actual names of the libraries. The cache creation program scans all of the directories that contain shared libraries, finds all of the shared libraries, extracts the SONAME from each one, and where there are multiple libraries with the same SONAME, discards all but the highest version number. Then it writes the cache file with SONAMEs and full pathnames so that at run time the dynamic linker can quickly find the current version of each library.

10.6 DYNAMIC LOADING AT RUN TIME

Although the ELF dynamic linker is usually called implicitly at program load time and from PLT entries, programs can also call it explicitly using dlopen() to load a shared library and dlsym() to find the address of a symbol, which is usually a procedure to call. Those two routines are actually simple wrappers that call back into the dynamic linker. When the dynamic linker loads a library by means of dlopen(), it does the same relocation and symbol resolution it does on any other library, so the dynamically loaded program can without any special arrangements call back to routines already loaded and refer to global data in the running program.

This permits users to add extra functionality to programs without access to the source code of the programs and without even having to stop and restart the programs. (This is useful when the program is something like a database or a Web server.) Mainframe operating systems have provided access to exit routines like this since at least the early 1960s, albeit without such a convenient interface, and it's long been a way to add great flexibility to packaged applications. It also provides a way for programs to extend themselves; there's no reason a program can't write a routine in C or C++, run the compiler and linker to create a shared library, then dynamically load and run the new code. (Mainframe sort programs have linked and loaded custom inner-loop code for each sort job for decades.)

10.7 MICROSOFT DYNAMIC-LINK LIBRARIES

Microsoft Windows also provides shared libraries, called dynamic-link libraries (DLLs) in a fashion similar to but somewhat simpler than ELF shared libraries. The design of DLLs changed substantially between the 16-bit Windows 3.1 and the 32-bit Windows NT and Windows 95. This discussion addresses only the more modern Win32 libraries. DLLs import procedure addresses using a PLT-like scheme. Although the design of DLLs would make it possible to import data addresses using a GOT-like scheme, in practice they use a simpler scheme that requires explicit program code to dereference imported pointers to shared data.

In MS Windows, both programs and DLLs are portable executable (PE) format files and are intended to be memory mapped into a process. Unlike Windows 3.1, where all applications share a single address space, Win32 gives each application its own address space, and executables and libraries are mapped into each address space where they are used. For read-only code this doesn't make any practical difference, but for data it means that each application using a DLL gets its own copy of the DLL's data. (That's a slight oversimplification, because PE files can mark some sections as shared data with a single copy being shared among all applications that use the file, but most data are unshared.)

Loading an MS Windows executable and the DLLs is similar to loading a dynamically linked ELF program, although in the MS Windows case the dynamic linker is part of the kernel. First the kernel maps in the executable file, guided by section information in the PE headers. Then it maps in all of the DLLs that the executable refers to, again guided by the PE headers in each DLL.

PE files can contain relocation entries. An executable generally won't contain them and so has to be mapped at the address for which it was linked. DLLs all contain relocation entries and are relocated when they're mapped in if the address space for which they were linked isn't available. (Microsoft calls runtime relocation *rebasing*.)

All PE files—both executables and DLLs—have an entry point, and the loader calls a DLL's entry point when the DLL is loaded, when the DLL is unloaded, and each time a process thread attaches to or detaches from the DLL. (The loader passes an argument to indicate why it's making each call.) This provides a hook for static initializers and destructors analogous to the ELF .init and .fini sections.

IMPORTED AND EXPORTED SYMBOLS IN PE FILES

PE supports shared libraries with two special sections of the file: .edata (since MSVC 4.2, exported symbols are in .rdata rather than .edata), for exported data, which lists the symbols exported from a file; and .idata, which lists the symbols imported into a file. Program files generally have only an .idata section, while DLLs always have an .edata section and may have an .idata section if they use other DLLs. Symbols can be exported either by symbol name or by *ordinal*, a small integer that gives the index of the symbol in the export address table. Linking by ordinals is slightly more efficient because it avoids a symbol lookup but is considerably more error prone because it's up to the person who builds a DLL to ensure that ordinals stay the same from one library version to another. In practice ordinals are usually used to call system services that rarely change and names are used for everything else.

The .edata section contains an export directory table that describes the rest of the section, followed by the tables that define the exported symbols (Figure 10.5). The export address table contains the relative virtual address

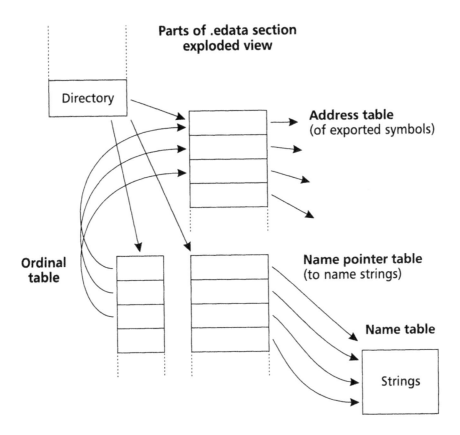

**Parts of .edata section
exploded view**

FIGURE **10.5** • Structure of .edata section.

(RVA) of the symbol (relative to the base of the PE file). If the RVA points back into the .edata section, it's a "forwarder" reference, and the value pointed to is a string naming the symbol to use to satisfy the reference (probably defined in a different DLL). The ordinal and name pointer tables are parallel, with each entry in the name pointer table being the RVA of the name string for the symbol and each entry in the ordinal table being the index in the export address table. (Ordinals need not be zero based; the ordinal base to subtract from ordinal values to get the index in the export address table is stored in the export directory and is most often 1.) Exported symbols need not all have names, although in practice they always do. The symbols in the name pointer table are in alphabetical order to permit the loader to use a binary search.

The .idata section does the converse of what the .edata section does, by mapping symbols or ordinals back into virtual addresses. The section consists of a null-terminated array of import directory tables, one per DLL from which

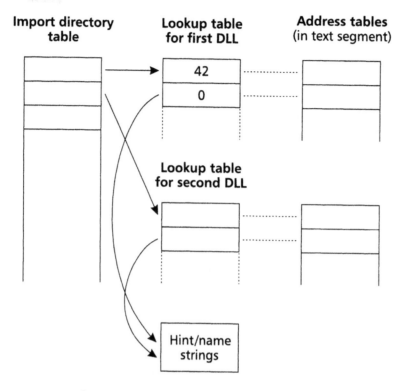

FIGURE 10.6 • Structure of .idata section.

symbols are imported, followed by an import lookup table per DLL, followed by a name table with hints (Figure 10.6).

For each imported DLL, there is an array of import addresses, typically in the program's text segment, into which the program loader places the resolved addresses. The import lookup table identifies the symbols to import, with the entries in the import lookup table being parallel to those in the import address table. The import lookup table consists of 32-bit entries. If the high bit of an entry is set, the low 31 bits are the ordinal of the symbol to import; otherwise the entry is the RVA of an entry in the hint/name table. Each hint/name entry consists of a 4-byte hint that guesses the index of the symbol in the DLL's export name pointer table, followed by the null-terminated symbol name. The program loader uses the hint to probe the export table, and if the symbol name matches, it uses that symbol; otherwise it binary-searches the entire export table for the name. (If the DLL hasn't changed since the program that uses the DLL was linked, or at least its list of exported symbols hasn't changed, the guess will be right.)

Unlike ELF imported symbols, the values of symbols imported by means of .idata are only placed in the import address table; they are not fixed up anywhere else in the importing file. For code addresses, this makes little difference. When the linker builds an executable or DLL, it creates in the text section a table of (misnamed) *thunks*, indirect jumps through the entries in the import address table, and it uses the addresses of the thunks as the address of the imported routine, which is transparent to the programmer. (The thunks as well as most of the data in the .idata section actually come from a stub library created at the same time as the DLL.) In recent versions of Microsoft's C and C++ compiler, if the programmer knows that a routine will be called in a DLL, the routine can be declared dllimport and the compiler will generate an indirect call to the address table entry, avoiding the extra indirect jump. For data addresses, the situation is more problematic, because it's harder to hide the extra level of indirection required to address a symbol in another executable. Traditionally, programmers just bit the bullet and explicitly declared imported variables to be pointers to the real values and explicitly dereferenced the pointers. Recent versions of Microsoft's C and C++ compiler also let the programmer declare global data to be dllimport and the compiler will generate the extra pointer dereferences, much like ELF code that references data indirectly through pointers in the GOT.

LAZY BINDING

Recent versions of MS Windows compilers have added delay-loaded imports to permit lazy symbol binding for procedures, somewhat like the ELF PLT. A delay-loaded DLL contains a structure similar to the .idata import directory table, but it is not in the .idata section so the program loader doesn't handle it automatically. The entries in the import address table initially all point to a helper routine that finds and loads the DLL and replaces the contents of the address table with the actual addresses. The delay-loaded directory table has a place to store the original contents of the import address table so the values can be put back if the DLL is later unloaded. Microsoft provides a standard helper routine, but its interfaces are documented and programmers can write their own versions if need be. MS Windows also permits programs to load and unload DLLs explicitly using LoadLibrary and FreeLibrary and to find addresses of symbols using GetProcAddress.

DLLS AND THREADS

One area in which the MS Windows DLL model doesn't work particularly well is thread local storage (TLS). An MS Windows program can start multiple threads in the same process; they share the process's address space. Each thread has a small chunk of TLS to keep data specific to that thread, such as pointers to data structures and resources that the thread is using. The TLS needs slots for the data from the executable and from each DLL that uses TLS. The MS Windows linker can create a .tls section in a PE executable that defines the layout for the TLS needed by routines in the executable and any DLLs to which it directly refers. Each time the process creates a thread, the new thread gets its own TLS, created using the .tls section as a template.

The problem is that most DLLs can either be linked implicitly from the executable or loaded explicitly with LoadLibrary. DLLs loaded explicitly don't automatically get .tls storage, and because a DLL's author can't predict whether a library will be invoked implicitly or explicitly, it can't depend on the .tls section.

MS Windows defines run-time system calls that allocate slots at the end of the TLS. DLLs use those calls rather than .tls unless the DLL is known to only be invoked implicitly.

10.8 OSF/1 PSEUDO-STATIC SHARED LIBRARIES

OSF/1, the ill-fated UNIX variant from the Open Software Foundation, used a shared-library scheme intermediate between static and dynamic linking. Its authors noted that static linking is a lot faster than dynamic linking because less relocation is needed and that libraries are updated infrequently enough that system managers are willing to endure some pain when they update shared libraries (although not the agony of relinking every executable program in the entire system).

So OSF/1 took the approach of maintaining a global symbol table visible to all processes, and it loaded all the shared libraries into a sharable address space at system boot time. This assigned all of the libraries addresses that wouldn't change while the system was running. Each time a program started, if it used shared libraries it would map in the shared libraries and symbol table and resolve undefined references in the executable using the global symbol table. No load-time relocation was ever required because programs were all linked to load in a part of the address space that was guaranteed to be available in each process, and the library relocation had already happened when they were loaded at boot time. When one of the shared libraries changed, the system just had to be rebooted normally, at which point the system loaded the new libraries and created a new symbol table for executables to use.

This scheme was clever, but it wasn't very satisfactory. For one thing, processing symbol lookups is considerably slower than processing relocation entries, so avoiding relocation wasn't that much of a performance advantage. For another, dynamic linking provides the ability to load and run a library at run time, and the OSF/1 scheme didn't provide for that.

10.9 MAKING SHARED LIBRARIES FAST

Shared libraries—and ELF shared libraries in particular—can be very slow. The slowdowns come from a variety of sources, several of which we mentioned in Chapter 8:

- Load-time relocation of libraries
- Load-time symbol resolution in libraries and executables
- Overhead resulting from PIC function prologue code
- Overhead resulting from PIC indirect data references
- Slower code resulting from PIC reserved addressing registers

The first two problems can be ameliorated by cacheing, the latter three by retreating from pure PIC code.

On modern computers with large address spaces, it's usually possible to choose an address range for a shared library that's available in all or at least most of the processes that use the library. One very effective technique is similar to the MS Windows approach. Either when the library is linked or the first time a library is loaded, tentatively bind its addresses to a block of address space. After that, each time a program links to the library, use the same addresses if possible (which means that no relocation will be necessary). If that address space isn't available in a new process, the library is relocated as before.

SGI systems use the term quickstart to describe the process of pre-relocating objects at link time or in a separate pass over the shared library. BeOS caches the relocated library the first time it's loaded into a process. If multiple libraries depend on each other, in principle it should be possible to pre-relocate and then pre-resolve symbol references among libraries, although I'm not aware of any linkers that do so.

If a system uses pre-relocated libraries, PIC becomes a lot less important. All the processes that load a library at its pre-relocated address can share the library's code whether it's PIC or not, so a non-PIC library at a well-chosen address can in practice be as sharable as PIC without the performance loss of PIC. This is basically the statically linked shared library approach from Chapter 9, except that in the case of address space collisions, rather than the program failing, the dynamic linker moves the libraries at some loss of performance. MS Windows uses this approach.

BeOS implements cached relocated libraries with great thoroughness, including preserving correct semantics when libraries change. When a new version of a library is installed, BeOS notes the fact and creates a new cached version rather than using the old cached version when programs refer to the library. Library changes can have a ripple effect. When library A refers to symbols in library B and library B is updated, a new cached version of library A will also have to be created if any of the referenced symbols in library B have moved. This does make the programmer's life easier, but it's not clear to me that libraries are in practice updated often enough to merit the considerable amount of system code needed to track library updates.

10.10 COMPARISON OF DYNAMIC LINKING APPROACHES

The UNIX/ELF and MS Windows/PE dynamic linking methods differ in several interesting ways. The ELF scheme uses a single name space per program, while the PE scheme uses a name space per library. An ELF executable lists the symbols it needs and the libraries it needs, but it doesn't record which symbol is in which library. A PE file, on the other hand, lists the symbols to import from each library. The PE scheme is less flexible but also more resistant to inadvertent spoofing: Imagine that an executable calls routine AFUNC (found in library A) and BFUNC (found in library B). If a new version of library A happens to define its own BFUNC, an ELF program could use the new BFUNC in preference to the old one, while a PE program wouldn't. This is a problem with some large libraries; one partial solution is to use the poorly documented DT_FILTER and DT_AUXILIARY fields to tell the dynamic linker which libraries this library imports symbols from, so the linker will search those libraries for imported symbols before searching the executable and the rest of the libraries. The DT_SYMBOLIC field tells the dynamic linker to search the library's own symbol table first, so that other libraries cannot shadow intralibrary references. (This isn't always desirable; consider the malloc hack described in Chapter 9.) These ad hoc approaches make it less likely that symbols in unrelated libraries will inadvertently shadow the correct symbols, but they're no substitute for a hierarchical link-time name space as Java has (Chapter 11).

The ELF scheme tries considerably harder than the PE scheme to maintain the semantics of static linked programs. In an ELF program, references to data imported from another library are automatically resolved, while a PE program needs to treat imported data specially. The PE scheme has trouble comparing the values of pointers to functions, because the address of an imported function is the address of the thunk that calls it, not the address of the actual function in the other library. ELF handles all pointers the same.

At run time, nearly all of the MS Windows dynamic linker is in the operating system, while the ELF dynamic linker runs entirely as part of the application, with the kernel merely mapping in the initial files. The MS Windows scheme is arguably faster, because it doesn't have to map and relocate the dynamic linker in each process before it starts linking. The ELF scheme is definitely a lot more flexible. Because each executable names the interpreter program (now always the dynamic linker, named ld.so) to use, different executables can use different interpreters without requring any operating system changes. In practice, this makes it easier to support executables from variant versions of UNIX—notably Linux and BSD—by making a dynamic linker that links to compatibility libraries that support nonnative executables.

EXERCISES

EXERCISE • 10.1

ELF shared libraries are often linked so that calls from one routine to another within a single shared library go through the PLT and have their addresses bound at run time. Is this useful? Why or why not?

EXERCISE • 10.2

Imagine that a program calls a library routine plugh() that is found in a shared library, and the programmer builds a dynamically linked program that uses that library. Later, the system manager notices that plugh is a silly name for a routine and installs a new version of the library that names the routine xsazq instead. What happens the next time the programmer runs the program?

EXERCISE • 10.3

If the run-time environment variable LD_BIND_NOW is set, the ELF dynamic loader binds all of the program's PLT entries at load time. What would happen in the situation in Exercise 10.2 if LD_BIND_NOW were set?

EXERCISE • 10.4

Microsoft implemented lazy procedure binding without operating system assistance by adding some extra cleverness in the linker and by using the existing facilities in the operating system. How hard would it be to provide transparent access to shared data, avoiding the extra level of explicit pointers that the current scheme uses?

PROJECT

It's impractical to build an entire dynamic linking system for our project linker, because much of the work of dynamic linking happens at run time rather than link time. Much of the work of building a shared library was already done in Project 8.3, in which we created PIC executables. A dynamically linked shared library is just a PIC executable with a well-defined list of imported and exported symbols and a list of other libraries on which it depends. To mark the file as a shared library or an executable that uses shared libraries, the first line is

```
LINKLIB lib1 lib2 ...
```

or

```
LINK lib1 lib2 ...
```

the libs are the names of other shared libraries on which this one depends.

PROJECT • 10.1

Starting with the version of the linker from Project 8.3, extend the linker to produce shared libraries and executables that need shared libraries. The linker needs to take as its input a list of input files to combine into the output executable or library as well as other shared libraries to search. The output file contains a symbol table with defined (exported) and undefined (imported) symbols. Relocation types are the ones for PIC files along with AS4 and RS4 for references to imported symbols.

PROJECT • 10.2

Write a run-time binder, that is, a program that takes an executable that uses shared libraries and resolves its references. It should read in the executable, then read in the necessary libraries, relocate them to non-overlapping available addresses, and create a logically merged symbol table. (You may want to actually create such a table, or you may use a list of per-file tables as ELF does.) Then resolve all of the relocations and external references. When you're done, all code and data should be assigned memory addresses, and all addresses in the code and data should be resolved and relocated to the assigned addresses.

ADVANCED TECHNIQUES

This chapter describes a grab bag of miscellaneous linker techniques that don't fit very well anywhere else in this book. Here we discuss special techniques required for C++, incremental linking approaches, link-time garbage collection, optimization and code generation, and, finally, the Java linking model.

11.1 TECHNIQUES FOR C++

C++ presents three significant challenges to the linker. One is its complicated naming rules, in which several functions can have the same name if they have different argument types. Name mangling solves this problem well enough that all linkers use it in some form or another.

The second challenge is global initializers and destructors: routines that need to be run before the main routine starts and after the main routine exits. This requires that the linker collect the pieces of initializer and destructor code—or at least pointers to them—into one place, so that startup and exit code can run it all.

The third, and by far the most complex, issue involves templates and extern inline procedures. A C++ template defines an infinite family of procedures, with each family member being the template specialized by a type. For example, a template might define a generic hash table, with family members being a hash table of integers, of floating-point numbers, of character strings, and of pointers to various sorts of structures. Because computer memories are finite, the compiled program needs to contain all of the members of the family that are actually used in the program, but it shouldn't contain any others. If the C++ compiler takes the traditional approach of treating each source file separately, it can't tell when it compiles a file that uses templates whether some of the template family members are used in other source files. If the compiler takes a conservative approach and generates code for each family member used in each file, it will usually end up with multiple copies of each family member, wasting space. If it doesn't generate that code, it risks having no copy at all of a required family member.

Inline functions present a similar problem. Normally, inline functions are expanded like macros, but in some cases the compiler generates a conventional out-of-line version of the function. If several different files use a single header file that contains an inline function and some of them require an out-of-line version, the same problem of code duplication arises.

Some compilers have used approaches that change the source language to help produce object code that can be linked by "dumb" linkers. Many recent C++ systems have addressed the problem head-on, either by making the linker smarter or by integrating the linker with other parts of the program development system. We look briefly at these latter approaches.

TRIAL LINKING

In systems stuck with simple-minded linkers, C++ systems have used a variety of tricks to get C++ programs linked. An approach pioneered by the original cfront implementation is to do a trial link, which will generally fail, then to have the compiler driver (the program that runs the various pieces of the compiler, assembler, and linker) extract information from the result of that link to finish the compiling and then relink (Figure 11.1).

On UNIX systems, if the linker can't resolve all of the undefined references in a link job, it still has the option of producing an output file that can be used as the input to a subsequent link job. The linker uses its usual library search

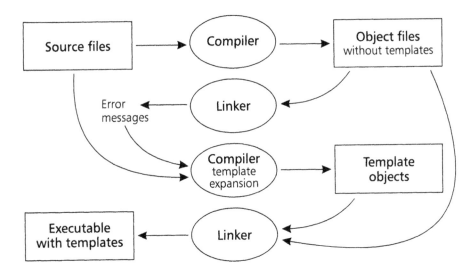

FIGURE **11.1** • Trial linking.

rules during the link, so the output file contains needed library routines as well as information from the input file. Trial linking solves all of the C++ problems above in a slow but effective way.

For global initializers and destructors, the C++ compiler creates in each input file routines that do the initialization and destruction. The routines are logically anonymous, but the compiler gives them distinctive names. For example, the GNU C++ compiler creates routines named _GLOBAL_.I.__4junk and _GLOBAL_.D.__4junk to do initialization and destruction of variables in a class called junk. After the trial link, the linker driver examines the symbol table of the output file, makes lists of the global initializer and destructor routines, and writes a small source file with those lists in arrays (in either C or assembler). Then in the relink the C++ startup and exit code uses the contents of the arrays to call all of the appropriate routines. This is essentially the same thing that linkers capable of handling C++ do; the process is just implemented outside the linker.

For templates and extern inlines, the compiler initially doesn't generate any code for them at all. The trial link has undefined symbols for all of the templates and extern inlines actually used in the program, which the compiler driver can use to rerun the compiler and generate code for them and then relink.

One minor issue is to find the source code for the missing templates, because it can be lurking in any of a potentially very large number of source files. cfront used a simple ad hoc technique, scanning the header files and guessing that a template declared in foo.h is defined in foo.cc. Recent versions of GCC use a repository that notes the locations of template definitions in small files created during the compilation process. After the trial link, the compiler driver need only scan those small files to find the source code for the templates.

Duplicate Code Elimination

The trial linking approach generates as little code as possible, then it goes back after the trial link to generate any required code that was left out the first time. The opposite approach is to generate all possible code, then to have the linker throw away the duplicates (Figure 11.2). The compiler generates all of the expanded templates and all of the extern inlines in each file that uses them. Each possibly redundant piece of code is put in its own segment with a name that uniquely identifies what it is. For example, GCC puts each piece in an ELF or COFF section called .gnu.linkonce.d.mangledname where mangledname is the mangled version of the function name with the type information added. Some formats identify possibly redundant sections solely by name, while Microsoft's COFF uses COMDAT sections with explicit type flags to identify possibly redundant code sections. If there are multiple copies of a section with the same name, the linker discards all but one of them at link time.

This approach does a good job of producing executables with one copy of each routine at the cost of very large object files with many copies of templates. It also offers at least the possibility of smaller final code than the other approaches. In many cases, the code generated when a template is expanded for different types is identical. For example, a template that implemented a bounds-checked array of <TYPE> would generally expand to identical code for all pointer types, because in C++, pointers all have the same representation. A linker that's already deleting redundant sections could check for sections with identical contents and collapse multiple identical sections to one. Some MS Windows linkers do this.

Database Approaches

The GCC repository is a simple version of a database. Over time, tool vendors are moving toward database storage of source and object code, as in the

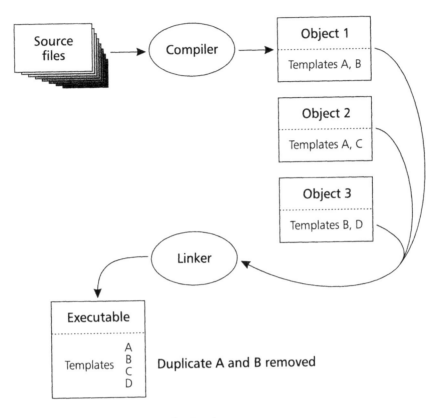

FIGURE **11.2** • Duplicate elimination.

Montana environment in IBM's Visual Age C++. The database tracks the location of each declaration and definition, which makes it possible after a source code change to figure out what the individual routine dependencies are and to recompile and relink just what has changed.

11.2 INCREMENTAL LINKING AND RELINKING

For a long time, some linkers have permitted incremental linking and relinking. UNIX linkers provide an -r flag that tells the linker to keep the symbol and relocation information in the output file, so that the output can be used as the input to a subsequent link.

IBM mainframes have always had a "linkage editor" rather than a linker. In the IBM object format, the segments in each input file—IBM calls the segments *control sections,* or csects—retain their individual identities in the output file. You can re-edit a linked program and replace or delete control sections. This feature was widely used in the 1960s and early 1970s when compiling and linking were slow enough that it was worth the manual effort needed to arrange to relink a program; only the csects that had been recompiled were replaced. The replacement csects need not be the same size as the originals; the linker adjusts all of the relocation information in the output file as needed to account for the different locations of csects that have moved.

In the mid- to late 1980s, Quong and Linton (see References) at Stanford did experiments with incremental linking in a UNIX linker to try to speed up the compile-link-debug cycle. The first time their linker runs, it links a conventional statically linked executable, then it stays active in the background as a daemon with the program's symbol table remaining in memory. On subseqent links, it only treats the input files that have changed, replacing their code in-place in the output file but leaving everything else alone other than fixing up references to symbols that have moved. Because segment sizes in the recompiled files usually don't change very much from one link to the next, they build the initial version of the output file with a small amount of slop space between the input file segments (Figure 11.3). On each subsequent link, so long as the changed input file segments haven't grown more than the slop amount, the changed file segments replace the previous versions in the output file. If they have grown past the end of the slop space, the linker moves the subsequent segments in the output file using their slop space. If more than a small number of segments need to be moved, the linker gives up and relinks from scratch.

Quong and Linton did considerable testing to collect data on the number of files compiled between linker runs in typical development activities and on the change in segment sizes. They found that typically only one or two files change, and the segments grow only by a few bytes if at all. By putting 100 bytes of slop space between segments, they avoided almost all relinking. They also found that creating the output file's symbol table, which is essential for debugging, was as much work as creating the segments and used similar techniques to update the symbol table incrementally. Their performance results were quite dramatic, with links that took 20 or 30 seconds to do conventionally dropping to half a second for an incremental link. The primary drawback

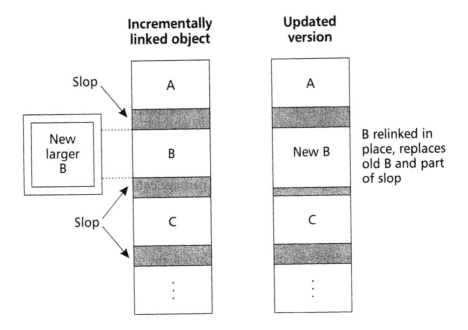

FIGURE **11.3** • Incremental linking.

of their scheme was that the linker used about 8MB to keep all of the symbols and other information about the output file, which at the time was a lot of memory (workstations rarely had more than 16MB).

Some modern systems do incremental linking in much the same way that Quong and Linton did. The linker in Microsoft's Visual Studio links incrementally by default. It leaves slop space between modules and also can in some circumstances move an updated module from one part of the executable to another, putting in some glue code at the old address.

11.3 LINK-TIME GARBAGE COLLECTION

Lisp and other languages that allocate storage automatically have for decades provided *garbage collection*, a service that automatically identifies and frees up storage that's no longer referred to by any other part of the program. Several linkers offer an analogous facility to remove unused code from object files.

Most program source and object files contain more than one procedure. If a compiler marks the boundaries between procedures, the linker can determine which symbols each procedure defines and which symbols each procedure references. Any procedure with no references at all is unused and can safely be discarded. Each time a procedure is discarded, the linker should recompute the definition/reference list, because the procedure just discarded might have had the only reference to some other procedure that can in turn be discarded.

One of the earlier systems to do link-time garbage collection is IBM's AIX. The XCOFF object files used in AIX put each procedure in a separate section. The linker uses symbol table entries to tell which symbols are defined in each section and relocation entries to tell which symbols are referenced. By default, all unreferenced procedures are discarded, although the programmer can use linker switches to tell it not to do garbage collection at all or to protect specific files or sections from collection.

Several MS Windows linkers—including CodeWarrior, the Watcom linker, and the linker in recent versions of Microsoft's Visual C++—can also do garbage collection. An optional compiler switch creates objects with packaged functions: each procedure is in a separate section of the object file. The linker looks for sections with no references and deletes them. In most cases, the linker looks at the same time for multiple procedures with identical contents (usually from template expansions, mentioned in Section 11.1) and collapses them as well.

An alternative to a garbage collecting linker is more extensive use of libraries. A programmer can turn each of the object files that are linked to a program into a library with one procedure per library member, then can link from those libraries so the linker pulls in procedures as needed, skipping the ones with no references. The hardest part is to make each procedure a separate object file. This typically requires some fairly messy preprocessing of the source code to break multiprocedure source files into several small single-procedure files, replicating the data declarations and include lines for header files in each one and renaming internal procedures to prevent name collisions. The result is a minimum-size executable, at the cost of considerably slower compiling and linking. This is a very old trick; the DEC TOPS-10 assembler in the late 1960s could be directed to generate an object file with multiple independent sections that the linker would treat as a searchable library.

11.4 LINK-TIME OPTIMIZATION

On most systems, the linker is the only program in the software building process that sees at one time all of the pieces of a program that it is building. That means that it has opportunities to do global optimization that no other component can do, particularly if the program combines modules written in different languages and compiled with different compilers. For example, in a language with class inheritance, calls to class methods generally use indirect calls because a method may be overridden in a subclass. But if there aren't any subclasses or there are subclasses but none of them override a particular method, the calls can be direct. A linker could make special-case optimizations like this to avoid some of the inefficiencies otherwise inherent in object-oriented languages. Fernandez at Princeton (see references) wrote an optimizing linker for Modula-3 that was able to turn 79% of indirect calls into direct calls in addition to reducing instructions executed by over 10%.

A more aggressive approach is to perform standard global optimizations on an entire program at link time. Srivastava and Wall (see references) wrote an optimizing linker that decompiled RISC architecture object code into an intermediate form, applied high-level optimizations such as inlining and low-level optimizations such as substituting a faster but more limited instruction for a slower and more general one, then regenerated the object code.

Particularly on 64-bit architectures, the speedups from these optimizations can be quite significant. On the 64-bit DEC Alpha architecture, the general way to address any static or global data or any procedure is to load into a register an address pointer to the item from a pointer pool in memory, then to use the register as a base register. (The pointer pool is addressed by a global pointer register.) DEC's OM optimizing linker looks for situations where a sequence of instructions refers to several global or static variables that are located close enough to each other that they can all be addressed relative to the same pointer; the linker rewrites object code to remove many pointer loads from the global pool. It also looks for procedure calls that are within the 32-bit address range of the branch-to-subroutine instruction and substitutes that for a load and indirect call. The OM linker also can rearrange the allocation of common blocks to place small blocks together, in order to increase the number of places where a single pointer can be used for multiple references. Using these and some other standard optimizations, OM achieves significant improvements in executables, removing as many as 11% of all instructions in some of the SPEC benchmarks.

The Tera computer compilation suite does very aggressive link-time optimization to support the Tera's high-performance, highly parallel architecture. The C compiler is little more than a parser that creates "object files" containing tokenized versions of the source code. The linker resolves all of the references among modules and generates all of the object code. It aggressively inlines procedures, both within a single module and among modules, because the code generator handles the entire program at once. To get reasonable compilation performance, the system uses incremental compilation and linking. On a recompile, the linker starts with the previous version of the executable, rewrites the code for the source files that have changed—which, as a result of the optimization and inlining, may be in code generated from files that haven't changed—and creates a new, updated executable. Few of the compilation or linking techniques in the Tera system are new, but to date it's unique in its combination of so many aggressive optimization techniques in a single system.

Other linkers have done other architecture-specific optimizations. The Multiflow VLIW machine had a very large number of registers; thus register saves and restores could be a major bottleneck. To improve performance, an experimental tool used profile data to figure out which routines frequently called which other routines. It modified the registers used in the code to minimize the overlapping registers used by both a calling routine and its callee, thereby minimizing the number of saves and restores.

11.5   LINK-TIME CODE GENERATION

Many linkers generate small amounts of the output object code, for example, the jump entries in the PLT in UNIX ELF files. But some experimental linkers do far more code generation than that.

The Srivastava and Wall optimizing linker discussed in Section 11.4 starts by decompiling object files back into intermediate code. (In most cases, if the linker wants intermediate code, it'd be just as easy for compilers to skip the code generation step, to create object files out of intermediate code, and to let the linker do the code generation. That's what the Fernandez optimizing linker discussed in Section 11.4 actually did.) The Srivastava and Wall linker can take all the intermediate code, do a big optimization pass over it, then generate the object code for the output file.

There are a couple of reasons that production linkers rarely do code generation from intermediate code. One is that intermediate languages tend to be related to the compiler's source language. While it's not too hard to devise an intermediate language that can handle several Fortran-like languages such as C and C++, it's considerably harder to devise one that can handle those and yet also handle less-similar languages such as COBOL and Lisp. Linkers are generally expected to link object code from any compiler or assembler, making language-specific intermediates problematic.

LINK-TIME PROFILING AND INSTRUMENTATION

Several groups have written link-time profiling and optimization tools. Romer et al. at the University of Washington wrote Etch, an instrumentation tool for MS Windows x86 executables (see references). It analyzes ECOFF executables to find all of the executable code in the main executable (which is typically intermixed with data) as well as in DLL libraries it calls. It has been used to build a call graph profiler and an instruction scheduler. The lack of structure in ECOFF executables and the complexity of the x86 instruction encoding were the major challenges to creating Etch.

Cohn et al. at DEC wrote Spike, an MS Windows optimization tool for Alpha NT executables. It performed both instrumentation (to add profiling code to executables and DLLs) and optimization (using the profile data to improve register allocation and to reorganize executables to improve cache locality).

LINK-TIME ASSEMBLER

An interesting compromise between linking traditional binary object code and linking intermediate languages is to use assembler source code as the object language. The linker assembles the entire program at once to generate the output file. Minix, a small UNIX-like system that was the inspiration for Linux, did that.

Assembler is close enough to machine language that any compiler can generate it; yet it is still at a high enough level to permit useful optimizations including dead code elimination, code rearrangement, and some kinds of strength reduction, as well as standard assembler optimizations such as choosing the smallest version of an instruction that has enough bits to handle a particular operand.

Such a system could be fast—because assembly can be very fast—particularly if the object language were really tokenized assembler code rather than full assembler source code. (In assemblers, as in other compilers, the initial tokenizing is often the slowest part of the entire process.)

LOAD-TIME CODE GENERATION

Some systems defer code generation past link time to program load time. Franz and Kistler (see references) created slim binaries, originally as a response to Macintosh fat binaries that contain object code for both older 68000 Macs and newer PowerPC Macs. A slim binary is actually a compactly encoded version of an abstract parse for a program module. The program loader reads and expands the slim binary and generates the object code for the module in memory, which is then executable. The inventors of slim binaries make the plausible claim that modern CPUs are so much faster than disks that program loading time is dominated by disk I/O and that even with the code generation step, slim binaries are about as fast to load as standard binaries because their disk files are small.

Slim binaries were originally created to support Oberon, a strongly typed Pascal-like language, on the Macintosh and later on MS Windows for the x86, and they apparently work quite well on those platforms. The authors also expect that slim binaries will work equally well with other source languages and other architectures. This is a much less credible claim: Oberon programs tend to be very portable due to the strong typing and the consistent run-time environment, and the three target machines are quite similar with identical data and pointer formats (except for byte order on the x86). A long series of "universal intermediate language" projects dating back to the UNCOL project in the 1950s have failed after gettting promising results with a small number of source and target languages, and there's no reason to think that slim binaries wouldn't have the same outcome. But as a distribution format for a set of similar target environments—for example, Macs with the 68000 or PPC; or MS Windows with the x86, the Alpha, or MIPS—it should work well.

The IBM S/38 and AS/400 have used a similar technique for many years to provide binary program compatibility among machines with different hardware architectures. The defined machine language for the S/38 and AS/400 is a virtual architecture with a very large single-level address space that is never actually implemented in hardware. When an S/38 or AS/400 binary program is loaded, the loader translates the virtual code into the actual machine code for whatever processor the machine on which it is running contains. The translated code is cached to speed loading on subsequent runs of the program. This has allowed IBM to evolve the S/38 and then the AS/400 line from a midrange system with multiboard CPUs to a deskside system using a PowerPC CPU, while maintaining binary compatibility throughout. The virtual architecture is very tightly specified and the translations are very complete, so programmers can debug their programs at the virtual-architecture level without reference to the physical CPU. This scheme probably wouldn't have worked without a single vendor's complete control over the virtual architecture and over all of the models of the computers on which it runs, but it's a very effective way to get a lot of performance out of modestly priced hardware.

11.6 THE JAVA LINKING MODEL

The Java programming language has a sophisticated and interesting loading and linking model. The Java source language is a strongly typed object-oriented language with a syntax similar to C++. What makes it interesting is that Java also defines a portable binary object code format, a virtual machine that executes programs in that binary format, and a loading system that permits a Java program to add code to itself as it runs.

Java organizes a program into *classes*, with each class in a program compiled into a logically (and usually physically) separate binary object code file. Each class defines the fields that each class member contains, possibly some static variables, and a set of procedures (methods) that manipulate class members. Java uses single inheritance, so each class is a subclass of some other class, with all classes being descendants from the universal base class Object. A class inherits all of the fields and methods from its superclass and can add new fields and methods, possibly overriding existing methods in the superclass.

Java loads one class at a time. A Java program starts by loading an initial class in an implementation-dependent way. If that class refers to other classes, the other classes are loaded on demand when they are needed. A Java application can either use the built-in bootstrap class loader that loads classes from files on the local disk, or it can provide its own class loader that can create or retrieve classes any way it wants. Most commonly, a custom class loader retrieves class files over a network connection, but it could equally well generate code as it runs or extract code from compressed or encrypted files. When a class is loaded as a result of a reference from another class, the system uses the same loader that loaded the referring class. Each class loader has its own separate name space, so even if an application run from a disk and one run over a network have identically named classes or class members, there's no name collision.

The Java definition specifies the loading and linking process in considerable detail. When the virtual machine needs to use a class, it first *loads* the class by calling the class loader. Once a class is loaded, the linking process includes *verification* that the binary code is valid and *preparation* (allocating the static fields of the class). The final step of the process is *initialization*, which runs any routines that initialize the static fields and which happens the first time that an instance of the class is created or a static function of the class is run.

STEPS IN JAVA LOADING AND LINKING

Loading and linking are separate processes because any class needs to ensure that all of its superclasses are loaded and linked before linking can start. Conceptually this means that the process crawls up and then down the class inheritance tree (Figure 11.4). The loading process starts by calling the classLoader procedure with the name of the class. The class loader produces the class's data somehow, then it calls defineClass to pass the data to the virtual machine. defineClass parses the class file and checks for a variety of format errors, generating an exception if it finds any. It also extracts the name of the class's superclass. If the superclass isn't already loaded, it calls classLoader recursively to load the superclass. When that call returns, the superclass has been loaded and linked, at which point the Java system proceeds to link the current class.

Class tree

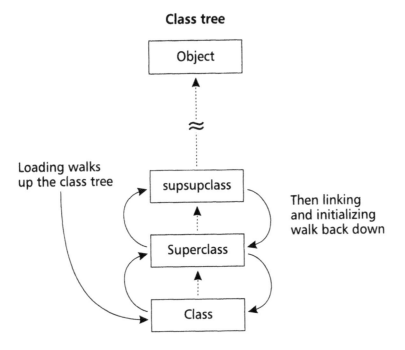

FIGURE **11.4** • Loading and linking a Java class file.

The next step, verification, makes a variety of static correctness checks, such as ensuring that each virtual instruction has a valid opcode, that the target of each branch is a valid instruction, and that each instruction handles the appropriate data type for the values it references. This speeds up program execution because these checks need not be made when the code is run. If verification finds errors, it throws an exception. Then preparation allocates storage for all of the static members of the class and initializes them to standard default values, typically zero. Most Java implementations create a method table at this point that contains pointers to all of the methods defined for this class or inherited from a superclass.

The final stage of Java linking is resolution, which is analogous to dynamic linking in other languages. Each class includes a *constant pool* that contains both conventional constants such as numbers and strings and the references to other classes. All references in a compiled class, even to its superclass, are symbolic and are resolved after the class is loaded. (The superclass might have been changed and recompiled after the class was, which is valid so long as every field and method to which the class refers remains defined in a compatible way.) Java allows implementations to resolve references at any time from the moment after verification to the moment when an instruction actually uses the reference (such as calling a function defined in a superclass or other class). Regardless of when it actually resolves a reference, a failed reference doesn't cause an exception until it's used, so a Java program behaves as though it uses lazy just-in-time resolution. This flexibility in resolution time permits a wide variety of possible implementations. An implementation that translates the class into native machine code can resolve all of the references immediately, so the addresses and offsets can be embedded into the translated code with jumps to an exception routine at any place where a reference can't be resolved. A pure interpreter might instead wait and resolve references as they're encountered when the code is interpreted.

The effect of this loading and linking design is that classes are loaded and resolved as needed. Java's garbage collection applies to classes the same way it applies to all other data, so if all references to a class are deleted, the class itself can get unloaded.

The Java loading and linking model is the most complex of any we've seen in this book. But Java attempts to satisfy some rather contradictory goals—portable type-safe code and also reasonably fast execution. This loading and linking model supports incremental loading, static verification of most of the type safety criteria, and class-at-a-time translation to machine code for systems that want programs to run fast.

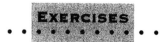

EXERCISES

EXERCISE • 11.1

How long does the linker you use take to link a fairly large program? Test your linker to see what it spends its time doing. (Even without linker source code you can probably do a system call trace, which should give you a pretty good idea.)

EXERCISE • 11.2

Look at the generated code from a compiler for C++ or another object-oriented language. How much better could a link-time optimizer make it?

What information could the compiler put in the object module to make it easier for the linker to do interesting optimizations? How badly do shared libraries mess up this plan?

EXERCISE • 11.3

Sketch out a tokenized assembler language for your favorite CPU to use as an object language. What's a good way to handle symbols in the program?

EXERCISE • 11.4

The AS/400 uses binary translation to provide binary code compatibility among different machine models. Other architectures—including the IBM 360/370/390, the DEC VAX, and the Intel x86—use microcode to implement the same instruction set on different underlying hardware. What are the advantages of the AS/400 scheme? Of microcoding? If you were defining a computer architecture today, which would you use?

 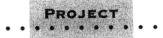

PROJECT • 11.1

Add a garbage collector to your linker. Assume that each input file may have multiple text segments named .text1, .text2, and so forth. Build a global definition/reference data structure using the symbol table and relocation entries and identify the sections that are unreferenced. You'll have to add a command line flag to mark the startup stub as referenced. (What would happen if you didn't?) After the garbage collector runs, update the segment allocations to squeeze out space used by deleted segments.

Improve the garbage collector to make it iterative. After each pass, update the definition/reference structure to remove references from logically deleted segments and run it again, repeating until nothing further is deleted.

REFERENCES

Apple Computer. "Inside Macintosh: MacOS Runtime Architectures." *developer.apple.com/techpubs/mac/runtimehtml/RTArch-2.html*.

AT&T. *System V Application Binary Interface*. UNIX Press/Prentice Hall, Upper Saddle River, NJ; 1990.

AT&T. *System V Application Binary Interface, Intel 386 Architecture Processor Family Supplement*. Intel order number 465681, 1990.

AT&T, *System V Application Binary Interface, Motorola 68000 Processor Family Supplement*. UNIX Press/Prentice Hall, Upper Saddle River, NJ; 1990.

Barlow, Daniel. "The Linux GCC HOWTO." 1996. *www.linux-howto.com/LDP/HOWTO/GCC-HOWTO.html*.

Cohn, Robert, David Goodwin, P. Geoffrey Lowney, and Norman Rubin. "Spike: An Optimizer for Alpha/NT Executables." In USENIX Windows NT Workshop, August 11–13, 1997.

Ellis, Margaret, and Bjarne Stroustrup. *Annotated C++ Reference Manual*. Addison-Wesley Longman, Reading, MA; 1990. Includes the C++ name mangling algorithm.

Fernandez, Mary. "Simple and Effective Link-Time Optimization of Modula-3 Programs." Programming Language Design and Implementation 95 Proceedings (*ACM SIGPLAN Notices*, vol. 30, no. 6, June 1996, pp. 102–115).

Franz, Michael, and Thomas Kistler. *Slim Binaries*. Department of Information and Computer Science, University of California at Irvine, Technical Report 96-24, 1996.

Fraser, Christopher, and David Hanson. "A Machine-Independent Linker." *Software Practice and Experience*, vol. 12, 1982, pp. 351–366.

Gries, David. *Compiler Construction for Digital Computers*. Wiley, NY; 1971. Contains one of the best available descriptions of IBM card image object format.

Hoffman, Paul. *Perl for Dummies*. IDG Books, Foster City, CA; 1998.

IBM. *MVS/ESA Linkage Editor and Loader User's Guide*. Order number SC26-4510, 1991. Also available at *www.ibm.com/*.

Intel. *8086 Relocatable Object Module Formats*. Order number 121748, 1981.

Intel. *Tool Interface Standard (TIS) Formats Specification for Windows Version 1.0*. Order number 241597, 1993. Describes PE format and debug symbols, although Microsoft has changed them since this came out.

Intel. *Tool Interface Standard (TIS) Portable Formats Specification Version 1.1*. Order number 241597, 1993. Also at *developer.intel.com/vtune/tis.htm*. Describes ELF, DWARF, and OMF for x86.

Kath, Randy. "The Portable Executable File Format from Top to Bottom." 1993. *premium.microsoft.com/msdn/library/techart/msdn_pefile.htm*.

Lindholm, Tim, and Frank Yellin. *The Java Virtual Machine Specification*. Second edition. Addison-Wesley Longman, Reading, MA; 1999.

Microsoft. *Portable Executable and Common Object File Format Specification, Revision 5.0*. October 1997. *premium.microsoft.com/msdn/library/specs/pecoff/microsoftportableexecutableandcommonobjectfileformatspecification.htm*.

Pietrek, Matt. "Peering Inside the PE: A Tour of the Win32 Portable Executable File Format." 1994. *premium.microsoft.com/msdn/library/techart/msdn_peeringpe.htm*.

Pietrek, Matt. *Windows 95 System Programming Secrets*. IDG Books, Foster City, CA; 1995.

Quong, Russell, and Mark Linton. "Linking Programs Incrementally." *ACM TOPLAS*, vol. 13, no. 1, 1991, pp. 1–20.

Romer, Ted, Geoff Voelker, Dennis Lee, Alec Wolman, Wayne Wong, Hank Levy, and Brian Bershad. "Instrumentation and Optimization of Win32/Intel Executables Using Etch." In USENIX Windows NT Workshop, August 11–13, 1997.

Schwartz, Randal. *Learning Perl*. O'Reilly, Sebastopol, CA; 1993.

Srivastava, Amitabh, and David Wall. "Link-Time Optimization of Address Calculation on a 64-bit Architecture." 1994. *www.research.digital.com/wrl/techreports/abstracts/94.1.html. SIGPLAN Notices*, vol. 29, no. 6, pp. 49–60.

Srivastava, Amitabh, and David Wall. "A Practical System for Intermodule Code Optimization at Link Time." 1993. DEC Western Research Lab TR-92.6, *www.research.digital.com/wrl/techreports/abstracts/92.6.html*.

Venners, Bill. *Inside the Java Virtual Machine*. Second edition. McGraw-Hill, New York;; 1999.

Wall, Larry, Tom Christiansen, and Randal Schwartz. *Programming Perl*. Second edition. O'Reilly, Sebastopol, CA; 1996.

INDEX

Printed and bound by CPI Group (UK) Ltd, Croydon, CR0 4YY

03/10/2024

01040342-0005